MOUNTAIN BIKING

Utah's Brian Head - Bryce Country

Gregg Bromka

Off-Road Publications
Salt Lake City, Utah
http://www.OffRoadPub.com

Cover photographs:
Katie and Mary: Twisted Forest–High Mountain Trail
Inset: Rocky Mountain columbine

Back Cover photographs:
Top: High Mountain
Left: Scout Camp Loop
Right: Thunder Mountain
Bottom: Sunset Cliffs

Cover design: Passey Design, Salt Lake City, Utah

First edition, first printing 1998
5 4 3 2 1
Printed in the United States of America
All text, illustrations, and photographs by the author.

Published by Off-Road Publications
1590 S. 1400 East
Salt Lake City, Utah 84105
http://www.OffRoadPub.com

ISBN: 0-9624374-3-3
Library of Congress Catalog Card Number: 98-067191

TABLE OF CONTENTS

Area of Coverage Map iv
Trail Map Legend v

PREFACE. vii
Acknowledgments viii

INTRODUCTION. 1
Getting Started 3
Life Beyond Mountain Biking 4

REGIONAL SETTING. 9
People, Places, and Passageways 9
Shape of the Land: Geology & Natural History 14

MOUNTAIN BIKING (Stuff You Should Know). 27
Trail Etiquette 27
Trail Access Policies 30
Caring for the Environment 31
Planning Your Trip 33
Trail Description Format 37
An Introduction to Topographic Maps 39
Warning and Disclaimer 40

BRIAN HEAD-AREA RIDES. 43
1 The Three Peaks 44
2 C Trail 48
3 Red Creek Reservoir 51
4 Yankee Meadow Reservoir 53
5 Brian Head Town Trail 56
6 Twisted Forest-High Mountain 59
7 Blowhard Mountain 62
8 Pioneer Cabins 65
9 Scout Camp Loop 68
10 Dark Hollow Trail–Second Left Hand Canyon 71
11 Brian Head Resort Mountain Bike Park 76
12 Lowder Ponds 81
13 Left Fork Bunker Creek 85
14 Right Fork Bunker Creek 89
15 Brian Head to Panguitch 92
16 Tour de Frog 97
17 Spruce Trail (Horse Valley Peak) 103
18 Birch Spring Knoll 107
19 Dead Lake 110
20 Red Desert–Tippets Valley 113
21 Virgin River Rim Trail 116
22 Navajo Lake Loop Trail 124

23 Cascade Falls 127
24 Ice Cave 129
25 Duck Creek ATV Trail System 132

BRYCE-AREA RIDES. 137
26 Casto Canyon 138
27 Losee Canyon 141
28 Cassidy Trail to Losee Canyon 144
29 Thunder Mountain 147
30 Tropic Reservoir 151
31 Sunset Cliffs I (Blue Fly Creek) 153
32 Sunset Cliffs II (Badger Creek) 157
33 Sunset Cliffs III (Blubber Creek) 159
34 Sunset Cliffs IV (Robinson Canyon) 162
35 Mill Creek Trail 165
36 Pink Cliff 168
37 Great Western Trail (East Fork Sevier River Section) 171
38 Daves Hollow–Whiteman Bench 175
39 Henderson Canyon Overlook 178
40 Powell Point 180
41 Barney Top 183

APPENDICIES. 189
I Rides According to Difficulty 189
II Master List of Rides 191
III Sources of Additional Information and Services 193
IV Book References 196

ABOUT OFF-ROAD PUBLICATIONS. 198

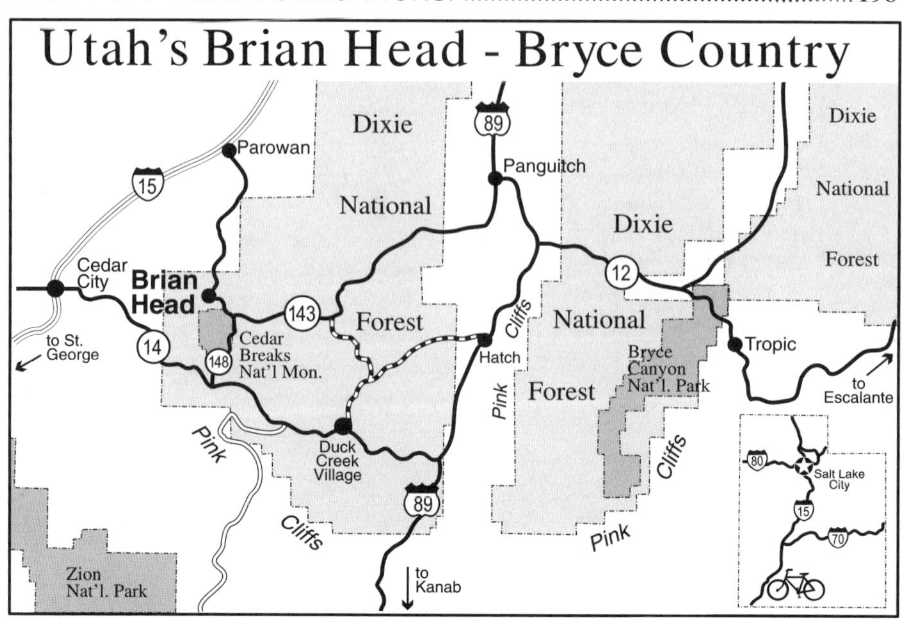

Trail Map Legend

Roads and Trails

Highway/paved road
(Main route; side route)

Light duty dirt road
(Main route; side route)

All-weather dirt road
(Main route; side route)

Doubletrack/Jeep road
(Main route; side route)

Singletrack/ATV trail
Main route; side route

Map symbols

Interstate highway

U.S. highway

State highway

FDR ## Forest Development Road

Ride locator number

Ride locator number (nearby)

Trailhead

Direction of travel

0.00 Mileage

No bicycles allowed

No motorized travel allowed

Hiking trail

Viewpoint

Peak--elevation in feet

Lake/pond

Spring

Logging area

City/town

Campground (developed)

Campground (primitive)

Picnic area/table

Ranger station Visitor center

Ranger field station

Building/house

Building/house (abandoned)

Excavation

Cemetary

Bridge/overpass

Fence/gate

Landing strip

Boat dock

Radar tower/ antenna

Ski resort

National Park/ Wilderness boundary

Power line

Ski lift

Interstate highway

Mike and Vince toe the edge of the Ashdown Gorge Wilderness on the Blowhard Mountain Trail.

Ride lots . . . Eat dirt . . .Live longer!

PREFACE

I first ventured to Brian Head in the late 1980s, encouraged by my buddies who gave glowing reports about a killer Labor Day mountain bike race called the Brian Header. They bragged about placing in the top three in their respective classes and about the loads of schwag they scored. (That's because Brian Head was relatively unknown at the time and few showed, so it was nearly impossible not to score in the top three.) Mostly, my fellow sprocket heads gloated over the outrageous race course—the *best* singletrack they had ridden.

On my initial visit, my pumpkin-orange '78 Datsun wagon labored up Parowan Canyon toward Brian Head, threatening to burst a gasket. I swerved erratically about the road because I was too busy gawking at the vermillion cliffs and weird rock formations breaking from the lush forests. "Awesome," I thought. As I crept into town, Brian Head seemed utterly deserted, except for the battered Jeep Scrambler belonging to Bill Murphy, proprietor of Brian Head Cross Country.

Murph graciously escorted me around the race course—Scout Camp Loop, I learned. We lollygagged. I snapped a few photos of the intense autumn colors and took mental notes when Murph spoke passionately of dreamy singletracks descending toward Panguitch Lake. But on Scout Camp's "back nine," I dropped Murph when I bolted down the twisting trail through the profuse aspens, hellbent on overtaking the imaginary race leader. Indeed, this is an outrageous race course.

A decade later, my aging Trooper labors and swerves up Parowan Canyon as I stare out the side window at the same rosy cliffs and bizarre hoodoos. I find that Brian Head hasn't changed much. The town still looks deserted, except that now there are a dozen cars parked in the ski resort's Giant Steps lot, each topped with bike racks. Apple Annie's General Store remains the only outpost for life's necessities: Spaghetti O's, bait and tackle, and cheap red wine. And the Wall Street Journal is still nowhere to be purchased in town. But today the annual Brian Header draws hundreds of racers, and you better be damn good to place third or better in your class.

Some claim Brian Head is destined to the same fate that has plagued Moab, where visiting mountain bikers clog the trails and where fat-tire fever nears hysteria. Doubtful. Brian Head will never eclipse Moab as the self-proclaimed center of the mountain biking universe. Sure, Brian Head is experiencing increased visitation, partly because it's the gateway to Cedar Breaks National Monument and partly because the word is out about the best alpine mountain biking between the Rockies and the Sierras. The past decade of growth (a term used lightly) has brought numerous improvements to the state of mountain biking at Brian Head, not detriments as those Cassandras once professed. And the first-time visitor to Brian Head will find the trails every bit as serendipitous as in years past. Brian Head will always be a humble yet brow-raising mountain biking destination for those who are tired of the same old dirt. Rest easy, Moab, Brian Head will gladly let you keep your crown.

Acknowledgments

Mountain Biking Utah's Brian Head–Bryce Country has been a multi-year endeavor that began with my first visit to Brian Head in 1988. While accumulating trail data over the years, I was introduced to and gathered information from many individuals who proved instrumental in shaping the future of mountain biking in this region. I, and mountain bikers who have benefitted from your efforts, applaud you.

Foremost, I am grateful to the Utah Travel Council, Garfield County Travel Council, Iron County Tourism and Convention Bureau, and Brian Head Chamber of Commerce for their visionary support of this project through their cooperative grants.

Bill Murphy, proprietor of Brian Head Cross Country, deserves endless accolades. Through his pioneering efforts, outcry for trail preservation and development, and genuine admiration for mountain biking, Murph helped put Brian Head on the map. He introduced me to the trails of Brian Head and welcomed me into his home.

A tip of the hat, rather helmet, goes to Kent Traveler of the Cedar City Ranger District, Carl Gillette of the Powell Ranger District, and the staff of the Escalante Ranger District for trail and forest information and for bolstering recreational opportunities on the Dixie National Forest.

Sincere thanks and handshakes go to Clark Kraus of Brian Head Resort for allowing me to cruise freely about the resort's Mountain Bike Park and tag along on many tours, Jean Seiler of Ruby's Inn for inviting me on the inaugural Brian Head to Bullfrog mountain bike tour ("Tour de Frog") in 1990, James Howells for proof reading, and Julie Jenkins for meticulous editing.

High fives to Katie and Mary for their patience and darling smiles while I shot the cover photograph; to Mike, Vince, and Jim for memorable rides and killer photos; and to fellow mountain bikers who did not shy from my camera's lens while I poached still more photos during many bike festivals.

I bow my head and worship the "Great Architect" for his (or her) imaginative creativity when conjuring up the Pink Cliffs, which impart striking color and form to southern Utah's High Plateaus.

Last, hugs and kisses to my wife and dearest friend, Tricia, for patience, love, and understanding.

Vince defies "Natural Selection" at the Parowan Canyon overlook.

INTRODUCTION

"Color Country" is the evocative tag that the tourism industry has applied to Utah's Brian Head–Bryce Country; "Utopia" is what mountain bikers call it. Brian Head–Bryce Country is a unique blend of alpine components encased in ornately eroded slopes painted in rose red, sunburst orange, and coral pink. Although the colors of these encompassing cliffs may suggest the desert, these highlands are void of the sweltering heat. Brian Head–Bryce Country is replete with cool, breezy summits and bounteous forests cut by creek-fed canyons.

Scenery reaches superlative degrees in nearby Cedar Breaks National Monument and Bryce Canyon National Park. Here the flesh-tone Pink Cliffs have been carved into colossal bowls stuffed with bizarre hoodoo formations that defy the imagination. But the Pink Cliffs' capacity to dazzle the eye is not restricted to the parks' boundaries, for the cliffs' erosional theme encompasses and unites Utah's Brian Head–Bryce Country. To the mountain biker, more so than to any other visitor, the Pink Cliffs are a constant companion—one that is forever charming and never tedious. But scenery alone does not make Brian Head–Bryce Country a premier mountain bike destination. The area's trails are superb.

Over the years, **Brian Head** has gained fame for its downhill singletrack trails that drop from alpine ridges through thick forests to warm valleys. Today, you can hop on the ski resort's Giant Steps Lift or ride a shuttle van to Brian Head Peak and let gravity be your accelerator. Dark Hollow–Second Left Hand Canyon, Left and Right Forks of Bunker Creek, and Blowhard Mountain are veritable test tracks for today's "freeride" bikes. Those who prefer to earn their downhills by first riding to mountain summits or who favor marathon cross-country treks will find Brian Head's trail network accommodating.

To say Brian Head is a biker-friendly town is an understatement. With only 100 permanent residents and four top-flight bike shops, Brian Head boasts the most bike shops per capita in the United States, if not the world.

If you're looking for a guided tour, mark your calender for Brian Head's two mountain biking festivals: Brian Head Bash (July) and Fall Colors Festival (September). These multi-day events include guided rides, shuttle services, a chairlift pass, door prizes, lunch on the trail, and evening activities. Your job is easy: pedal and have fun.

If competition is your forte, roll up to the starting line at one of three mountain bike races: the Utah Summer Games (June), the Brian Header (July), and the 12-Hour Mountain Bike Relay Race (September). Each has gained increased popularity over the years and draws hundreds of participants. There are categories for all abilities and ages.

Bienvenido, Bienvenu, Benvenuto—Welcome to Brian Head.

Duck Creek Village, which is a stone's throw from Brian Head, hosts a nexus of trails centered about the newly developed Virgin River Rim Trail. Intended for non-motorized use, the 33-mile trail hugs the rim of the Markagunt Plateau where you can peer at corrugated cliffs below and spy Zion National Park in the distance. Tackle the entire route or explore numerous side trails that connect with the Navajo Lake Loop Trail.

Since snow lingers at Brian Head well into late spring and returns early in autumn, **Cedar City** offers opportunities for riding "off season" as well as during summer. During the times of the year when the Brian Head Resort's chairlifts carry skiers rather than bikers, you can carve turns on the mountain in the morning and pedal in the dirt around Cedar City in the afternoon.

As this guidebook's title suggests, the **Bryce** area east of **Panguitch** is an untapped reservoir overflowing with mountain biking opportunities. There are nearly as many rides in the Bryce area as there are around Brian Head. Although the trails within Bryce Canyon National Park are closed to bicycles, nearby Red Canyon and the East Fork Sevier River valley beckon the mountain bike purist. Scenery in these areas approaches national-park caliber, and the countless trails and jeep roads welcome mountain bikers without limitations. Like Brian Head Peak, from which you have a top-of-the-world view of Cedar Breaks National Monument, Table Cliff Plateau, northeast of Bryce, affords a bird's-eye vantage of Grand Staircase–Escalante National Monument.

In addition to world-class trails and stunning scenery, Utah's Brian Head–Bryce Country offers extensive amenities to round out your visit. Overnight accommodations range from campgrounds to cozy bed and breakfast inns to deluxe motels and

Bikers congregate during the annual Brian Head Bash.

hotels. Dining is a blend of take-out service, home-style cafes, and restaurants that offer gourmet cuisine. And access to the area is easy via state and federal highways and via airline service to Cedar City.

Whether you're looking for a mellow route suited for the entire family, a remote backcountry adventure, or a training ride that will make your quadriceps scream, you'll find it in this guidebook. But in addition to raw trail data, this guidebook strives to instill you with undying reverence for the unique natural setting of Utah's Brian Head–Bryce Country.

Do you want more? Look for trail updates and information on new rides in Brian Head–Bryce Country on the internet—**http://www.OffRoadPub.com/trailnews**

Getting Started

How do you determine the ride that's right for you? Start by scanning the Table of Contents. Pick a route that sounds enticing, flip to that chapter, and read about it. The most logical approach, however, is to study Appendix I: Ride According to Difficulty, where all routes (and options) are organized by the location and the degree of difficulty. If you're like the Odd Couple's Felix Unger, who must have order in his life, then turn to Appendix II: Master List of Rides, and simply knock off the trails one by one, alphabetically. If you're from out of town, you may need additional information on services, accommodations, and events to complete your visit. For this, turn to Appendix III: Sources of Additional Information to find a long list of agencies, businesses, and tourism organizations that can answer all of your biking and travel-related questions. Last, if want to learn more about the area, you'll find a list of related books in Appendix IV: References. Most of these books can be found at local libraries, gift shops, and travel information centers throughout Utah.

Life Beyond Mountain Biking

If your forte is not mountain biking, or if your posterior simply needs a rest, Utah's Brian Head–Bryce Country offers an array of activities geared for all interests and ages.

Brian Head is a haven for summertime activities that complement any mountain bike outing. Learn about the Markagunt Plateau's diverse flora, fauna, geology, and history on the weekly Nature Walk, hosted by a representative of the Dixie National Forest. Astronomers and those who "wish upon a star" can take a closer look at the heavens at the annual Star Gazing Party, which begins with and indoor slide show and culminates with telescope viewing atop Brian Head Peak. Bikers of a different sort wheel into town for the Thunder on the Mountain Motorcycle Ride. After touring the countryside on open wheels, you are invited to a dance, a dinner, and a pancake breakfast. Even though the summer's days are cool at Brian Head, the heat will be on during the annual Chili Cook Off. Brian Head's fire department will be poised to douse the culinary flames. Finally, autumn is a special time to visit Brian Head. Fall foliage, complemented by evergreen forests and vermillion cliffs, will seduce your camera's lens. Have you ever seen groves of flaming red aspens? You will at Brian Head. Autumn would not be compete without the traditional Oktoberfest Celebration. Dance to reveling oom-pah bands, quaff Bavarian brew, and feast on German cuisine.

Culture and history await in **Cedar City**. Each summer, Cedar City is transformed into a modern-day Camelot when the Utah Shakespearean Festival visits the campus of Southern Utah University. Theater goers can choose from several plays by the English language's most famous playwright or from other classic and contemporary productions. The Festival's Adams Memorial Theater is an accurate replica of Shakespear's famed Globe Theater. In addition to the professionally produced plays, patrons can mingle with the cast, juggle with jesters, and dance a jig during the outside Greenshows, which precede the evening curtain calls. The Royal Feaste is a seven course meal presented by your Elizabethan hosts where patrons dine in the style of the day, with their hands!

Ponder the rugged lifestyle of Mormon pioneers at the Iron Mission Museum in Cedar City. The state park chronicles the development of Iron County during the 1850s, when missionaries developed the nearby iron mines to establish Mormon self-sufficiency. The park also houses one of the west's largest collection of horse-drawn wagons.

Panguitch is the gateway to Bryce Canyon National Park, but it hosts numerous activities and attractions right in town. The Paunsagunt Western Wildlife Museum exhibits more than 300 animals from North America displayed in their natural habitat, plus exotic game from Africa, India, and Europe. The museum houses a collec-

A pre-theater Green Show at the Shakespearean Festival.

tion of artifacts from western Native American tribes, including pottery, metates, pestals, mortars, arrowheads, and bead work. The Panguitch Playhouse offers a chuck wagon dinner followed by western entertainment performed by the Panguitch Players. If you think mountain biking is a rough and tumble activity, then hold on to your helmet during the Panguitch Invitational High School Rodeo, which draws participants from 40 states and Canada. On a calmer note, visit the Quilt Walk Festival. The show includes quilt displays, demonstrations, quilting classes, and related crafts.

Anglers will relish Brian Head–Bryce Country's many lakes, reservoirs, and streams that are stocked with fish. You can troll the placid waters of Yankee Meadow Reservoir, Panguitch Lake, Navajo Lake, or Tropic Reservoir in search of rainbow, brown, brook, and cutthroat trout. If you would rather tie a fly than cast from a dingy, then work the banks of Duck Creek, Mammoth Creek, Sevier River, or East Fork Sevier River.

National Parks

If you are a cross-training mountain biker and hiker or if you are just a casual tourist, then schedule time to explore nearby Bryce Canyon National Park and Cedar Breaks National Monument.

Bryce Canyon National Park is not a canyon at all but a series of crescent-shaped amphitheaters stamped into the Pink Cliffs, which ring the forested Paunsagunt Plateau. Bryce defies description and must be seen to be fully appreciated. When you do view Bryce, your imagination will run wild and conjure up all sorts of images: medieval castles topped with spires, lance-totting sentinels, crenulated pinnacles, gables

Hiking at Bryce Canyon National Park.

and pagodas, terraces of crumbling columns, collapsed turrets, and even platoons of Turkish soldiers in pantaloons. But these intricate shapes and detailed forms are just part of Bryce Canyon. The park's vivid palette of colors changes throughout the day, and watching the sun rise and ignite Bryce Canyon bedazzles the eye and brings a swell of heart-felt emotion. Don't be content with viewing Bryce from the rim-edge overlooks either. Descend any one of its numerous trails and become immersed in its beauty. Hikes range from easy walks to strenuous jaunts to overnight backpacking endeavors.

Also carved from the Pink Cliffs, Cedar Breaks National Monument is more than "Bryce Canyon in the making," for it boasts its own unique characteristics. The great rock amphitheater is one gigantic Roman coliseum, measuring 3 miles wide and 2,000 feet deep. Glowing orange hues prevail but are blended with stripes of lavender, vermillion, yellow, and cream. Motorists can peer over the rim from numerous designated pullouts. Hikers can pursue three trails for more intimate interludes. The 2-mile Wasatch Ramparts Trail descends along the south rim past ancient bristlecone pines to a stunning view of the Cedar Breaks amphitheater. The 2-mile Alpine Pond Trail stays high on the east rim and loops through the quiet forest to a secluded pond. Experienced hikers and backpackers can venture down the Rattlesnake Trail through Cedar Breaks to the Ashdown Gorge Wilderness below.

However, if mountain biking is the name of your game, then pump up the knobby tires because fat is where it's at. There are enough biking opportunities here to keep you returning to Utah's Brian Head–Bryce Country for years.

Brian Head Peak rises above Cedar Breaks National Monument.

REGIONAL SETTING

People, Places, and Passageways

The names of places, features, and passageways are a reflection of the people who venture through and inhabit a region. Utah is endowed with over 22,500 geographic names that reference a fascinating blend of religious, secular, Native American, geologic, and natural history. By applying a name to a physiographic feature, regardless of how grand it is, one runs the risk of trivializing the feature. But by reducing it to human terms the feature can be more easily comprehended and remembered. But what's in a name?

The naming of Utah's places dates back centuries to a time when Native Americans inhabited the West without abandon. The archaic Fremont Indians named the various aspects of the land they inhabited, no doubt. But the Fremonts did not have a written language, so any geographic names they applied vanished when this ancient people mysteriously disappeared from central and southern Utah about 1300 A.D. Insight to the Fremont's lifestyle and history must be interpreted from the pottery shards, clay figurines, and mystical rock art they left behind. Did the Fremont Indians record the names of places in the enigmatic images pecked into the rock at Parowan Gap?

In historic times, Native Americans recorded life's experiences, expressed interludes with nature, and described shapes and colors by naming the features they encountered and the places they visited. "Unka-timpe-wa-wince-pock-itch" translates from the Paiute Indian language to "red rocks standing like men in a bowl," which describes the spire-packed amphitheaters of Bryce Canyon National Park with simplistic accuracy. They called present-day Cedar Breaks National Monument "Un-cap-i-cun-ump" or "circle of red or painted cliffs." Again, these native people lacked the ability to record the names of places because they had not developed a cohesive written language. Instead, native place names became "preempted, anglicized, or bastardized" by European intruders, states John W. Van Cott, author of *Utah Place Names.* This was largely out of ignorance because immigrants commonly spelled native words phonetically. The Indian word for water, for example, was spelled "Pa," "Pa'a," "Pah," "Paw," or Pai." Consequently, preserving place names in the native language seemed nearly hopeless.

Despite the immigrants' contempt for the native language, Indian names, or derivatives thereof, have been generously bestowed upon Utah. Panguitch Lake, a rich source of sustenance for the Paiute Indians, means "big" or "heavy fish." Markagunt

Fremont Indian petroglyphs at Parowan Gap

and Paunsagunt Plateaus are native words meaning "highland of trees" and "place or home of the beavers," respectively. Paragonah, the Mormon hamlet located a few miles north of Parowan, was the term the Piede Indians (a clan of the Paiutes) used in reference to nearby Little Salt Lake. The present day spelling is a modernized version of what explorer John C. Fremont called Paragoona, which he adapted from the native word paragoons or "marsh people." Although Anglos have since displaced Native Americans, relegating them from boundless territories to confined reservations, place names with native origin have endured Utah's history and provide us with lasting insight of their lifestyle and ancestry.

The first written account of European place names in Utah stems from the explorations of the Spanish padres Domínguez and Escalante. While pursuing a land route between missions in present day New Mexico and California during 1776, the expedition first crossed northern Utah's mountainlands but later retreated through southern Utah's torrid deserts. They applied geographic names to their rudimentary maps throughout their travels.

The Sevier River (originating south of Panguitch) was called "Ava-pa-noquint" by the Paiutes, meaning "big quiet waters" or "big placid river," notes an entry in the Utah Historical Society Archives. But when Domínguez and Escalante arrived they named it Rio de Santa Isabel, perhaps in reference to the angelic meadows through which its headwaters flow. Later, Spaniards traveling the Old Spanish Trail through central Utah renamed it Rio Severo or Rio Savarah, which describes the difficult land and alkaline lake into which the river eventually drains. Several accounts state it was named for or by General Sevier, although there are claims that Sevier never visited the area. Perhaps it was named for Harrison Sevier, an early pioneer settler. An entry in the Archives suggests it should have been called Crooked Creek, for the way Orsen W. Huntsmen described it in his diary: "The river is so crooked, a snake would break its trail if it tried to follow it."

The Virgin River finds its headwaters on the south rim of the Markagunt Plateau. But the Domínguez and Escalante party, who first encountered the stream east of Zion National Park where it bubbled with hot sulfur springs, penned it Rio Sulfúreo de las Pirámidas. Spaniards who later ventured through the region applied the biblical connotation, Rio Virgin, which was then anglicized to its present usage.

Not long after Spaniards made inroads through Utah, trappers, explorers, and pioneers ventured west in the mid 1800s to pursue promises of untold fortunes, to reconnoiter uncharted terrain, and to lay claim to endless tracts of land. The Mormons, more than any other group of European immigrants, readily labeled the peaks, valleys, waterways, passages, and settlements throughout southern Utah's High Plateaus.

Upon the directive of Latter Day Saint prophet Brigham Young in 1849, a scouting party lead by Parley P. Pratt set out from Great Salt Lake City to survey the prospect of establishing settlements in southwestern Utah. They found Little Salt Valley (Parowan) to have good soil, reliable water sources, and an abundance of timber in the nearby mountains. But before Parowan received its present-day name, it was first called Little Salt Lake City, in reference to nearby Little Salt Lake; then it was called Louisa for Louisa Beeman, one of the first Mormon women to consent to polygamy. But Parowan was derived, in part, from the native word "pah-o-an," in reference to the bad or saline water of Little Salt Lake.

The scouts also confirmed reports of iron ore in the hills east of Cedar Valley (so named for the abundant "cedars" or junipers growing in the valley). In little time, the church organized the "Iron Mission" (thus Iron County's name) and called upon Great Salt Lake City's devoted members to establish a string of settlements southward along the Old Spanish Trail. (Today, Interstate 15 follows part of this historic trade route). Cedar City, settled after Parowan as southwestern Utah's second town, was established at the mouth of Coal Creek (state highway 14) when coal was discovered on the slopes of the Markagunt Plateau. (Although Cedar City overshadows Parowan as an economic center today, Parowan remains the seat of Iron County.) Mormon settlements then sprung up in Santa Clara and St. George. And, ironically, the Mormons first procured land from the Paiute Indians to build a fort at Las Vegas.

These intrepid pioneers built their communities from scratch, for there were no lumber yards, mercantiles, or supply depots for hundreds of miles. The resources

Pioneeer Cabins at Brian Head.

they needed to erect and sustain their communities came from the generosities of nature; thus the pioneers reaped the bounty of the plateaus. Lumber mills, dairy pastures, and reliable fishing holes became a primary focus. Those who established these sites or homesteaded nearby named the creeks, canyons, peaks, and meadows. Bunker Creek, Lowder Ponds, Lars Fork, and Tippets Valley on the Markagunt Plateau bear the names of Mormons who ventured from the valley to the highlands. Similarly, Casto, Losee, and Henderson Canyons and Daves Hollow on the Paunsagunt Plateau bear pioneer names, as do the town of Bryce and nearby Bryce Canyon National Park.

Brian Head Peak, named by pioneers, has a far more illustrious history. Originally, Brian Head Peak was called Monument Peak because a survey monument was erected atop the summit in the late 1800s. Its present name stems from two competing origins. According to pioneer lore, the peak received its misspelled named for a nineteenth century geologist named Bryan. A second account claims that Marion Gudmudson named the peak after William Jennings Bryan, who was a popular politician and orator of the late 1800s. An entry in the Utah Historical Society Archives extends this later claim. It notes how the timberline circling the sloping peak resembles a man's balding head, apparently that of William Jennings Bryan's.

These southern Utah settlements struggled to survive despite the wealth of natural resources the valleys and plateaus provided. Winters were often severe, crop failures weakened morale, skilled workers were few, and the competition from encroaching railroads weakened the iron mines' profitability. Skirmishes with Native Americans heightened when the ever-encroaching Mormons continually appropriated native lands.

The faltering pioneer history of Panguitch reflects such hard times. Shortly after Parowan and Cedar City were established, a party crossed the Markagunt Plateau to settle in the Sevier River Valley. Their first winter was the harshest, and they fought off starvation by rationing already meager supplies. Panguitch blossomed slowly to a quaint community of only 70 families by 1865. Then, escalating troubles between Mormons and Native Americans forced the town's abandonment. Panguitch would not be resettled until five years thereafter, nearly 15 years after its first occupation. Today, Panguitch is gateway to Bryce Canyon National Park and the hub of Garfield County. (Garfield County was named in 1882 for President James A. Garfield.)

Not long after the Mormons arrived in the Great Salt Lake Valley in 1847, waves of transcontinental travelers washed over Utah. Many were following the call of Brigham Young; others sought to exploit the mines, forests, ranges, and waterways of the West. They, too, named the land. Even those who gained infamy for their lawless acts, like Butch Cassidy and the Wild Bunch, are recognized in Utah's place names.

Yet 20 years after the coming of the Saints, the region known as the Colorado Plateau, of which the High Plateaus form the western sector, remained a great mystery. Until 1869, maps of the western frontier typically showed southern Utah and northern Arizona as a large blank scrawled with the words "unexplored." Uncovering the mysteries of the Colorado River and the land it embraced became the mission of Major John Wesley Powell who, during the years of 1869 and 1871–1872, successfully navigated the Colorado through the Grand Canyon.

On the coattails of Powell came government-apportioned survey parties, whose duty was to compile scientific studies of the various aspects of the Colorado Plateau. Powell and his crew mapped northward from the Grand Canyon across the Utah–Arizona border to the base of Utah's High Plateaus. A. H. Thomson surveyed the canyonlands west of the Colorado River while C. K. Gilbert studied the Henry Mountains. Captain Clarence E. Dutton was assigned to the High Plateaus. As they mapped, they named. Color was everywhere and the names they applied expressed the predominant hue: The Pink, White, Gray, and Vermillion Cliffs of southern Utah each comprise a rung of the what Dutton coined the Grand Staircase. In addition to studying the geology and geography of southern Utah, Powell et al. had a penchant for native ethnology, and they were eager to apply Indian names to the lands they surveyed. The Markagunt and Paunsagunt Plateaus of southern Utah and the Shivwits, Kaibab, and Coconino Plateaus of the Grand Canyon District are of Native American origin. These scientists-cum-adventurers were quick to transform lifeless buttes, towers, and promontories into enchanting temples, alters, and shrines by applying evocative names with mythical, classical, and religious connotations, states C. Gregory Crampton in *Land of Living Rock*. And being pioneers in their own right, they were not shy to honor themselves and their cohorts: Powell Point on the Table Cliff Plateau and Mount Dutton on the nearby Sevier Plateau.

These great surveys provided the impetus for establishing the governmental land management agencies of today, including the Forest Service, the Bureau of Land Management, and the National Park Service. These agencies have played a key role in generating and maintaining place names on public lands. Chessman Ridge, The

Bartizan, Jericho Ridge, and Wasatch Rampart came into being with the creation of Cedar Breaks National Monument in 1933.

By the beginning of the twentieth century, most of the places, features, and settlements of Utah, including those of the High Plateaus, had been named and recorded. Still, the process is never-ending and continues today. Original place names are periodically renamed; the names of ghost towns struggle to survive; towns and outposts pop up along the shores of new reservoirs while others disappear from inundation; and local, state, and national parks are dedicated in the spirit of preserving history or natural resources. One of the most recent applications of Utah place names came in 1996 with the creation of the nation's newest national monument: Grand Staircase–Escalante National Monument.

So what's in a name? As Clarence Dutton was quick to note over a century ago in *Report on the Geology of the High Plateaus of Utah*, ". . . he who runs may read if his eyes have been duly opened . . ." The mountain biker who rides with "eyes open" will find the trails of Utah's Brian Head–Bryce Country are more than a mere network of dirt paths: they are windows to the past and a collection of Utah's rich history. The names of places and passageways bind the human spirits of past and present with that of nature.

Shape of the Land: Geology & Natural History

Three of the nation's most pronounced physiographic regions converge upon Utah: the Central Rocky Mountains (the Wasatch and Uinta Mountains in the north), the Colorado Plateau (canyon country in the southeast and extreme southwest), and the Basin and Range (the west desert's alternating mountains and valleys). A fourth topographic region, Utah's High Plateaus, forms a transition zone between the Colorado Plateau and the Basin and Range. This band of eight lofty tablelands rises to elevations between 8,000–11,000 feet and fills the state's central and south-central territories. They display both layer-cake sedimentary geology, typical of the Colorado Plateau, and uplift along north-south trending faults, characteristic of the Basin and Range. Many are capped with a veneer of volcanic rocks that emanated from both local and regional centers. Of the High Plateaus, the southernmost assemblage is especially striking. Here the Markagunt, Paunsagunt, and Table Cliff Plateaus are rimmed mutually by the colorful and ornately eroded Pink Cliffs. Major John Wesley Powell named the Pink Cliffs during his explorations of the Colorado River in 1869 and 1871–1872, but his protégé, Captain Clarence E. Dutton, studied them in detail a decade later and published his findings in 1880 in *Report on the Geology of the High Plateaus of Utah.*

Dutton systematically surveyed the High Plateaus and made revelations about their geology and structure that endure today. He surmised that the great landmasses of the High Plateaus were mere remnants of the "immense denudation" of the adjacent Colorado Plateau to the south and east. Their very existence, he concluded, stemmed from the fact ". . . that the brunt of erosion throughout the [Colorado Plateau] is directed against the edges of the strata and not against the surfaces." Can-

Jim overlooks Zion National Park and the Grand Staircase from the Pink Cliffs at Strawberry Point.

yons and cliffs are the trademarks of the Colorado Plateau rather than broad pene-plains. But Dutton was quick to note that flat surfaces are not lacking, for the eye is forever falling upon

> . . . a vast expanse of nearly level terraces, bounded by cliffs of strange aspect, which are truly marvelous . . . They wind about in all directions, here throwing out a great promontory, there receding in a deep bay, but continuing on and on until they sink below the horizon, or swing behind some loftier mass, or fade out in the distant haze.

Nowhere is the principal of headward erosion more evident than it is in, what Dutton coined, the Grand Staircase. The Staircase is a series of broad terraces, each terminated by a line of cliffs, retreating to the north and rising in elevation from the brink of the Grand Canyon to the southern rim of the High Plateaus. When Dutton's eyes fell upon the Grand Staircase, he described the "sublime spectacle" with words more characteristic of a poet than of a student of science.

> We stand upon the great cliff of Tertiary beds [Pink Cliffs] which meanders to the eastward till lost in the distance, sculptured into strange and even startling forms, and lit up with colors so rich and glowing that they awaken enthusiasm in the most apathetic. Standing among evergreens, knee-deep in succulent grass and a wealth of Alpine blossoms, fanned by chill, moist breezes, we look over

"Clansmen in hiding:" the Kaiparowits Formation in Parowan Canyon.

> terraces decked with towers and temples and gashed with cañons to the desert which stretches away beyond the southern horizon, blank, lifeless, and glowing with torrid heat . . . Thirty miles away the last descent falls upon . . . an unbroken slope to the brink of the Grand Cañon.

Five massive sedimentary sequences comprise the Grand Staircase, and each has been named for the predominant hue of its exposed rocks. Stepping northward across the Kaibab Plateau from the rim of the Grand Canyon, the Chocolate Cliffs, also called the Belted or Shinarump Cliffs, form the first riser. These banded dark brown and tan rocks were deposited near the muddy margin of a shallow, oscillating sea during the early Triassic Period, about 225 million years ago.

The Vermillion Cliffs (Jurassic Period) rise above the Chocolate Cliffs. Marked by sheer walls colored rusty brown and flaming red, these 160–200 million-year-old sediments heralded in, what geologist William L. Stokes called, the great Red Bed Age. During this time, the ancient marine sea receded from Utah and was replaced by river flood plains, deltas, and coastal dunes.

Above the Vermillion Cliffs, the White Cliffs are the tallest scarps of the Grand Staircase. These Jurassic-age rocks, 135–165 million years old, form massive towers and beehive domes in Zion and Capitol Reef National Parks. They are the great petrified sand dunes that once drifted pervasively across southern Utah. Mountain bikers who have ridden Moab's famed Slickrock Trail know this rock as the Navajo Sandstone and revel in its sandpaper traction and wave-like form.

The Gray Cliffs are of such soft stone that they form a sequence of steep hills rather than perpendicular cliffs. These interbedded sandstones, siltstones, and mudstones were deposited 100–130 million years ago during the Cretaceous Period. Many individual formations constitute the Gray Cliffs, but as a group they record the advance and retreat of a fairly shallow sea. As you drive up Cedar Canyon/UT 14 or Parowan Canyon/UT 143, you'll recognize this sequence for its drab color, stringers of shale and coal, and strange dunce-cap shaped outcrops of pebbly sandstone.

Last, the vivid Pink Cliffs mark the top step of the Grand Staircase and are the focus of Utah's Brian Head–Bryce Country. Unlike the lower formations, which originated as either terrigenous or shallow marine deposits, these Tertiary-age, 60 million-year-old limestones accumulated as soft ooze on the floor of a freshwater body. The main basin of ancient Flagstaff Lake was centered over the present day Uinta Basin in northeastern Utah, but an elongate bay, called Lake Claron, extended southward and covered much of the High Plateaus. The limey mud and silt that piled up on the lake's floor formed the Claron Formation and is revealed today as the Pink Cliffs.

Continuing northward from the Pink Cliffs and across the summits of the High Plateaus, you encounter volcanic rocks that cap the sedimentary stack. Black, basaltic lava flowed from local volcanic vents or was ejected from cinder cones. These desolate magmatic rocks interrupt the plateau's charming forest, most notably around Navajo and Panguitch Lakes. A very different igneous rock crowns Brian Head Peak and the Sidney Peaks ridge. These Tertiary-age ash flows and breccias were more silicic, viscous, and thicker than the runny basalt lavas and were exploded from larger composite or stratosvolcanoes, perhaps from the vicinity of the Tushar Mountains 60 miles to the north. Although their weathered surface is dark gray, a cleanly fractured plane reveals a pale purple tint and tiny, distinct crystals.

Although the rock chapters of the Grand Staircase span nearly 200 million years of the earth's history, the shape of Utah's Brian Head–Bryce Country did not evolve until very recently in geologic time. The placid scene in southern Utah, post-dating Lake Claron, was one of low-lying uplands and open valleys. Erosion and deposition occurred at slow rates. About 25 million years ago, the entire western United States began to rise in response to widespread tectonic forces. The land over Utah and Nevada, bowed gently upward, and the earth's crust stretched until it broke along huge north-south trending faults. Horst and graben topography developed over Nevada, characterized by linear mountain ranges separated by broad valleys, and the Wasatch Fault began its slow, steady displacement.

This period of rifting and uplift broke the land mass over southern Utah and hoisted the plateaus to alpine elevations. If you were to slice the earth's crust from Cedar City to Bryce (geologists call this a cross section), you would find that each plateau (the Markagunt, Paunsagunt, and Table Cliff) is separated by normal or rift faults. The relative movement across these faults is up on the east side and down on the west side. Thus, each plateau reaches its maximum elevation to the west and dips gently eastward. As southern Utah rose, erosion attacked cliff edges with ferocity.

Headward erosion gnaws at the rim of Bryce Canyon National Park.

Water is the master sculptor of the Pink Cliffs. It wears down the bedrock physically with a slow, relentless process. As rain falls, the impact of droplets dislodges individual grains of sand and washes them down slope. As runoff coalesces, flowing water can carry larger volumes of material or cause catastrophic erosion to exposed bedrock. Because these plateaus are high in elevation and are subject to frequent freezing and thawing, water that has seeped into cracks and pore spaces expands and contracts causing the rock to heave.

Water can alter the chemistry of a rock, as well, by dissolving or changing its mineral components. The Pink Cliffs are largely made of limestone, and the calcareous minerals are easily dissolved by water. But water does not attack these minerals uniformly. Chemical variations and impurities make different layers of rock more resistant or susceptible to weathering. The Pink Cliffs' classic "hoodoo" formations are the product of differential erosion where "hats" of resistant rock rest atop softer, more easily eroded layers. Repetitive columns of hoodoos occur when vertical joints are widened and deepened. In this badlands topography, erosion acts so quickly that thick, mature soil never forms, which further accelerates the process of erosion. Studies have shown that the rim of Bryce Canyon National Park is receding at a geologically rapid rate of 9–48 inches per century.

Climate

The elevation of Utah's Brian Head–Bryce Country ranges from a low of 5,990 feet in Parowan to a high of 11,307 feet atop Brian Head Peak, for a net change of a vertical mile. As a rough gauge, the temperature decreases approximately three degrees Fahrenheit for every 1,000 feet in elevation gain. So during midsummer, when

Storm clouds brew over the Markagunt Plateau.

daytime highs top 90 degrees in Parowan and Cedar City, temperatures atop Brian Head Peak barely break 70 degrees. Most of Utah's Brian Head–Bryce Country lies between 7,000–10,000 feet where the climate is ideal for mountain biking. Nighttime temperatures are pleasant at lower elevations, but above 8,000 feet, evening temperatures can be chilly. At Brian Head, elevation 10,000 feet, nights are often cold with temperatures dropping into the low 40s. Campers should have warm clothes and thick sleeping bags.

Utah is the second driest state in the nation; only Nevada receives less annual precipitation. Dry weather is the norm, but rainfall is not uncommon on southern Utah's High Plateaus. The abrupt rise of these flat-topped mountains effectively blocks eastward flowing storm tracts, and the rising warm air cools quickly to produce billowing cumulus clouds packed with moisture. Rain generally occurs as erratic afternoon storms, but wet weather can linger for several days when strong low-pressure systems dominate the region. When clouds build and storms threaten, temperatures can drop dramatically, and rain may become mixed with hail and even snow during summer months. It would behoove the bicyclist to pack rain wear at all times, even when the morning's sky is cerulean and cloud free.

Flora

A wide variety of plants inhabit Utah's Brian Head–Bryce Country, and their temperature-and moisture-dependant habitat can be an accurate gauge of elevation. The majority of Brian Head–Bryce Country falls within two life zones: the Transitional Life Zone (5,500 feet to 8,000 feet), also called the submontane belt, and the Canadian Life Zone (8,000 feet to 10,000 feet), commonly referred to as the mon-

Bristlecone pine (left); manzanita (right).

tane forest belt. Brian Head and Cedar Breaks National Monument enter the Subalpine Life Zone above 10,000 feet, and only Brian Head Peak rises above timberline to the Alpine–Tundra Life Zone.

At the lowest elevations within the Transitional Life Zone, only the most tenacious plants survive the warm, dry environment. Open fields are covered with black sage, rabbitbrush, and bunch grasses. Rolling hillsides are peppered with Utah juniper and pinyon pine—the state's most popular trees. Both grow 10 to 30 feet tall and form rounded, bushy crowns. Juniper is easily recognized by its green scaley branches, white-blue berries, and fibrous wood. Pinyon has short, stout needles and its cones produce delicious pine nuts. Gamble oak and bigtooth maple form dense thickets in shaded recesses and in gullies that receive intermittent runoff; cottonwoods and willows thrive in moist riparian areas.

Rising in elevation to the upper Transitional and lower Canadian Life Zones, at about 8,000 feet, the juniper and pinyon community (j/p for short) gives way to more robust trees. Of the conifers, the mighty ponderosa pine grows in pure stands on sunny slopes or mingles with Douglas-fir on shaded aspects. Both grow to majestic heights of up to 150–200 feet and are known for their fine lumber qualities. Ponderosa pine is easily recognized by its deeply furrowed, reddish-brown bark and four-to eight-inch long needles in bundles of two or three. The trunk of a mature ponderosa can reach five feet in diameter and its branches are widely spaced and massive. The bark of the Douglas-fir is also thick and furrowed but green-brown in color. Its large branches tend to droop, forming a pointed, narrow crown, and its short, flat, flexible needles are dark yellow-green or blue-green and grow in two rows. The cones of the Douglas-fir hang downward, which is contrary to other fir trees. Where the Pink Cliffs' pebbly limestone forms the soil's crust, greenleaf manzanita creates a charming ground cover, commonly in association with ponderosa pine. Its wavy, low-spreading branches are garnet red and tipped with glossy, bladed leaves. In the spring, manzanita is graced with pale pink flowers.

Fir-spruce-aspen forests are indicative of the cooler, moist climate of the Canadian Life Zone between 8,000–10,000 feet. The quaking aspen is the most common

Aspen leaves are cradled in the boughs of a subalpine fir.

deciduous tree and is emblematic of the Rocky Mountains. Its heart-shaped leaves, supported by thin flat stems, flutter in the slightest breeze and create a babble of summery noise. The bark is soft, smooth, and gray-white and often records the initials of passersby or the emphatic signature of a curious bear. Aspen leaves turn golden during autumn, but isolated stands turn deep orange to fiery red. White fir, Douglas-fir, and blue spruce grow mutually amidst aspens, and the deep shadows cast by the forest community inhibit the growth of shrubs or herbaceous plants.

As the Canadian Life Zone grades to the Subalpine Life Zone near 10,000 feet, the variety of trees is reduced to those that can withstand harsher conditions. Subalpine fir is the classic Rocky Mountain evergreen and forms narrow, graceful spires. The bark is often shiny silver-gray and its needles are short and stout with white lines on the top and bottom of each. Engelmann spruce grows to a tall, narrow conical shape with drooping branches. Its rust-colored bark develops a mottled appearance when coin-size patches flake away. Its needles give off an unpleasant skunk-like odor when crushed.

The bristlecone pine is the most amazing tree inhabiting Utah's Brian Head–Bryce Country. Bristlecones are considered the oldest living organism in the world; several specimens have been found to approach 5,000 years in age. They are found throughout the Southwest on high, barren, wind-swept slopes, and their gnarled shapes have been sculpted by wind, time, and other harsh environmental factors. On southern Utah's High Plateaus, major stands grow on the immature, pebbly limestone soils associated with the Pink Cliffs. Bristlecone pines are characterized by their multi-stemmed, malformed shape and by their twisted roots that sprawl across the ground's surface. Their wood is solid and dense. Their needles form charming, compact clusters at branch tips and resemble the bushy tail of a fox or a bottle brush. Bristlecones are often confused with the limber pine, which also grows in harsh ridge-top environments. But the limber pine is well named because its branches are highly flexible and can be bent into a knot without breaking.

Brian Head Peak and Sidney Peaks are the only locations in Brian Head–Bryce Country that rise above timberline to the Alpine Tundra Life Zone. Cool summers and long, severe winters inhibit mature soil formation and make the summit a place of dwarf plants and wind-resistant shrubs. Subalpine fir and Engelmann spruce grow in small isolated patches, and persistent ridge-top winds bend the limbs into "krumholz" or flag-shaped form. Common juniper is a low, sprawling, tangled bush that forms a basal mat around fir and spruce.

Why are the trees dying?

While biking the trails around Brian Head, you'll quickly notice that the forest is losing one of its most valued resources—trees. Since 1995, logging activity has increased dramatically, not because of man's hunger for lumber, but because man is trying to thwart the devastating effects of insect infestation. Spruce trees, in particular, are turning brown, losing their needles, and dying because they are infested with bark beetles. These insects, smaller than a grain of rice, are a natural part of the forest's ecosystem but have recently become an epidemic. A combination of natural factors over the years has weakened the trees' built in defenses to resist beetle attacks.

Bark beetles attack trees by boring through the bark and laying their eggs in tunnels they have chewed in the cambium, the layer beneath the bark. When the larvae hatch from the eggs, they feed on the cambium. The resulting burrows, called galleries, encircle the trunk and prevent the flow of water and nutrients to the tree, causing it to die.

Can anything be done? The spruce beetle could be allowed to run its course. But most of the trees in the infested area would die and eventually blow down. This would significantly alter the forest's ecosystem, adversely affect scenic qualities, and create a forest fire hazard. The Dixie National Forest is pursuing an alternate approach to reducing the beetles' impact by harvesting and removing the infested trees. Also, thinning overpopulated stands of trees may promote healthier trees by reducing competition for sun and nutrients. By promoting tree diversity through planting strategies, the beetles' food supply can be interrupted because beetle species feed on specific trees. The immediate result will be unsightly. But by addressing the problem now, the forest might be saved for future generations to enjoy.

Columbine (left); Indian paintbrush (right).

How does this effect recreation? Logging activities may alter or close trails and roads temporarily, but they will be reopened or rehabilitated as soon as possible. Bulletin boards, located at trailheads and at trail junctions, will inform you of current logging activity and of the status of trails; otherwise, inquire at any local bike shop. Be aware of helicopters hauling logs overhead.

Wildflowers endow Utah's High Plateaus; their blossoms brighten the mountain meadows and complement the striking color of the Pink Cliffs. Of the many species that bloom throughout the summer months, a few are especially attractive.

The eye-catching paintbrush is perhaps the most easily recognized flower in Utah despite its 14 species. It ranges from dry Upper Sonoran deserts to alpine tundra and varies in color from bright red to orange to sulfur yellow. Its narrow, wavy, colorful bracts top individual stems and resemble soft bottle brushes.

Several species of the sunflower family populate open meadows and produce bursts of bright yellow color. Mules ear, arrowleaf balsamroot, and heartleaf arnica, display common attributes: lance-shaped ray flowers surrounding a button of disk flowers. The name of each plant is indicative of the shape of its green basal leaves.

Fleabanes (daisies) and asters, both members of the sunflower family as well, are easily recognized by their disk-shaped arrangement of pale blue to bright purple ray flowers around a flat head of yellow disk flowers. The fleabanes bloom earlier than the asters and are distinguished from asters by their 70–100 ray flowers. Asters bloom throughout summer and often into early autumn. Sweethearts traditionally pick the ray flowers until one remains, which tells if love is true.

Reaching three feet in height, the bushy bluebell seeks moist, sheltered slopes and huddles among groves of trees at higher elevations. Drooping pendant blossoms at the tips stems resemble clusters of miniature hand bells.

Geraniums come in several species and colors and inhabit a wide range of environments from the juniper-pinyon community to the fir-spruce-aspen zone. These beautiful herbaceous perennials sport five beak-like flowers with conspicuous veins that guide pollinators to the nectar at the base of the petals. The white Richardson

An exhibit at the Paunsagunt Wildlife Museum.

geranium inhabits higher, moist elevations among fir and spruce; whereas the rose-lavender sticky geranium seeks a lower habitat.

The Colorado columbine brings a joyous response to any wildflower seeker. Its white central flowers curve inward as scoops and have long spurs pointing backward as counterweights. The petal-like sepals surrounding the flowers flare outward and are often tinted pale blue. These graceful flowers are found at higher elevations in moist environments.

Atop Brian Head peak, cushion phlox forms small tufts with tiny, huddled, white flowers. The diminutive tushar paintbrush, with its bright red leafy bracts, adds explosive color to the sullen rocky slopes.

Fauna

Wildlife abounds in both the Transitional and Canadian Life Zones. Scurrying among the brush are a variety of rodents, including the Uinta chipmunk, the golden-mantled ground squirrel, and the deer mouse along with the black-tailed jack rabbit. Prairie dogs stand watch over the grassy plains north of Bryce Canyon National Park. They appear statuesque while standing guard next to their burrows, but with a chirp and flip of the tail they warn the colony of approaching predators and then dart underground. The beaver is rarely seen in the open but its handiwork is evident in the mounded branches that dam streams. The hunters of the forest are sly and mostly nocturnal. Spying a coyote, badger, bobcat, or gray fox during the day is a rare treat.

Larger mammals find refuge among the alpine forest during the summer and migrate to lower, warmer elevations during winter. Mule deer commonly venture out to open meadows to forage, especially in Bryce Canyon and Cedar Breaks where they are protected from hunters. Pronghorn antelope inhabit the Paunsagunt Plateau's grassy plains west and north of Bryce Canyon National Park. The pronghorn is the fastest animal in the Western Hemisphere and is a close second behind the cheetah.

It can burst to a speed of 70 miles per hour or sustain 30 miles per hour for several miles. The unique, shiny black horns curve backward and inward in the shape of a heart with a short stub, or prong, on the leading edge. Elk are rarely seen but are known to inhabit the southern reaches of the East Fork Sevier River valley. Stirring a bedded herd brings a flurry of stampeding hooves and thrashing antlers. Cougar, also called puma or mountain lion, are few and elusive. They actively keep deer populations in check but are considered a nuisance when their native territory overlaps that of the ever-encroaching cattle and sheep.

Overhead, swifts and swallows dart for insects among the cliffs. The white-throated swift is likely the fastest flying bird in North America with diving speeds approaching 200 miles per hour. About the size of sparrow, the swift's long slender wings, curved backward like a scimitar, allow for high speed flight and sharp cuts. Woodpeckers and nuthatches are active among the trees; open meadows lure robins, bluebirds, and meadowlarks; and hummingbirds frequent sweet wildflowers in meadows or brightly colored feeders dangling from porches. Clark's nutcrackers are conspicuous birds because of their gray-black plumage and noisy demeanor. In picnic areas and parks, they appear tame, if not brash, and will pluck food from the plate of an unsuspecting picnicker. Perhaps the most familiar animal of flight is the common raven, which soars the sky in its Darth Vaderish plumage searching for small prey or for scraps left over from another's kill.

Pikas and yellow-bellied marmots make their homes among the bouldery cliffs and talus slopes near timberline. The pika resembles a tan-colored, tail-less guinea pig but is actually a relative of the rabbit. Well camoflaged and eluvise, the pika's presence is made known by a series of peculiar short squeaks that mimick the distant bleating of a young goat. The marmot, on the other hand, is amusing and highly visible. This rolly-polly relative of the groundhog often can be seen in the morning and late afternoon hours sunning itself on a rocky perch. When alarmed, it produces a familiar high-pitched chirp, darts into the rocky cover, and often resurfaces moments later to take a survey.

Mary emerges from aspens on the Scout Camp Loop.

MOUNTAIN BIKING (Stuff you should know)

Trail Etiquette

Webster defines *etiquette* as "... the forms [and] manners established by convention as acceptable or required for social relations ..." Etiquette, therefore, applies to tea parties as well as backcountry travel. When it comes to mountain biking, trail etiquette is a subject that cannot be overemphasized because your every action has an impact on the trail, on the environment, and on how you are perceived by others.

The following is a modified version of the "Rules of the Trail" by the International Mountain Bike Association (IMBA). Although it may seem lengthy, it boils down to basic common sense: *Ride Aware, Be Prepared, and Share the Trail.*

1. Ride on Open Trails Only

Respect trail and road closures and access restrictions (ask if not sure), avoid possible trespassing on private land, and obtain appropriate permits and authorization as may be required. Federal and state wilderness areas are closed to bicycles. Bikes must stay on established roads and designated bike trails in national parks.

2. Leave No Trace

Be sensitive to the dirt beneath you and practice *low-impact* cycling. Even on open trails, you should not ride under conditions where you will leave evidence of your passing, such as on certain soils shortly after rainfall. Avoid riding during muddy conditions. Bike tires can leave a groove in wet soils that will channel water flow and accelerate trail erosion. Stay on the trail and do not create new ones. Riding cross-country is destructive to vegetation and may tempt others to follow.

Pack out what you pack in, plus a little extra left behind from those less thoughtful than you.

3. Control Your Bicycle

Lack of attention for even a second can cause disaster. Excessive speed poses a safety threat to your fellow trail users; there is no excuse for it. Be ready to stop *safely,* and without skidding, at any instant.

Shortcutting switchbacks, skidding while descending or stopping, spinning your rear tire when climbing, and riding around water bars are examples of "bad form."

Bob shows good form cornering by keeping his wheels rolling and by not skidding.

Perfect your riding techniques and show them off to others. Riding skillfully is *cool*; riding recklessly is *lame*.

4. Always Yield the Trail

Make known your approach well in advance. A friendly greeting (or a bell) is considerate and works well. Show your respect when passing others by slowing to a walking pace or stopping alongside the trail. Anticipate that other trail users may be around corners or in blind spots.

5. Never scare animals

All animals are startled by an unannounced approach, a sudden movement, or a loud noise. This can be dangerous for you, for others, and for the animals. Give animals extra room and time to adjust to you. Running livestock and disturbing wild animals is a serious offense. Leave gates as you found them or as marked.

When encountering horses, use special care. If overtaking a horseback rider from behind, make your presence known well in advance (with a spoken greeting) and ask to pass. Wait for the horse and rider to pull off the trail safely; then pass slowly. Ask the rider for instructions, if you are uncertain what to do. When meeting a horse head on, pull your bike off the trail (preferably to the downhill side), and avoid making sudden movements or loud noises.

6. Plan ahead

Know your equipment, your ability, and the area in which you are riding, and prepare accordingly. *Be self-sufficient* at all times. Wear a helmet, keep your bicycle in good mechanical condition, and carry the necessary supplies for changing weather

Only you can prevent . . .
trail closures!

or other conditions. A well-executed trip is a satisfaction to you and not a burden or offense to others.

7. Respect Other Trail Users

Show courtesy and respect to all trail users, at all times. We all are members of the trail community, who are seeking the therapeutic value the backcountry offers. We all must learn to share.

Set a good example. Stop, dismount, and talk to fellow trail users. Your motivations are no different than those of other trail users, regardless of your method of travel. Show that you understand other trail users' needs, desires, and fears. Aim for a clean, quiet backcountry experience. Keep the trail as natural as possible.

Granted, this may seem like a lot to remember when your sole objective is to pedal through the woods for a while. If anything, remember this one point every time you ride: Just because you *can* doesn't mean you *should!*

Trail Access Policies

United States Forest Service and Bureau of Land Management

The Dixie National Forest and the Bureau of Land Management maintain an open policy toward mountain bikes. Bicycles are allowed on established trails and roads unless otherwise posted. Be aware that trails and roads may not be constructed or maintained specifically for bicycles and that you may encounter other trail users, including motor vehicles on some routes.

National Parks and Monuments

Bicycles are considered vehicles and are restricted to established roads that are open to motorists or to bicycle specific paths. Bicyclists must travel to the far right side of the road in single file and obey all traffic rules of motorized use. All foot and pack trails are closed to bicycles. Bicyclists may be required to pay a park entrance fee and to carry the receipt at all times.

Wilderness Areas

In the Wilderness Act of 1964, Congress defined wilderness as an area

> . . . where the earth and its community of life are untrammeled by man, where man himself is a visitor who does not remain . . . which generally appears to have been affected primarily by the forces of nature, with the imprint of man's work substantially unnoticeable.

Also, the Act contends that wilderness areas

> . . . offer outstanding opportunities for solitude or primitive and unconfined recreation . . . and may contain ecological, geological, or other features of scientific, educational, scenic, or historic value.

A long-standing argument has been whether mountain bikes are or should be allowed in designated wilderness areas. Proponents claim that bicycles cause no more degradation to the environment than foot traffic and far less than horses. They also assert that mountain bikes, although a mechanized form of travel powered by the human body, do not lessen the aesthetic quality of the wilderness experience sought by others. Regardless of the argument, mountain bikes are *not* allowed in designated wilderness areas as stated (indirectly) in the Wilderness Act:

Prohibition of Certain Uses:

> . . . there shall be . . . no use of motor vehicles, motorized equipment or motorboats, no landing of aircraft, no other form of mechanical transport . . . within any such [wilderness] areas.

Wilderness Areas offer much more than playgrounds for backpackers and equestrians. These areas are ecologic reservoirs, which provide habitat for plant and animal species that are intolerant to human impact. Great satisfaction can be gained simply knowing that these tracts of land remain unspoiled and that conservation practices are an important aspect of our society.

Instead of squabbling over access policies in wilderness areas, perhaps mountain bikers should learn to love wilderness areas for being sanctuaries of non-mechanized travel. Their very existence strengthens the claim that mountain bike access should be actively provided for on roads and trails on *non*-wilderness public lands. So if you have any energy left over from a long day's ride, get involved on a local level to secure current access privileges, to bolster the claim for the development of new trails, and to lend a helping hand during trail maintenance projects.

Ashdown Gorge Wilderness Area is the only federal wilderness area within this guidebook's area of coverage. Violators are subject to citation.

Brian Head Resort

Brian Head Resort operates and maintains its Mountain Bike Park from the Giant Steps base area. Mountain bikers must be aware that maintenance operations may occur at any time and in any area. Be especially watchful of any activity on slopes above you. All lifts, structures, and buildings are private property. Stay on trails designated as open to mountain bikes, obey all signs restricting travel, and do not trespass across lands posted closed to recreational uses or across private property in summer cabin areas. Stay clear of snowmaking equipment (pipes, valves, etc.).

Resort Rules:

- Helmets are required at all time when bicycling on the resort's trails
- Always ride in control
- Avoid biking alone
- Be aware of hikers on the trails and yield the right-of-way
- Littering will result in loss of lift pass
- Downhill riders always have the right-of-way
- Ride on marked and designated trails only
- Attach lift ticket to hand brakes or derailleur cables
- Tread lightly; locking brakes erodes trails
- Smoking is not permitted on the lift or on the trails

Caring for the Environment

"*Don't Waste Utah*," is the frank but effective slogan of the Utah Department of Transportation's beautification campaign. Whether you are mountain biking, hiking, backpacking, car camping, or picnicking, keep the area you are visiting beautiful and unspoiled for future visitors. It takes little added effort and virtually no extra time to "*Leave No Trace*."

Campsite Selection:

Whenever possible, camp at developed federal, state, or private campgrounds. Amenities, including water taps, picnic tables, fire pits, tent pads, trash pickup, and outhouses, are worth the nominal fee. If you camp in the backcountry, choose a site in a wooded area and, preferably, a site that has been used previously. Camping in meadows damages delicate plant life and is aesthetically unpleasing. Also avoid riparian areas because the community of water-loving plants along streams is precious to wildlife.

Cooking:

Use a gas camp stove whenever possible rather than building a ground fire. If you must use a ground fire, use an existing fire pit instead of building a new one. If you must build a new fire pit, dig through twigs, needles, and sod until cool, moist soil is reached. Make sure there are no tree roots exposed in the bottom of the pit. A rock ring around the pit does little to prevent ashes from spreading, so resist building one. Collect only dead or down wood and think small. Bonfires are dangerous, especially during midsummer when forests are dry. Burn the fire to ashes and douse heavily with water until dead and cold. Finally, cover the cold ashes with the soil that was originally removed from the pit. (National parks prohibit the collection of firewood, even of dead wood that has fallen to the ground.)

Keep a clean campsite:

Items such as cans, bottles, and aluminum foil do not burn and their presence in a fire pit may cause subsequent campers to build new ones. Carry plastic bags in your vehicle and pack out all trash if garbage collection is not available.

Washing:

Never wash (body, bike, or cooking utensils) in a lake, pond, or stream. The introduction of mud, soaps, sunscreens, bike lubricants, and oils can pollute water sources that are critical for animals. Carry wash water away from the source, dispose of dirty water in a small hole, and cover it with dirt. Biodegradable soaps are most effective when rinsed off on land where soil bacteria can degrade it.

Trash:

If you made room in your fanny pack or vehicle to bring stuff in with you, then you certainly have the means to *pack it out*. Remember, the little things add up: candy wrappers, fruit peels, nut shells, pop tops, cigarette butts, etc. These items do not decompose readily. Carry a garbage bag in your vehicle for camp waste. On the trail, carry a zipper-top bag for leftovers and to help keep packs mess-free.

Human Waste:

Bears do it, cows do it, and soon enough you'll have to do it. Use trailhead facilities whenever possible; otherwise, pick a location several hundred feet away from water sources, trails, campsites, and other uses; then dig a small hole six to twelve inches deep in fertile soil, shallower in desert soils. Tissue paper should be packed out. (Burning tissue paper and burying it is acceptable, but it's a fire hazard.) Cover the pit with soil, leaves, and twigs.

Planning Your Trip

The trails in Utah's Brian Head–Bryce Country range from short jaunts just out of town to remote backcountry treks. While it is reasonable to adjust your preparedness for each ride, never underestimate your need for water and food, the prospect of rapidly changing weather, and the possibility of having to address a mechanical or health-related emergency.

Water and Food

Water and food are essential to life, and the lack of either one can turn the most blissful ride into an agonizing nightmare. Play it safe and overestimate your consumption of both; the added weight is trivial. Besides, if you have a little extra, you may be a lifesaver for someone who did not plan as carefully as you. Remember the old cyclists' axiom: Eat before you feel hungry, drink before you feel thirsty. Consume food and water at regular intervals, rather than one large binge midway through the ride.

Bike Maintenance and Gear

Because of their intended use under rough trail conditions, mountain bikes require regular maintenance. Check and clean your equipment before and after every ride. Repair or replace worn or broken parts immediately. Barring major overhauls, regular maintenance is easy and requires a minimal investment in tools and time. Learn the basic on-trail repair techniques (or ride with someone who has). Don't wait for a mishap on the trail to realize how little you know about your bike.

Tools and Repair Equipment:

Some people ride with just the shirt on their back, others seem to pack a complete hardware store. At the least, carry the "basic tool kit," which can be stuffed easily into a small under-the-saddle pack:

- Tire levers
- Patch kit
- Spare tube
- Frame-mount pump or compressed air cartridge

Now consider these extras:

- Multipurpose tool
- Chain tool
- Crescent wrench, pliers, or vise grips
- Flat head and/or Phillips screwdrivers
- Hex and socket wrenches
- Spoke wrench
- Duct tape
- Pocket knife

Still more stuff:

Spare brake and derailleur cables, chain lube, sunscreen, lip balm, water purification tablets, toilet paper, and zipper-top baggies for left over snacks.

A word of advice:

If you ride with a group, share the load, but stay close together or regroup often. It does little good for the lead rider to be carrying the pump and patch kit if another rider is a mile behind with a flat. If you ride solo, you may have to carry the whole works.

Accessories:

- Lock
- Cyclometer
- Camera
- Emergency Gear:
- Waterproof matches or lighter
- Compass and map
- Flashlight or headlamp
- Plastic whistle
- Emergency blanket
- First aid kit

Clothing

Clothing is a personal matter. Whether biking on or off road, the variation in cycling fashion is staggering—from no fashion (cut-off shorts, T-shirt, and running shoes) to pricey high zoot (aero helmets, color coordinated lycra, designer goggles, and shoe-pedal binding systems). Consider function as well as style.

- Helmet: Today's helmets are incredibly lightweight, well ventilated, and utterly vogue. (It fits your head better than the handlebars or rear rack.) Like the American Express Card, "Don't leave home without it."
- Padded bicycling shorts and gloves: Whether skin-tight lycra or cargo style, padded bike shorts cushion the bumps and prevent chaffing and blistering where you need it most.
- Shirt: A cotton T-shirt suffices during warm, dry weather. During cool or damp weather, synthetic materials like polypropylene, lycra, or a combination blend wick moisture away from your skin and dry quickly.
- Shoes: Lightweight hiking boots or mountain biking shoes have semi-rigid soles that provide support both in the pedals and on the trail.
- Extra layers: Layering is the key to maintaining a comfortable body temperature and preventing excessive perspiration while exercising, especially in cool or damp weather. Wear layers of synthetic materials next to the skin (polypropylene, lycra, CoolMax, or the like) and a nylon or breathable-

Some routes in Brian Head-Bryce Country take you to remote places that receive few visitors; prepare accordingly.

weatherproof shell on the outside. Cotton sweat pants and sweaters are poor choices for rainy weather.

- Rainwear: Afternoon thunderstorms are common in the High Plateaus, even if the morning sky is cloud free. Pack along lightweight rainwear or at least a garbage bag—just cut three holes for your head and arms.
- Eye wear: Not only are sunglasses and sport shields designed to be highly fashionable (an important feature for many bikers), they protect your sensitive eyes from the sun's harmful rays, passing branches, and flying debris. Make sure glasses are fastened securely with a retention strap.
- Sunscreen: For those who insist on riding as scantily clad as possible (to avoid embarrassing tan lines), sunscreen is a must. All the High Plateaus are at high elevation, and exposed skin can burn in less than one hour. Use a sunscreen with a minimum SPF (sun protection factor) of eight.

Potential Hazards

Health-related problems can result from lack of preparedness, inadequate physical conditioning, and plain misfortune. Weather conditions in the High Plateaus can vary between the extremes, depending on the season: sweltering heat in the lower valleys to cool, moist forests at middle elevations to frigid, wind-swept tundra atop ridges and peaks. Plan for current and forecasted weather conditions.

Lightning:

During summer, afternoon thunderstorms are common and they can be violent. Don't be fooled by the morning's cerulean sky. If lightning is proximal and strikes are frequent, get off ridges quickly. Seek shelter at lower elevations in valleys, between boulders in rocky slopes, or in heavily forested areas. Avoid shallow caves, open meadows, lone trees, or isolated tree clusters. Separate yourself from your bike. Then sit on a small rock with just your feet and buttocks touching the rock, preferably with insulating material in between you and the rock (foam pad or pack). Clasp your hands around your knees. If you are struck, the lightning may pass around your heart because of the insulation.

Sitting out a storm is a viable option. In many cases storms pass quickly, and your ride can be resumed. But think ahead by packing along rainwear. The best protection against being caught in a thunderstorm is to start your ride early and complete it by mid-afternoon.

Hypothermia:

The lowering of the body's core temperature is not just a winter-related health threat because air temperature does not have to dip below freezing for exposure to occur. Frigid mountain rains, wind blowing across exposed or wet skin, and lack of food and water can attenuate the onset of hypothermia. Symptoms of mild hypothermia include feeling deep cold or numbness, shivering, poor coordination, slowing of pace, and slurred speech. As hypothermic conditions worsen, a person may develop blueness in the skin, fingers, or lips; severe fatigue; irrationality and disorientation; and decreased shivering followed by stiffening of muscles.

Treat a hypothermic victim by seeking shelter and warmth. Remove wet clothes and replace with dry clothing, or cover the victim with wind-proof materials to prevent additional evaporative heat loss. Encourage the victim to ingest of warm fluids (non-alcoholic) and food or to move at a slow, steady pace to raise body temperature.

Heat exhaustion:

The opposite of hypothermia is *hyper*thermia (raised body temperature), which is caused by exposure to hot environments and over exertion. Blood vessels in the skin become so dilated to promote internal cooling that blood to the brain and other vital organs is reduced to inadequate levels. Symptoms include nausea, dizziness, mild confusion, headache, slight temperature elevation, and dehydration. The hyperthermic victim may or may not be sweating, and the skin may be cool to the touch. Cool the victim immediately by seeking shade and shelter. Wet the victim and fan vigorously, and encourage drinking cool fluids (non-alcoholic).

Altitude sickness:

Ascending to high elevations (nearly all of the High Plateaus) without acclimating may produce headaches, fatigue, loss of appetite, drowsiness, and apathy. (It's about the same feeling as a hangover.) Treatment includes rest, adequate consumption of fluids and food, and pain relievers. If you're visiting from low elevations, proceed very slowly at first or allow an extra day to adjust to the new environment.

Bad Water:

Water does not have to be visually polluted to be bad. Even the clearest mountain streams may be unhealthy to drink because of mine wastes, bacteria and viruses, or a single-celled organism called *Giardia lamblia*. This microorganism causes intestinal distress in the way of severe diarrhea, nausea, cramps, and loss of appetite. In short, it will make your life miserable for weeks if not treated medically. It becomes introduced to surface waters from animal and human waste. To be safe, avoid all surface waters and carry plenty of water with you. There are three effective ways to treat questionable water: boil it for 10–15 minutes, purify it through a filtration device, or disinfect it with chemicals (Potable Aqua, Globaline, or iodine).

Hunting Season:

Big-game hunting season in Utah runs from early September through the end of October, and much of the High Plateaus are prime deer and elk habitat. Hunters wear neon orange for a reason. You should do the same if you insist on biking off-road during the autumn hunt. Avoid the opening and closing days of hunting season, stay on main dirt roads, and forfeit remote singletracks.

Trail Description Format

Trail descriptions have been developed to provide the reader/rider with specific information in an easy-to-read format. Each description begins with a data box that provides the route's specifications. For those who want "just the facts . . .," this may be all that is needed. Next is an introductory paragraph, set in italics, which offers an enticing summary of the route. The main body of the description is where you'll find specific directions to guide you through the route, embellished with additional highlights.

Category Headings

- *Location:* General location of the route from the nearest town or city.
- *Length:* Total miles to complete the ride. Mileages noted in the description as bold (**mX.X**) correspond to mileages marked on trail maps.
- *Configuration:* Out-and-back: You ride from the trailhead to a distant location and return to the trailhead by retracing your tracks on the same path. Mileage is for the entire round trip.
- *Loop:* You ride from the trailhead to a distant location and return to the trailhead via a different route (or continuation of the same route). You always move forward across new terrain. Mileage is for the entire loop.
- *Point-to-point:* You ride from the trailhead to a distant location, where the route ends. Mileage is for the one-way trip from the trailhead to the trail's end. This type of route requires a vehicle shuttle. Don't forget your car keys!
- *Surface: Pavement:* Primary or secondary paved road. *All-weather road:* Improved dirt and gravel road—suitable for passenger cars. *Double-track:*

Infrequently maintained or unimproved dirt road, usually restricted to high clearance and/or four-wheel-drive vehicles—a "jeep" road. *ATV trail:* A narrow "doubletrack" open to ATV (all-terrain vehicles) and motorcycles. *Singletrack:* A narrow single path, i.e., a maintained or primitive hiking trail or a game trail.

- *Physical Difficulty:* Physical difficulty is subjective and reflects the amount of physical exertion required to complete a ride. Difficulty is relative *only* to other rides in the Brian Head—Bryce area, not to rides in other locations or states. *Novice:* Route is generally suitable for bikers who are new to the sport, ride infrequently, and/or possess only basic off-road riding skills. *Intermediate:* Route is generally suitable for bikers who ride periodically, possess good riding skills, and are usually game for a small adventure. *Advanced*: Route is generally suitable for strong bikers who ride on a regular basis, are acclimated to high elevations, and possess advanced bike-handling skills. Typically, these rides *go places. Expert*: Route is reserved for elite riders who have attained an indefatigable level of physical fitness and have Zen-like handling skills.
- *Technical Difficulty:* This is a measure of the level of bike handling skill needed or the likelihood that a rider will have to touch a foot down ("dab") or dismount to clear obstacles. Technical difficulty is based on, but not limited to, loose or embedded rocks, unusually steep ascents or descents, short radius turns, sand, ruts, fallen trees or limbs, exposed tree roots, water bars, and water crossings. Levels are low, moderate, high, and extreme.
- *Elevation Changes:* The high and low elevations for a route are given along with their respective locations. The trailhead elevation is given if it is different from the route's high or low elevation. **Gain** is the sum of all uphills encountered along the entire ride, *not* simply the difference between the highest and lowest elevations. For example, an undulating ridge ride (point-to-point) may have a low elevation of 9,000 feet at the trailhead and a high elevation of 10,000 feet at the trail's end. In between, however, there may be several climbs of 500 feet each. The *gain* for this ride far exceeds the net difference between the high and low elevations. Similarly, **loss** is the total amount of descending on a trail.
- *Maps:* United States Geological Survey topographical maps (1:24,000 scale) are listed. Trail maps are modified replications of topographic maps.
- *Land Status:* This category tells the ownership of the land through which the route passes.
- *Common abbreviations:*
  I-#: Interstate highway
  US #: Federal highway
  UT #: Utah state highway
  FDR #: Forest Development Road
  GWT: Great Western Trail

The **Options** category offers variations to the main route or additional biking opportunities in the area. The **Notes** category gives additional information pertinent to the route or area, including unusual hazards and cautions, applicable fees or permits, trail restrictions, nearby services, etc. **Access** provides concise directions on how to reach the trailhead.

An Introduction to Topographic Maps

He had bought a large map representing the sea,
Without the least vestige of land:
And the crew were much please when they found it to be
A map they could all understand.

Lewis Carrol
The Hunting of the Snark
"Fit the Second, Stanza 2"

In whatever form, maps are simply drawings of the earth's surface: its physical and cultural features. The trail maps in this guidebook are reproduced (and modified) *topographic maps* published by the United States Geological Survey. Understandably, "topos" can be confusing at first glance because they seem to have more lines than a spider's web. But the information they provide about distance *and* elevation change (topography) is indispensable. From a topo map, you can determine how long a hill is and how steep it is.

The trademark of topographic maps is "contour lines." These continually curving lines represent points of equal elevation above sea level. The "contour interval" (stated at the bottom of the map) tells how many vertical feet are between successive contours. The contour interval is usually 40 feet on 7.5 minute, 1:24,000 scale topographic maps, where 1 inch on the map equals 24,000 inches on the ground (.38 mile). On 1:100,000 scale metric topographic maps, the contour interval is 50 meters. Huh?

Envision an island. The shoreline around the island has an elevation of zero feet above sea level; mark it as the zero contour line. If the water level rises, successive shorelines would mark new contours, or levels of equal elevation. But instead of marking an infinite number of shorelines as the water rises gradually, mark a new shoreline (contour) when the water rises, let's say, every 10 vertical feet (contour interval). When viewed from directly overhead, you would see concentric shorelines, or contours, each marking an elevation change of 10 feet.

Now, pull out the calculator and look at a 1:24,000 scale topographic map. If a one-mile-long trail crosses four contours, you'll climb 160 vertical feet (assuming the map's contour interval is 40 feet). The grade is about 3 percent (vertical rise divided by horizontal distance multiplied by 100). That's an easy hill. If another one-

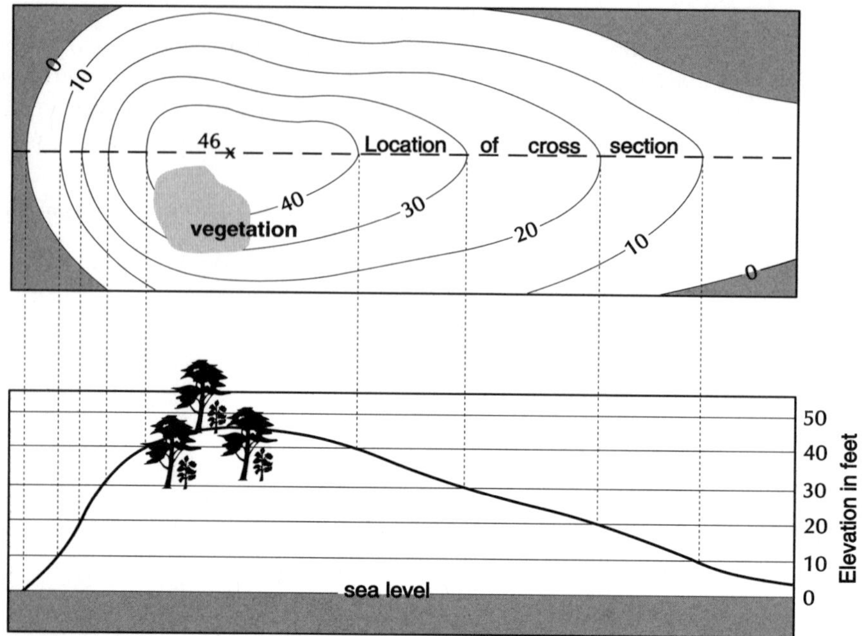

A basic topographic map.

mile-long trail crosses 40 contours, you'll climb 1,600 feet: a 30-percent grade. Yikes, where's the chairlift?

Remember these key points when viewing topographic maps: The closer together the contour lines, the steeper the slope. If contour lines merge into a single line, i.e., contour lines lie on top of each other, the hill has become a vertical cliff. Contour lines form Vs in valleys and gulches, and the apex of the V always points upstream. Where contour lines form pseudo-concentric circles (bull's-eyes), the smallest circle in the middle is the top of the hill or mountain.

Warning and Disclaimer

This guidebook is exactly that, a guide. It is not intended to be all inclusive or a substitute for good judgement and common sense. Mountain biking has inherent risks and dangers. Hazards, whether natural or man-made, whether mentioned in this book or not, can present themselves at any moment and under a variety of situations or may occur where one did not exist previously. Be aware of logging activity, heavy machinery, and helicopter tree hauling in the area or adjacent to trails.

Since it is impossible to estimate someone else's ability or attitude, to note constantly changing trail conditions, to foresee all hazards, or to accurately forecast seasonal or daily weather, each reader/rider must use his/her best judgement in determining where, when, and under what circumstances to ride a particular route, not

Tuck and roll . . . tuck and roll!

only to ensure his/her own safety and the safety of others but also to minimize environmental impacts. Pick your route objectively and plan accordingly; then *ride at your own risk!*

All routes presented in this book were deemed open to bicycles at the time of publication; *however*, access privileges, management policies, and land status may change without notice. The reader/rider agrees to obey all signs and policies regulating trail access, to obtain expressed permission to cross private lands, and to assume all responsibility and consequences resulting from the failure to do the above mentioned. In the case where trails cross private property, the landowners make no claim that the trails or any portions of their property are free of hazards.

Tom leads the way down the Dark Hollow Trail.

BRIAN HEAD-AREA RIDES

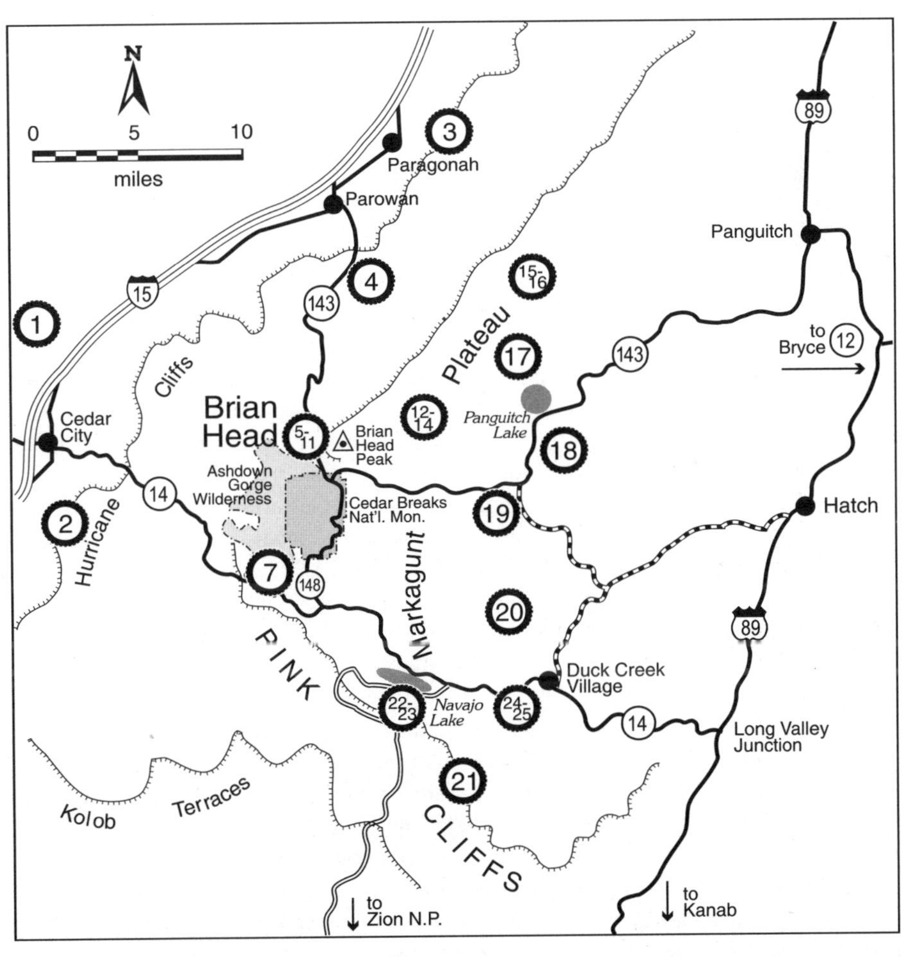

1 The Three Peaks

Location:	12 miles northwest of Cedar City
Length:	8 miles
Configuration:	Loop (counterclockwise)
Tread:	Doubletrack (optional singletrack)
Physical Difficulty:	Intermediate (one short, steep hill then gentle climbs on sandy doubletracks; route-finding and route-following skills required)
Technical Difficulty:	Low to moderate (dirt and sand doubletracks; one rocky descent)
Elevation Changes:	High: 6,140 feet (north end of loop) Low: 5,680 feet (trailhead and at south end of loop) Gain: 750 feet
Maps:	USGS 1:24,000 scale: The Three Peaks, Utah
Land Status:	Bureau of Land Management (Cedar City District)

Rising above Cedar Valley to the west, a trio of granitic knobs announces the beginning of the Basin and Range Province, which covers western Utah and and all of Nevada. The terrain of the Basin and Range is a repetitious pattern of narrow north-south trending mountain ranges separated by bleak, parched, table-smooth valleys. Some may find it to be a wasteland; mountain biker's find it to be a treasure for off-season riding.

The route below is a simple introduction to many days worth of riding at the Three Peaks. The loop follows doubletracks throughout and crosses a few of the desert singletracks that locals brag about. To fully experience the potential of the area, tag along with the Color Country Cycling Club on their next outing to the Three Peaks. They will convince you that singletrack doesn't have to pass through alpine forests to be exciting. Or sign up for the Utah Summer Games because the Three Peaks was the venue for its mountain biking race course in 1998.

From the parking area among the granite boulders, return to the dirt access road and turn right, heading due west toward a prominent peak labeled 6404 on the 1:24,000 scale topographic map. After 0.7 miles, fork right at a Y junction and pass a wire fence with its post tops painted white. (You may notice some cement slabs in the roadbed.) Ignore upcoming doubletracks forking from the main road. As you round the north side of peak 6404, you come to another Y junction. Actually, this is the eastern corner of a large triangular junction of three doubletracks. Fork right then right again at the northern tip of the triangular junction, and take the doubletrack northward. In the distance, you will see this doubletrack rising up onto low knolls about a mile away. That's your goal, so ignore doubletracks that attempt to steer you otherwise. One-half mile from the triangle junction, a narrow singletrack crosses your road. That's the Utah Summer Games cross country race course. You can pursue this trail back to the parking area after completing this loop. Climb the steep, rocky road up the knolls and collect your bearings (**m2.4**). (A singletrack forking right from atop the knolls is the Utah Summer Games downhill course.)

Now descend north then west, and pass below an old mine's tailings pile. (The road is rocky and rough.) Stay on this evident doubletrack until you arrive at a T junction with the "west side" road (**m3.4**). Whew! Did you make it?

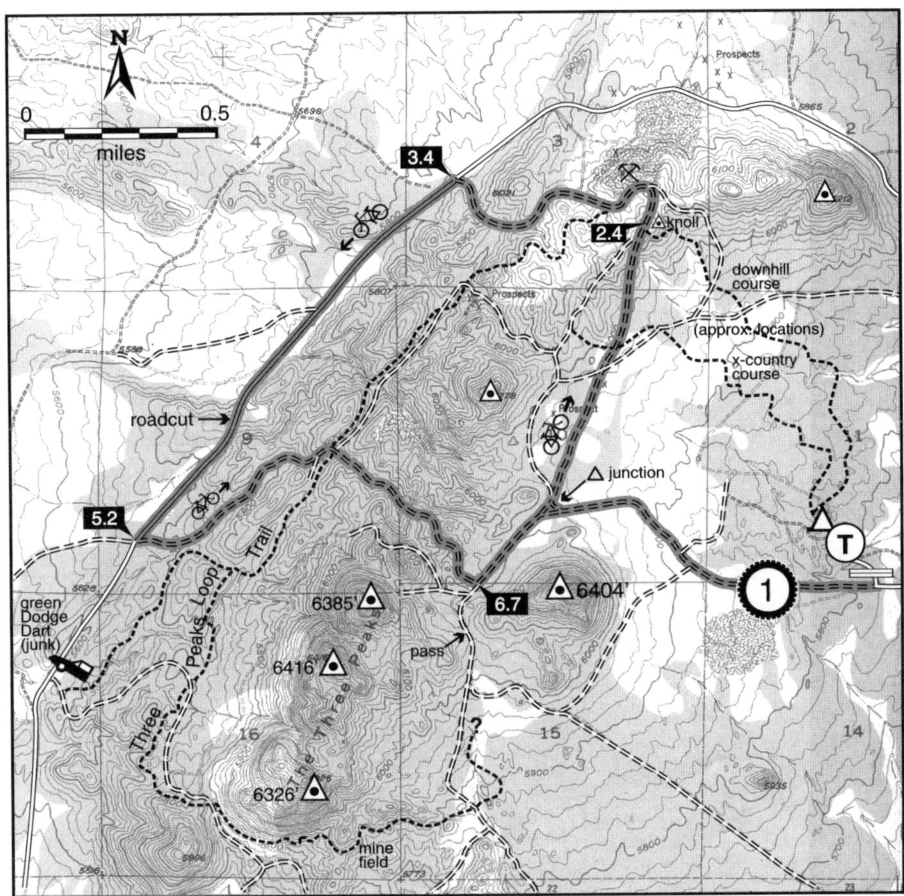

USGS 1:24,000 scale: The Three Peaks (20 foot contour interval).

Enjoy the easy pedaling southward on the smooth, wide dirt road; then climb a short hill through a road cut. After one-half mile of descending, turn left toward the Three Peaks on a doubletrack that crosses the west side road at an angle (**m5.2**). The track follows up a dry wash, crossing it several times. Just short of 1 mile up, a seldom traveled doubletrack forks sharply right. Ignore it but make note of it. As your road curves right immediately thereafter, look for a singletrack crossing the road. Look real hard. That's the Three Peaks Loop Trail (see Option). Continue slogging eastward up the dry, sandy wash until you come to a Y junction (**m6.7**). Head north around the west side of peak 6404 and return to the large triangular junction you encountered earlier. Return to the trailhead by backtracking or exploring the Utah Summer Games race course.

If you choose the latter, you're on your own. The course is difficult to map, virtually impossible to describe, but rates high on the fun-hog meter. You'll slash sagebrush and crash juniper boughs like a ski racer rounding slalom gates. A few

Lonnie and Mike outrun boiling storm clouds on the Three Peaks Loop Trail.

miles later, you'll wind up at the parking area after reconnoitering a maze of doubletracks.

Option: The Three Peaks Loop Trail

If you possess the uncanny knack of sniffing out primitive trails and relish the technical conditions associated with them, then you will love this 3-mile section of the Three Peaks Loop Trail. If you are tentative about pedaling faint cattle paths through nondescript sagebrush, then you will get lost for sure. Keep this one point in mind: the trail always crosses a doubletrack when it intersects one. Also, watch for telltale signs of the trail when it appears most faint: tire tracks, cairns often made of two small rocks, and rows of pebbles lining the tread sporadically.

Now, assuming you turned off correctly from the main route above, take the tire-wide path southward. Cross the dry wash after one-half mile and come to a Y junction lined with small rocks and marked with a cairn; fork left. (The right fork, the Green Dart Trail, descends toward the west side road.)

Follow parallel to and above the dry wash; and then cross it. The next mile is a test of your trail-finding skills. On the southwest flank of the Three Peaks, the trail crosses a prominent doubletrack that descends southeastward away from the peaks. Again, cross the doubletrack. Henceforth, the trail is easier to follow because it is often lined with rocks or marked with algae-green dots of paint. It wraps around the peaks' southern flank, climbing intermittently. Cross another doubletrack (not on the topo map) and enter the "mine field," where you must cant-and-ratchet through granite knuckles. One-half mile thereafter, the trail intersects a dirt road, the best since you started. Although the Loop Trail crosses the road and continues, it is even harder to follow. So take the dirt road uphill for one-half mile to a low pass on the south side of peak 6404. Now wrap around the west side of peak 6404 and return to the triangle junction you encountered earlier in the ride. Retrace your tracks to the parking area or explore the Utah Summer Games race course.

Specs.: 3 miles; 400-foot gain (approximate)

Notes & Precautions:

Save the Three Peaks for off-season; it's deathly hot in the summer. Singletrack trails are primitive and poorly marked. The Bureau of Land Management may develop these trails in the future.

Trailhead Access:

From Cedar City, drive north on Main Street and cross under I-15 at Exit 62. Travel north on Minersville Highway/UT 130 for 3 miles; then turn left/west on Midvalley Road (4800 North). Cross Lund (3100 West) after 3 miles, staying west on Midvalley Road (all-weather dirt) and crossing sage plains. Beyond the intersection with 4300 West (mailboxes and garbage bins), Midvalley Road becomes lightly improved and is suitable for passenger cars when dry. One mile after passing under the power lines, the road dips through a shallow hollow—the first downhill so far. Turn right 0.3 mile thereafter at a gap in the corner of a wire fence. Take the main track left to the granite boulders and park near the two, tall, wooden posts.

For more Information:
Cedar Cycle
38 E. 200 South
Cedar City, UT 84720
(435) 586-5210

Color Country Cycling Club
P.O. Box 416
Cedar City, UT 84720
(435) 586-7567

2 C Trail

Location:	10 miles east of Cedar City
Length:	4.5 miles
Configuration:	Point-to-point
Tread:	Singletrack
Physical Difficulty:	Novice to intermediate
Technical Difficulty:	Moderate (hairpin turns require precise handling or occasional dismounts; soft dirt with loose and imbedded rocks in tread)
Elevation Changes:	High: 8,400 feet (trailhead: Kolob road on Cedar Mountain)
	Low: 6,050 feet (trail end: Cedar City)
	Loss: 2,350 feet
	Gain: 100 feet (at most)
Maps:	USGS 1:24,000 scale: Cedar City and Flanigan Arch, Utah (trail is not shown)
Land Status:	Bureau of Land Management (Cedar City District)

The C Trail is a downhiller's delight. Except for two short uphill spurts, you could pop off your chain and virtually glide down from Cedar Mountain to Cedar City. But if you carry too much speed into any of the rough, angular turns (it's easy to do), odds are you'll pitch over the handle bars and become an ornament dangling from a tree. If you cruise at a slower pace, you'll enjoy a bird's eye view of Cedar City, overshadowed by the Hurricane Cliffs, and you'll be entertained by critters scampering through the brush.

Don't be hasty in your departure because the scenery and history of the area warrant your attention. The C Trail received its name from Cedar Mountain, thus the white-washed C on the mountain's slope. Mormon pioneers cut timber from Cedar Mountain to construct homes and buildings when Cedar City was founded in 1851. The C trail was dedicated in June 1996 to commemorate the Bureau of Land Management's 50th anniversary and Utah's statehood centennial.

The trail itself crosses the Hurricane Fault, which separates the Colorado Plateau Province (to the east) from the Basin and Range Province (to the west). The tectonic forces that broke the earth's crust are evident in the Red Hill far below at the mouth of Cedar Canyon. Here, huge blocks of layered sedimentary rocks have been tilted, broken, and juxtaposed. Westward across Cedar Valley, you can spot several iron mines, after which Iron County was named.

Directions are quite simple—head downhill through 100 turns. Along the way, you'll swoop around big bends at full speed and shake your bootie through little squigglers. But the majority are short-radius turns caked with loose dirt and pebbles that require counter balancing, prudent braking, and precise tire placement. A few turns require a track stand while bunny hopping to negotiate without dabbing a foot. If you accept the challenge and try to ride as many as possible, your handling skills will improve tenfold after just one ride.

About 2 miles down, be leery of a sharp right-hand turn in a wooded hollow. You'll have to slam your gears into granny mode for the hill that follows. Even if you are quick with the shifters, you'll be forced to walk up the pitch. But at least you

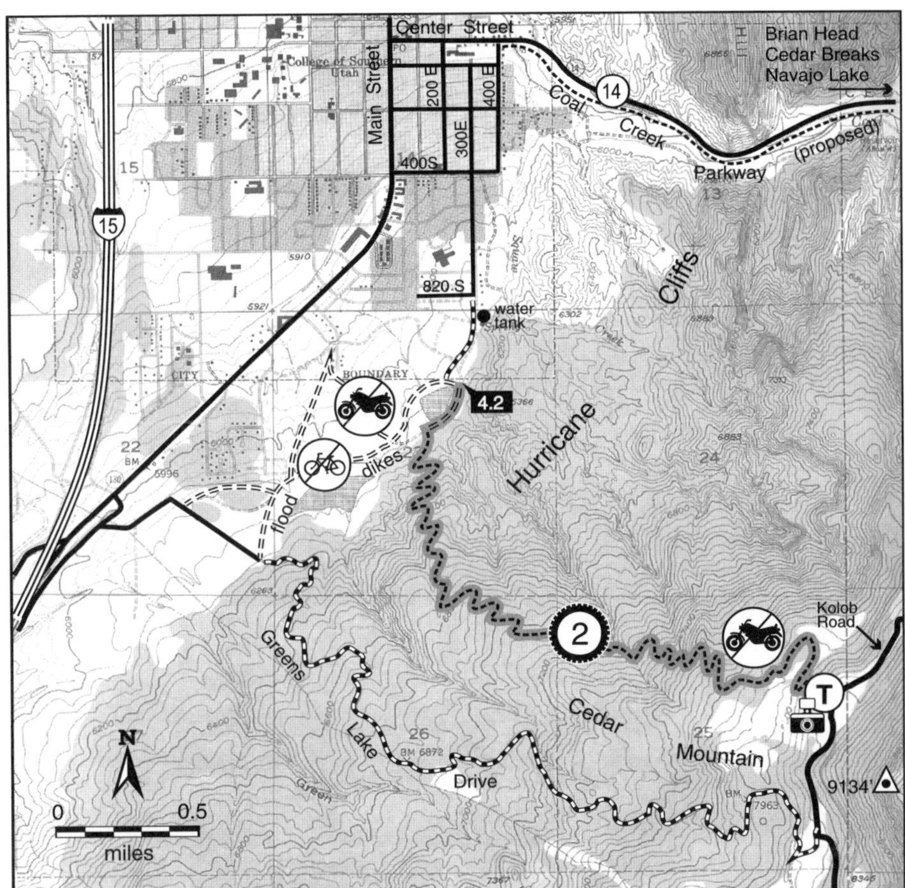

USGS 1:24,000 scale: Cedar City (40 foot contour interval).

won't be floundering in your big chain ring when you hop back on the saddle. When you reach the lower trailhead, fork right/north and take the dike road toward the water tank to reach the parking area.

Option: C Trail (out-and-back, er, *up*-and-back)

Locals are quick to note that riding up the C Trail is a "good workout." Because the trail has an average 10-percent grade, only your smallest gear will get a workout. The trail is mostly rideable. However, you'll be forced to walk countless turns unless, of course, you are a trials guru with Herculean legs. This out-and-back option is not intended for those who relish lounging on the chairlift at Brian Head Resort's Mountain Bike Park.

Specs.: 9 miles; 2,400-foot gain

Tilted strata of Red Hill can be seen from the C Trail.

Option: Cedar Canyon (loop)

A more realistic approach for those without a shuttle is to pedal 5 miles up Cedar Canyon on UT 14, and then climb 4.6 miles up the paved Kolob road to the upper C Trail trailhead. The highway is relatively easy. (Be cautious of traffic since the shoulder is very narrow.) The Kolob road, with its average 8 percent grade, will make you sweat. Pack along a lightweight jacket because the temperature on Cedar Mountain can be considerably cooler than it is in the valley, especially when you're drenched with perspiration.

Specs.: 16 miles; 2,400-foot gain

Option: Greens Lake Drive (loop)

If you frown upon letting your knobbies touch pavement, then this is the way to the upper trailhead. The climb is steady and steep, if not utterly mundane, with segments of gravel and washboard. From the lower parking area, return to the water tank and take residential roads left/west to Main Street. Pedal the pavement south and turn left on Old Highway 91, located just before the I-15 interchange. Curve right, and then turn left on Greens Lake Drive. Pavement to turns to an all-weather road at 550 West. Up you go.

Beyond the green water tank, a cautionary road sign warns motorists of 10 percent grades and sharp curves. (Heavy sigh!) Lower your head and grind out the miles. Half way up, Greens Lake Drive becomes Cedar Highlands Drive and passes exclusive homes. When you reach the paved Kolob Road, take it left a few hundred yards to reach the upper trailhead.

Specs.: 10 miles; 2,350-foot gain

Notes & Precautions:

This trail was built and intended for foot traffic; mountain bikers simply adopted the route. Thus, C Trail is not a race course. Ride attentively and courteously. Slow to a walking pace when approaching pedestrians or horseback riders, and always yield to other trail users.

Trailhead Access:

Lower trailhead: From the intersection of Main and Center Streets in Cedar City, take Center Street/UT 14 east and turn right on 200 East. Turn left on College Avenue then right on 300 East, and follow 300 East to 820 South, where pavement ends. Park here or take the dirt road south past the water tank to where it bends left and ends at a barricaded turnaround. The trailhead (proper) is about one-half mile south along the doubletrack. Upper trailhead: From the intersection of Main and Center Streets, take Center Street/UT 14 up Cedar Canyon 5 miles. Just before Milt's Steak House, turn right on the Kolob road up Right Fork Creek and drive 4.6 miles to the C trailhead.

3 Red Creek Reservoir

Location:	Paragonah (5 miles north of Parowan)
Length:	23.5 miles
Configuration:	Loop (clockwise)
Tread:	All-weather roads, doubletracks
Physical Difficulty:	Intermediate to advanced (steady, moderate climb up Little Creek Road; a few steep grades on rocky doubletrack approaching the route's high point; blazing-fast descent)
Technical Difficulty:	Low to moderate (minor gravel and washboards on Little Creek Road; rough, rocky doubletrack approaching the route's high point; some gravel and ruts on descent from the reservoir)
Elevation Changes:	High: 8,460 feet (junction with Horse Valley road) Low: 5,840 feet (trailhead: Paragonah) Gain: 2,620 feet
Maps:	USGS 1:24,000 scale: Cottonwood Mountain, Paragonah, and Red Creek Reservoir, Utah
Land Status:	Bureau of Land Management (Cedar City District) and Dixie National Forest (Cedar City Ranger District)

During the spring, you can carve some turns on the ski runs at Brian Head Resort in the morning, and then pedal this route in the afternoon. This lower-elevation ride begins in Paragonah, a sleepy hamlet that time forgot, and ventures through the colorful Hurricane Cliffs to the Markagunt Plateau's hinterlands. The route's namesake reservoir is stocked with trout and is a popular destination for anglers. During the warm summer months, you can refresh after the long climb by soaking your toes in Red Creek Reservoir or by taking the proverbial "Nestea plunge." The return leg to town is a speedy descent on a curvy doubletrack.

From the center of town, pedal north on Main Street/UT 271 for 0.7 mile, and then turn right on 700 North (all-weather road) toward Little Creek Road. (The junction is marked by a lonely stand of cottonwoods.) Cross the farm fields that fill the

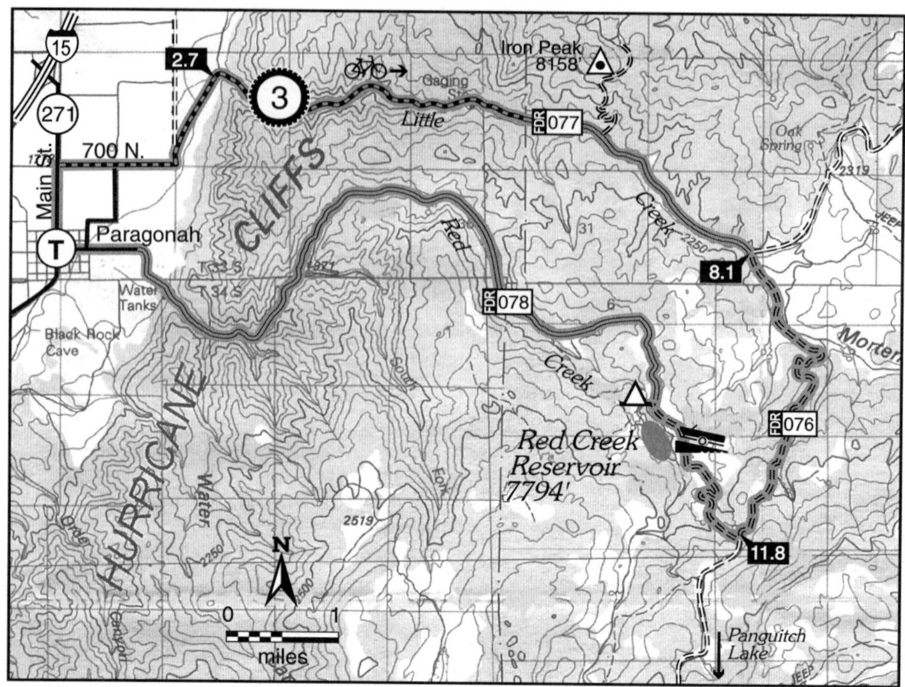

USGS 1:100,000 scale: Panguitch (50 meter contour interval).

valley, and bend left/north to follow along the base of the colorful sandstone foothills. (Do not take the doubletrack alongside the fence.) The sharp transition from featureless valley to steeply rising foothills is a sure indicator of faulting. Here, the Hurricane Fault has buckled the earth's crust and produced a seemingly impenetrable ridge running south to the Utah-Arizona border east of St. George.

Pass a small sign that indicates this route was part of the Old Spanish Trail from 1829–1848; then bend right and enter the Hurricane Cliffs on Little Creek Road/ FDR 077 (**m2.7**). The all-weather road rises gently but steadily up the redrock canyon for 5.5 miles. Notice how the surface of the road changes color from red-brown to gray. This color shift signifies a change in the surface geology from sandstone to volcanic rocks. Gradually, the forest changes from temperate-loving juniper, pinyon, and oak to pines, fir, and aspens, which prefer cooler climes higher up. Where the canyon widens, you'll see volcanic-capped Little Creek Peak to the northeast, rising to over 10,000 feet. Fork right on FDR 076, following a sign for Red Creek Reservoir and Panguitch Lake (**m8.1**).

After crossing the small pasture, the road narrows to doubletrack and rises steeply in stair-step fashion for nearly 4 miles. Just when you begin to lose patience with the rough conditions on each riser, the road levels and smooths but then repeats in this manner several times. The climb is complete when you reach the junction with the Horse Valley road (**m11.8**). Fork right on FDR 078, and descend the steep, pebbly doubletrack to Red Creek Reservoir. Pull up a piece of lakeshore for an afternoon

Cooling off at Red Creek Reservoir.

siesta or go for a breath-taking plunge. Finish off the loop by descending from the reservoir. The Red Creek road is a giant slalom course for fat tires, but use caution because patches of pebbles slide beneath your tires like ball bearings. Be alert to oncoming traffic because the road is one lane and motorists invariably shortcut turns. Upon breaching the Hurricane Cliffs, cool down on an easy stretch back to the center of town.

Notes & Precautions:

Paragonah offers no visitor services. Parowan offers all services, except a bike shop. Brian Head and Cedar City have the closest bike shops. Motorists may be encountered on Little Creek Road and the Red Creek road; motorists are less likely on the doubletracks near the route's summit.

Trailhead Access:

From I-15, take Exit 82 for Paragonah (5 miles north of Parowan and 27 miles south of Beaver). Travel south on UT 271 for 1.5 miles to the center of Paragonah. Park at your discretion. (The L.D.S. church parking lot is a good trailhead.)

4 Yankee Meadow Reservoir

Location: 5 miles south of Parowan, 9 miles north of Brian Head
Length: 13.5 miles
Configuration: Loop (clockwise)
Tread: All-weather road, doubletrack
Physical Difficulty: Intermediate (steady climbs)

Technical Difficulty:	Low (washboards and gravel on First Left Hand Canyon road, imbedded rocks near the summit, loose pebbles and ruts on Second Left Hand Canyon road)
Elevation Changes:	High: 9,000 feet (Second Left Hand Canyon above reservoir)
	Low: 6,600 feet (UT 143 at First Left Hand Canyon)
	Gain: 2,400 feet
Maps:	USGS 7.5 minute: Brian Head, Parowan, and Red Creek Reservoir, Utah
Land Status:	Dixie National Forest (Cedar City Ranger District)

Try this mid-elevation ride during the spring and the fall when trails on higher ground are snowbound. Although this loop does not follow the region's famed singletracks, it does showcase the area's awe-striking geology and fanciful rock formations. Yankee Meadow Reservoir is a fine location for a lunch break before rocketing down Second Left Hand Canyon. If you're a mountain biker/angler then pack your rod and reel because the reservoir is well-stocked with rainbow and cutthroat trout. This is a great out-and-back ride if lingering snow drifts prevent you from looping down Second Left Hand Canyon.

From UT 143, pedal up the First Left Hand Canyon road to the Vermillion Castle Campground. Here pavement turns to an all-weather road, which can develop washboards during prolonged dry spells and high vehicle use. The warm, dry climate at this low elevation suits juniper and pinyon, which are peppered about the canyon's sunny slopes. If you are geologically inclined, you'll recognize that the Kaiparowits Formation's gray-tan sandstone conglomerates comprise the basal unit in the canyon. Typically, these rocks erode to dunce cap-shaped hoodoos. As you pedal up the canyon, you move stratigraphically higher to the Claron Formation—the pervasive orange, pink, and white limestones that rim southern Utah's plateaus. The Grand Castle and Noah's Arc, north and south of the road, exemplify the glowing color and erosional characteristics of this formation.

After about a mile of moderate to steep climbing, the canyon opens to wind-rippled meadows bound by groves of quaking aspen. The charcoal-black palisades of the Sidney Peaks ridge loom overhead, and Brian Head Peak tops the Markagunt Plateau to the south.

Continue climbing to Yankee Meadow Reservoir (**m7.0**). When you've refueled your motor or hooked your quota of trout, continue climbing past the reservoir and enter the pine and fir woods. The road degrades to doubletrack spattered with small rocks, but pedaling is fairly easy. Where the road first curves left, step onto the knobby rocks nearby for an overview of Parowan Canyon and of the upcoming descent through Second Left Hand Canyon. Continue grinding your granny gears up several turns to the junction with the Second Left Hand Canyon road/FDR 048 (**m9.2**), signed "Parowan 8 miles (right)." Congratulations, you've made the "grade," so to speak.

From here gravity takes over with a vengeance: you'll reach highway speeds if you don't clamp down hard on the brake levers. Blaze past the Paradise Springs and Hendrickson Lake trailheads, while power sliding around sweeping turns. If you coast at a slower pace and lift your eyes from the road beneath your front wheel, you'll discover a lush, moist ecosystem thriving streamside. But a different world

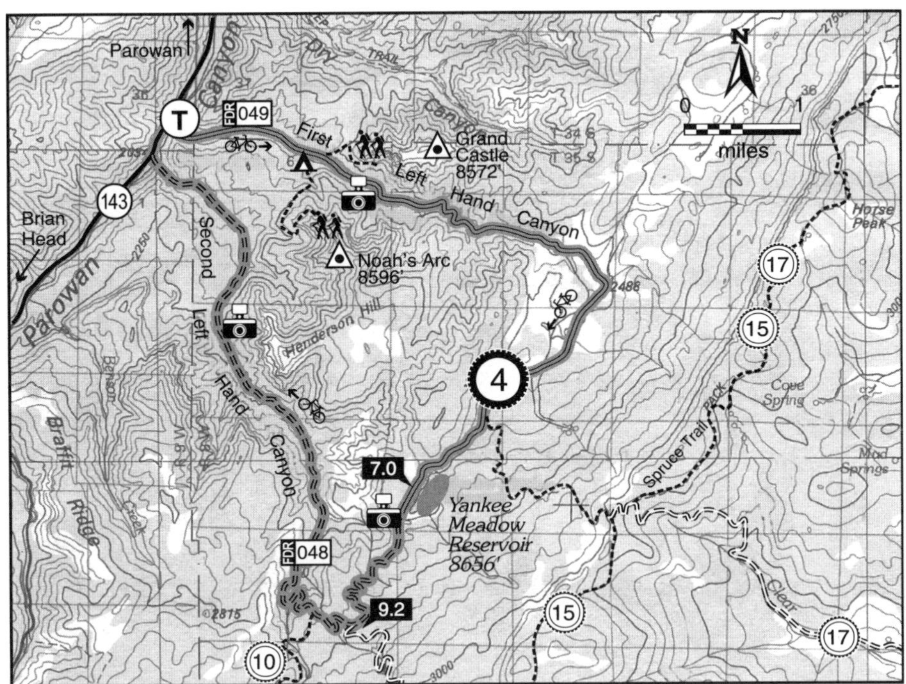

USGS 1:100,000 scale: Panguitch (50 meter contour interval).

exists away from the creek, one of dispersed ponderosa pines that cling tenaciously to steep, crumbly, limestone slopes. Only Dr. Seuss could conjure up these peculiar shapes: pedestals, anvils, teed-up golf balls, cone heads, and pyramids.

Two miles after exiting Second Left Hand Canyon, you come to the infamous Center Creek ford. Be prudent by checking the creek's depth before committing, or hurl yourself into the mix on a kamikaze bombing run. Either way, your toes will get soaked at the very least. Upon reaching UT 143, coast 0.5 mile to First Left Hand Canyon.

Notes & Precautions:

Be aware of motorists on the First Left Hand Canyon road; it provides the main access to Yankee Meadow Reservoir and the surrounding range lands. Traffic on Second Left Hand Canyon is infrequent and is generally restricted to high-clearance vehicles because of the rough, rutted conditions. The Center Creek ford at the bottom of Second Left Hand Canyon is usually rideable, but flow rates may rise dramatically during spring runoff and during storms. The Vermillion Castle Campground is a Forest Service fee area.

Trailhead Access:

From Parowan, take Center Street/UT 143 toward Brian Head. Drive 5 miles to First Left Hand Canyon/FDR 049, and park along the highway next to Center Creek

The Pink Cliffs enclose First Left Hand Canyon.

Reservoir. (From Brian Head, drive 9.1 miles down UT 143 to First Left Hand Canyon.) Alternatively, drive 1.3 miles up the First Left Hand Canyon road, and park at Vermillion Castle Campground.

5 Brian Head Town Trail

Location:	Brian Head
Length:	5.5 miles
Configuration:	Loop
Tread:	Machine-made dirt trail
Physical Difficulty:	Novice to intermediate (mostly gentle hills and descents)
Technical Difficulty:	Low (packed dirt with loose stones here and there)
Elevation Changes:	High: 9,970 feet (UT 143 at Sugarloaf Mountain Road)
	Low: 9,540 feet (trailhead: Navajo Lift)
	Gain: 430 feet
Land Status:	Dixie National Forest (Cedar City Ranger District) and private property (Brian Head Resort and Brian Head Town)

If you need to get from here to there around Brian Head, don't pedal the highway. Instead, ride the Town Trail. Completed in 1997 after many years of on-and-off construction, the Town Trail encircles Brian Head and provides convenient access to the many businesses and lodges along the way. But the Town Trail is more than an off-road link from door to door, it offers a quick retreat from the paved world into Brian Head's peaceful natural surroundings.

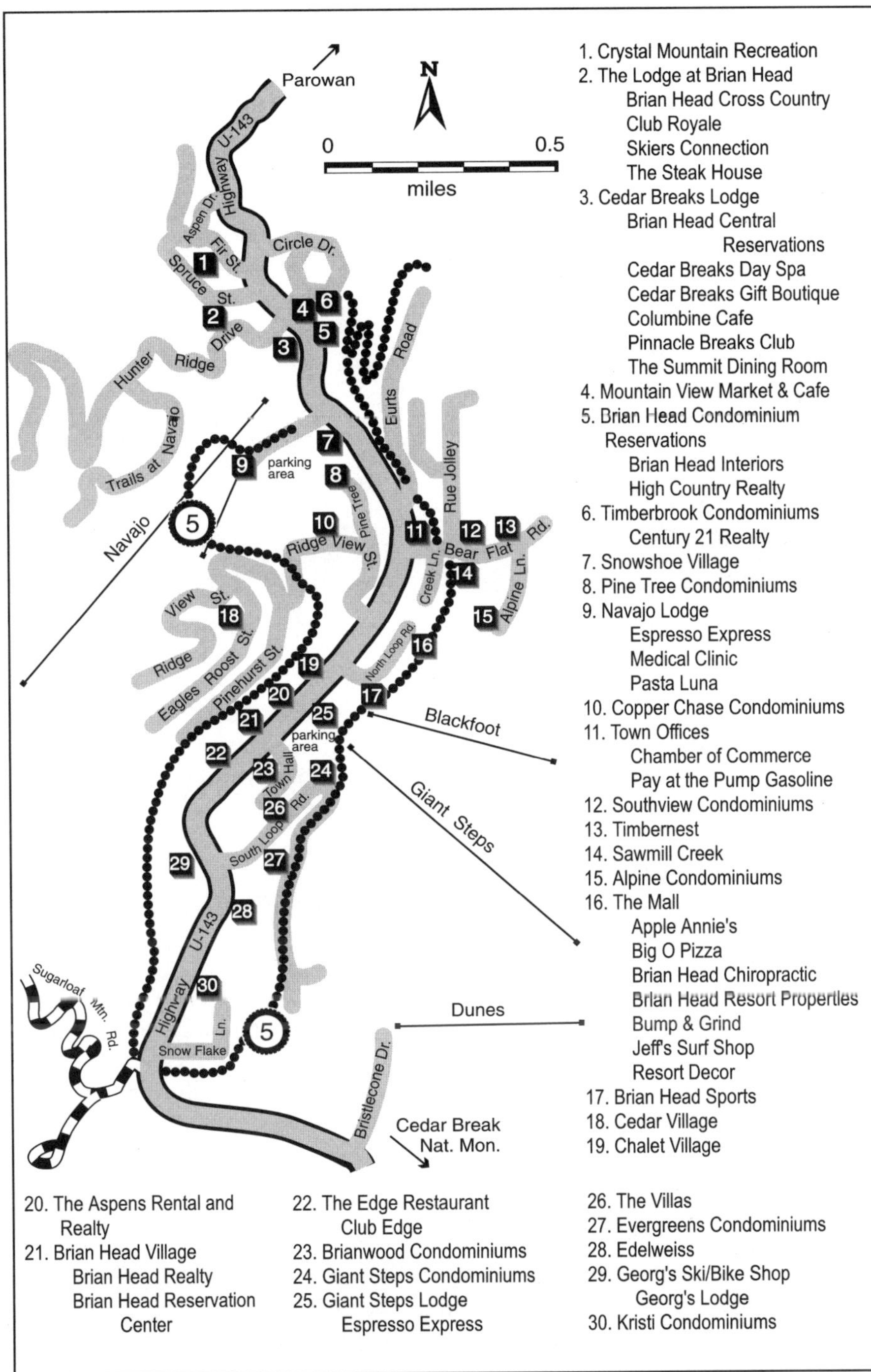

Map of Brian Head.

A group of bikers takes a break alongside Parowan Creek on the Town Trail.

For the full loop effect, start the Town Trail at Navajo Lodge and ride clockwise. The climbing is a bit more gentle on the east side of town. Cross the highway near Mountain View Market and Cafe and duck into the trees to escape civilization for a spell. The trail weaves through sun-dappled woods and crosses Parowan Creek before popping up onto Burt's Road. Take the path along the edge of Burt's road back toward highway 143; then veer left and go around the Brian Head town offices. Cross Bear Flat Road and wind behind the Mall until you reach Giant Steps Lodge. Past the lift and lodge, the trail follows South Loop Road for a bit then leaves the road and enters the trees. For a while, you'll pass through timber that has been logged to control the local bark beetle infestation. Cautiously cross highway 143 at Sugarloaf Mountain Road, and give a high-mountain yodel because you conquered the climb.

Now for the descent. Cross the meadow alongside the highway, and then wind behind Georg's Ski and Bike Shop and the Edge Restaurant. Follow Pinehurst Road, dart into the trees, cross Ridgeview Street near Chalet Village, and culminate the loop by coasting downhill across bunny slopes back to Navajo Lodge.

Notes & Precautions:

Don't leave the toddlers behind. The trail's six-foot-wide tread can accommodate a tag-along bike trailer. Use caution where the Town Trail crosses paved roads, especially highway 143 near Navajo Lodge and Sugarloaf Mountain Road. Pedestrians and horseback riders have the right of way. Slow to a walking pace or pull to the side of the trail when encountering bipeds and quadrupeds.

The Town Trail is not a race course, although it was used for the 12-hour mountain bike endurance race in 1997. If you're hellbent on full-throttle downhilling, head over to the resort's mountain bike park at Giant Steps Lift.

Trailhead Access:

You can access the Town Trail from just about anywhere in Brian Head—that's the whole idea. Still, main access points are the Navajo Lodge, Giant Steps Lodge, and Sugarloaf Mountain Road.

6 Twisted Forest–High Mountain

Location:	Brian Head
Length:	12.5 miles
Configuration:	Out-and-back
Tread:	All-weather road, doubletrack
Physical Difficulty:	Novice to intermediate (rolling terrain with gradual climbs, but one short agonizing hill near the route's beginning/end)
Technical Difficulty:	Low (minor gravel on dirt roads, some roots and ruts on the High Mountain jeep road)
Elevation Changes:	High: 9,940 (High Mountain)
	Low: 9,600 (trailhead: Brian Head Cross Country)
	Gain: 1,700 feet
Maps:	USGS 1:24,000 scale: Brian Head and Flanigan Arch, Utah
Land Status:	Dixie National Forest (Cedar City Ranger District)

Twisted Forest evokes childhood fairy tales of foreboding woodlands where spellbound country folk spent eternity. This Twisted Forest, on the contrary, is open, sunny, and brightly colored, and it welcomes curious travelers. When you walk through it, you'll mingle with some of the earth's oldest living species: bristlecone pines, which can live for over 2,000 years. The half-mile hike across the Twisted Forest takes you to a cliff-edge view of Cedar Breaks National Monument, Ashdown Gorge Wilderness, and Brian Head Peak. But don't be content here; pedal a few miles farther to High Mountain for an equally impressive panorama.

Head out from Brian Head Cross Country in the Lodge at Brian Head by coasting 0.2 miles down UT 14 toward Parowan. Turn left on Aspen Drive, bend right on Fir Street, and climb a short but crushing hill to Navajo Ridge. Where the pavement ends atop the hill (near Columbine Circle), stay on the main dirt road through the cabin subdivision, ignoring side roads. (Follow a small and utterly unobtrusive orange arrow nailed to a tree that is tagged "Dry Lakes.")

Bomb down off the ridge; then glide out of the woods, across the sage flats, and under the power lines to the junction with the Dry Lakes road (**m1.8**). Keep in mind, you must conquer this beast of a hill upon returning. If your legs are not willing to turn the cranks, don't fret; it's a quick and "mostly painless" walk with your bike in tow.

Turn left on the Dry Lakes road and enjoy easy pedaling through dense aspen groves blanketed with lush ferns and thick grasses. After 1 mile, the Dry Lakes road merges with the Sugarloaf Mountain road/FDR 265; stay straight on Sugarloaf. In a

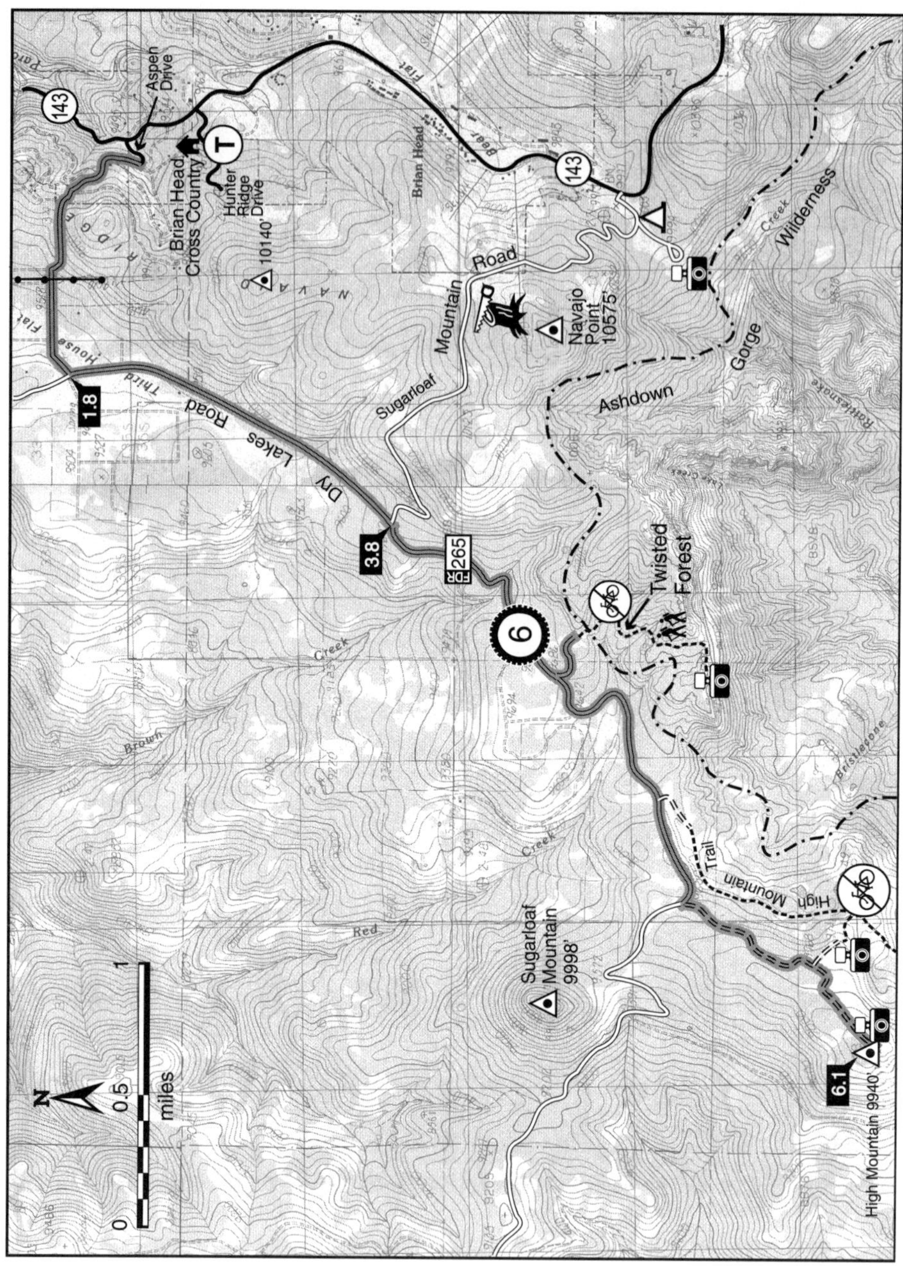

USGS 1:24,000 scale: Brian Head and Flanigan Arch (40 foot contour interval).

clearing 1 mile farther, fork left on a doubletrack (**m3.8**) and take it 0.25 mile to the Twisted Forest trailhead. Read the informative signs about bristlecone pines and local history; then stash your bike and take to foot. (Bikes are not allowed because the Twisted Forest is part of the Ashdown Gorge Wilderness.)

There's not much of a trail to follow through the Twisted Forest—you're free to hike wherever you please. To reach the Cedar Breaks viewpoint, set your bearings

Heading up to High Mountain.

east by southeast and your distance to about one-half mile. You'll know when to stop! Although bristlecones appear arthritic and feeble—with tangled roots, contorted limbs, and weathered bark—they are sturdy and stoic. Hug one and feel its time-worn energy. Bristlecones are found locally throughout the western mountain states and the highlands of the southwest in micro-ecosystems defined by specific elevation, climate, and soil type.

Return to the Sugarloaf Mountain road and continue south. Pass the turnoff for High Mountain Trail (wilderness access), and then pump up a short hill. Where the road curves right, fork left on the High Mountain jeep road and pedal up through the aspens. (If there is no sign marking the junction, look for a snowmobile decal tacked to a tree.) Exit the trees, and fork left to reach the viewpoint. Or continue uphill 0.4 mile to the summit of High Mountain (**m6.1**). Burn through lots of film if you're packing a camera; otherwise, gaze pensively until the salmon-colored cliffs and verdant forests are etched permanently in your mind. Enjoy the sunset, and then race back to town before darkness falls.

Option: Sugarloaf Mountain Road

An alternate route to the Twisted Forest is via the Sugarloaf Mountain road, which forks from UT 143 1 mile south of Brian Head Mall. Here the climb around Navajo Point on route to the Twisted Forest, is easier than the climb via Aspen Drive. But on the return leg, the climb around Navajo Point is long, steep, and drawn out. Also, logging activity has made this section of the Sugarloaf Mountain road less than visually appealing.

Notes & Precautions:

Time this ride for sunset when the Twisted Forest and Cedar Breaks National Monument are ignited with fiery color. The Twisted Forest is within the Ashdown Gorge Wilderness; bikes are prohibited. Since you must hike through the Twisted Forest, wear shoes that are comfortable for walking as well as pedaling. Use extreme caution along steep slopes and cliffs in the Twisted Forest. The limestone surface may crumble and break away. Sheep commonly graze the meadows of High Mountain.

Trailhead Access:

Start this ride at Brian Head Cross Country and Bike Shop in The Lodge at Brian Head, located on Hunter Ridge Drive.

7 Blowhard Mountain

Location:	10 miles south of Brian Head
Length:	7.5 miles
Configuration:	Point-to-point
Tread:	Singletrack
Physical Difficulty:	Moderate (mostly downhill; one modest climb around Wood Knoll)
Technical Difficulty:	Moderate to high (loose rocks and hairpin turns on narrow, steep trail descending off Blowhard Mountain; rocks, root drops, narrow tread in Moots Hollow; periodic dismounting)
Elevation Changes:	High: 10,600 feet (trailhead: Blowhard Mountain)
	Low: 7,600 feet (trail end: Moots Hollow)
	Gain: 200 feet
	Loss: 3,000 feet
Maps:	USGS 1:24,000 scale: Navajo Lake and Flanigan Arch, Utah (route is not shown)
Land Status:	Dixie National Forest (Cedar City Ranger District)

Blowhard Mountain Trail has been touted by locals and praised by national magazines for its camera-seducing scenery, extreme trail conditions, and big vertical drop. But in years past, Blowhard was an "outlaw ride" because it nipped the Ashdown Gorge Wilderness Area. Today, rerouted away from the wilderness, Blowhard Trail is perfectly legally, and it has maintained its stunning scenery plus a good chunk of its infamous singletrack to boot. The views of Ashdown Gorge and Cedar Breaks National Monument are surreal. Portions of the trail, especially the initial descent, are downright scary. The remainder is a joyous ride through lush forests broken by captivating views.

The classic Blowhard Mountain Trail is a 4-mile, point-to-point drop to the Crystal Springs road off UT 14 in Cedar Canyon. A new section of trail, constructed by the Cedar City Ranger District in 1996, extends the route another 3.5 miles to Moots Hollow for a total distance of 7.5 miles, as described below.

From the trailhead, circle counterclockwise around Blowhard Mountain on a new section of trail. Under the power lines, turn right at a large cairn, and then drop through steep, mostly rideable switchbacks. The brilliant color flashing through the

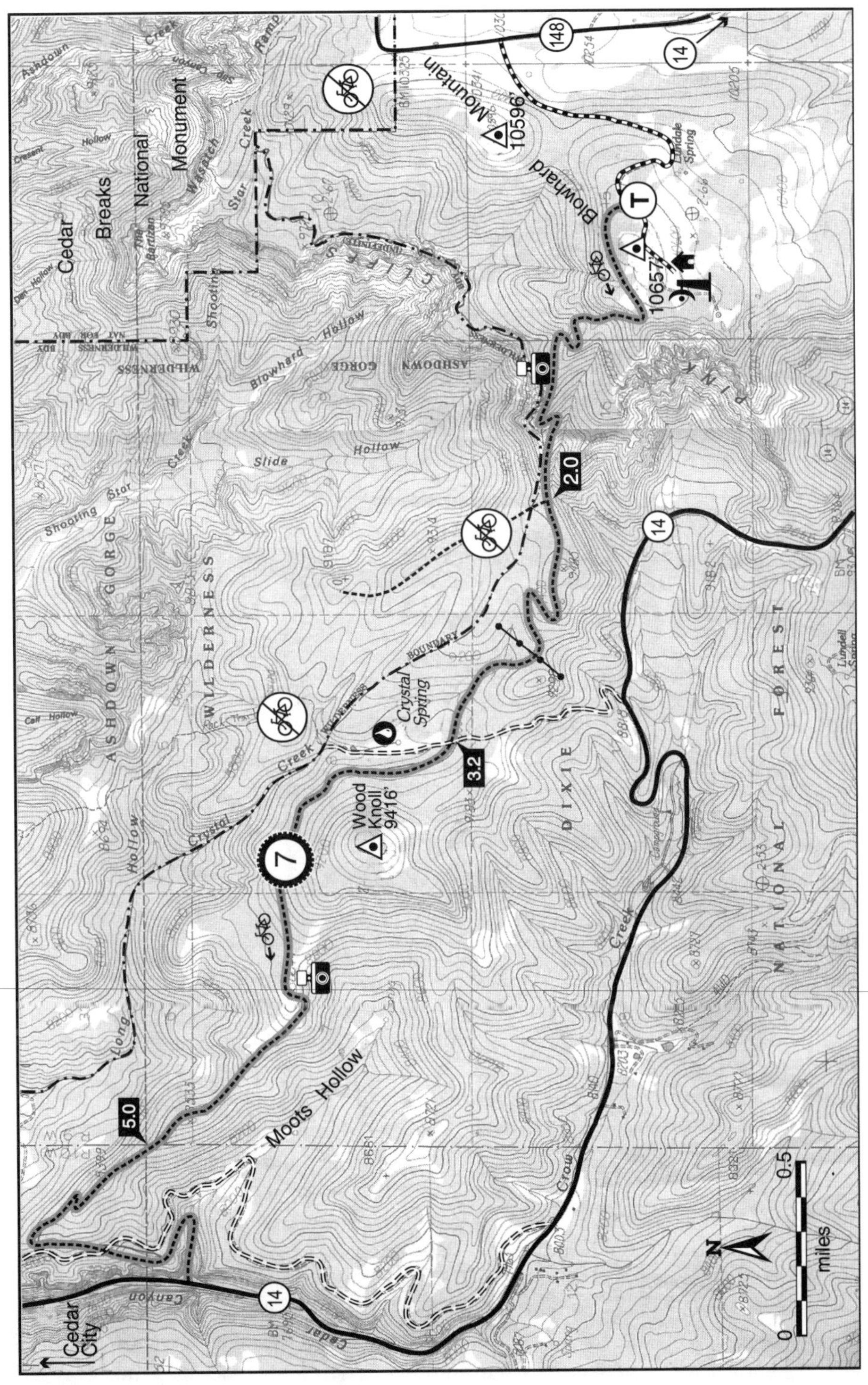

USGS 1:24,000 scale: Navajo Lake and Webster Flat (40 foot contour interval).

Mike peers into Ashdown Gorge from the Blowhard Mountain Trail.

trees hints that a spectacular show is ahead. Hang your butt *way* off the back of your saddle if you attempt to ride the quick but frightful pitch ahead. Afterward, the trail follows a knife-edge ridge overlooking ornately adorned amphitheaters of Asdown Gorge Wilderness and Cedar Breaks National Monument. Those suffering from vertigo might opt not to "toe the line" of the ridge because of the nearly 1,000 feet of vertical emptiness beneath you. Across the way, Brian Head Peak, Navajo Point, and High Mountain watch over the Breaks. Lower Ashdown Gorge, although sullen in color, is a mighty chasm into which the flaming formations funnel.

Follow along the ridge a few hundred yards, and then dive down the furrowed path over pebbly limestone and through angular turns. Ride what you can, but don't let machismo cloud sound judgement. Even expert riders can expect to dismount periodically. Beyond the Potato Hollow Trail junction (**m2.0**), the trail weaves through an opaque forest where sunlight has difficulty reaching the wooded deck. A mile farther, zoom down the power line doubletrack to the Crystal Springs road (**m3.2**). The trail brushes by Crystal Springs itself (enclosed by a log fence on your right) and then crosses the dirt road, continuing to Moots Hollow. (If you follow the dirt road to the right by mistake, you'll reach the Ashdown Gorge Wilderness boundary and have to backtrack. If you take the dirt road to the left, you'll climb a modest hill and then descend to UT 14 in Cedar Canyon. The latter is the "classic" Blowhard tour.)

The trail rises moderately through thick trees as it circles around Wood Knoll. Descend to and roughly follow a divide between upper Moots Hollow and Long Hollow where you can view Cedar Canyon and Kolob Plateau to the south and Ashdown Gorge to the north.

Cross the national forest boundary (**m5.0**), bank down switchbacks high above Long Hollow, and catch a fleeting glimpse of Ashdown Gorge, Brian Head Peak, and Cedar Breaks. Pass a sign for Blowhard Trail, and then descend to the doubletrack in Moots Hollow. The trail crosses the dirt road and culminates by following a rock ledge before plunging into lower Moots Hollow gorge. Use caution exiting the trail because it pops out suddenly on the shoulder of UT 14.

Notes & Precautions:

Avoid this route when it is wet or even damp, especially the short stretch on the Moots Hollow road. When wet, your wheels will become concrete doughnuts if you dare ride, and your shoes will turn to cement slippers if you portage. If you choose to loop back to the trailhead by pedaling up UT 14 in Cedar Canyon, use extreme caution; traffic can be heavy and the shoulder is all but non-existent. Do not park near or pedal around the FAA radar towers on Blowhard Mountain.

Trailhead Access:

From Brian Head Mall, drive 4 miles south on UT 143. Turn right on UT 148 for Cedar Breaks National Monument, and pass the visitor center. Blowhard Mountain road is 0.3 mile south of the national park/national forest boundary, marked solely by a stop sign. The signed trailhead is 1 mile up the all-weather road, before the FAA radar towers and work stations. Park off the road. To arrange a shuttle, drive south on UT 148 to UT 14. Crystal Springs road (signed) is 4.7 miles west on UT 14, between mileposts 13 and 14. Moots Hollow trailhead (unsigned and virtually invisible) is 8.7 miles west on UT 14 from the junction with UT 148, about 0.2 mile east/uphill of milepost 9. (Look for two pair of aspens at the mouth of a narrow gulch creasing the towering cliffs on the road's north side. Really. Park at the roadside pullouts.)

8 Pioneer Cabins

Location:	Brian Head	
Length:	5.3 miles	
Configuration:	Loop (clockwise)	
Tread:	Singletrack, doubletrack, all-weather road, pavement	
Physical Difficulty:	Novice (gentle and moderate hills)	
Technical Difficulty:	Low (gravel on Burts Road, some rocks on doubletracks)	
Elevation Changes:	High:	9,800 feet (between Pioneer Cabins and Bear Flat Road)
	Low:	9,600 feet (trailhead: Brian Head Cross Country)
	Gain:	500 feet
Maps:	USGS 1:24,000 scale: Brian Head, Utah (route is not shown)	
Land Status:	Dixie National Forest (Cedar Ranger District) and private property	

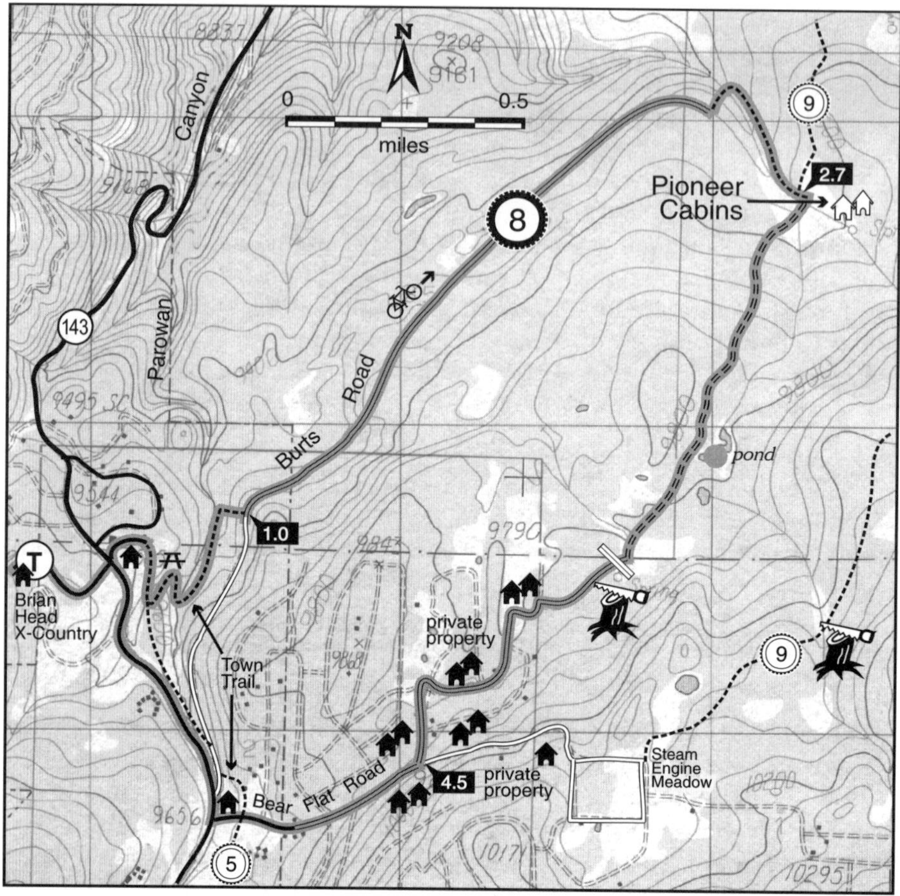

USGS 1:24,000 scale: Brian Head (40 foot contour interval).

The Pioneer Cabins loop is perfect for first-time bikers, families with children, or those needing to acclimate their lungs and legs to high elevations before embarking on more lengthy rides. The route begins on the newly constructed Town Trail and then passes two antiquated log cabins once occupied by homesteaders in the late 1800s. You culminate the loop by winding through modern-day cabins before racing back to Brian Head Cross Country on the highway.

From Brian Head Cross Country in the Lodge at Brian Head, coast down Hunter Ridge Road, cross UT 143, and pedal around Timber Brook Village Condominiums. Ignore the dirt road forking left; it leads to a private home. The Town Trail branches from the paved driveway behind the condos near the garages. Once on route, fork left following a sign for "bike trail" and enter the muffled, richly scented woods. Descend gradually through rustling aspens and stoic fir, and then pass a picnic table perched on a rock ledge above Parowan Creek. Ahead, cross a footbridge spanning

On route to Pioneer Cabins via the Town Trail.

the creek and continue weaving gently through the trees. A sharp, steep right-hand turn followed by short uphill require nimble handling and quick shifting. Turn left on "Burts Road to Nowhere" (**m1.0**), and undulate over low hills for about 1 mile to its end in the middle of, well, nowhere. The route continues as doubletrack to a creek crossing and then narrows to singletrack, which rises up a widening meadow bound by aspens on the left and conifers on the right.

As you near the top of the sloping meadow, trail signs will direct you to the right and across the field (**m2.7**). (A left turn takes you on the Scout Camp Loop in a clockwise, backward, direction.) But first, walk to the top of the meadow to visit the trail's namesake dwellings. These log shacks, built in the 1870s, were inhabited by pioneers who operated a dairy during the summer months. By about 1910, the dairy and cabins were abandoned. Now they are home to a cluster of aspens that have grown right through the roof.

Return to the trail junction, cross the field, and enter the trees to continue the loop on doubletrack. You'll have to climb a few rocky hills along the way, but the tranquility of these woods makes the effort painless. Pass a secluded, marsh-rimmed pond, and then break out of the trees to a meadow marked by a broken log fence. Go through two steel gates, which define private property, and enter woods that have been logged because of beetle infestation. Turn left at two upcoming intersections (the latter being a four-way junction followed by a notably rocky hill), and pass summer homes of varying design. Upon intersecting Bear Flat Road at a T junction (**m4.5**), turn right and coast downhill to UT 143. Return to Brian Head Cross Country via the highway, or peel off from the highway near the Burts Road junction for one last jaunt on the Town Trail back to the lodge.

Notes & Precautions:

Portions of this route cross private property. Please stay on track to avoid trespassing. Be aware of logging activity in this area.

Trailhead Access:

Begin at Brian Head Cross Country, located in the the Lodge at Brian Head on Hunter Ridge Road.

9 Scout Camp Loop

Location:	Brian Head
Length:	11 miles
Configuration:	Loop (counterclockwise)
Tread:	Singletrack, all-weather roads
Physical Difficulty:	Intermediate (rolling singletrack; two short, tough climbs)
Technical Difficulty:	Moderate (constantly twisting trail; short, rocky descents; one short, brutal climb loaded with rocks)
Elevation Changes:	High: 10,100 feet (Steam Engine Meadow) Low: 9,200 feet (Thunder Ridge Scout Camp) Gain: 1,400 feet Trailhead: 9,600 feet (Brian Head Cross Country)
Maps:	USGS 1:24,000 scale: Brian Head, Utah (most of trail is not shown)
Land Status:	Dixie National Forest (Cedar Ranger District) and private property

Scout Camp Loop is a Brian Head classic and has been the traditional course of the Brian Header Mountain Bike Race for over a decade. On Scout Camp, you trade the sweeping panoramas touted by other Brian Head rides for superlative singletrack engulfed by profuse aspen and fir. The first half is mostly a leisurely cruise on undulating trail that dodges, dips, and squeezes through dense timber. But on the "back nine," as you return to the trailhead from the scout camp, your legs are put to work on a variety of climbs ranging from gradual to gnarly. But all is fair in love and singletrack, and despite the required effort you'll love this singletrack.

From Brian Head Cross Country, coast down Hunter Ridge Road, cross UT 143, and go around Timber Brook Village Condominiums to pick up the Brian Head Town Trail. Follow the section for ATVs to the right and alongside the highway, cross "Burts Road to Nowhere" (all-weather road), and continue on the Town Trail to paved Bear Flat Road.

Mumble and grumble up Bear Flat Road, where pavement turns to rock-studded dirt. It's a tough little climb, especially at these elevations, because the oxygen-thin air seems to cut your fitness level in half. (Ignore spur roads leading to private homes.) After the road bends right and rises up one last pitch, fork left to enter Steam Engine Meadow (**m1.8**). The old rusted boiler marks the site of a sawmill that operated from about 1910–1930. Turn left/north at the steam engine, and follow the doubletrack into the trees, where the path narrows to a singletrack.

Dart through the woods like a slalom racer curving around ski gates, weighting the outside pedal to maximize your tire's bite. Shift gears precisely to maintain a smooth, steady cadence. Feather your brakes in anticipation of changing terrain to keep tires rolling fluidly without locking up. Whoa! Watch out for boulders and ruts that booby trap some turns; they'll buck those who are daydreaming. (Recent logging activity may alter your blissful experience.)

Skirt the edge of a small field, and then enter the more-expansive Muñoz Meadow. (Dark Hollow Trail joins from the right, exiting the conifers.) Here the trail veers from the meadow's center to its forested perimeter and descends steadily about 1

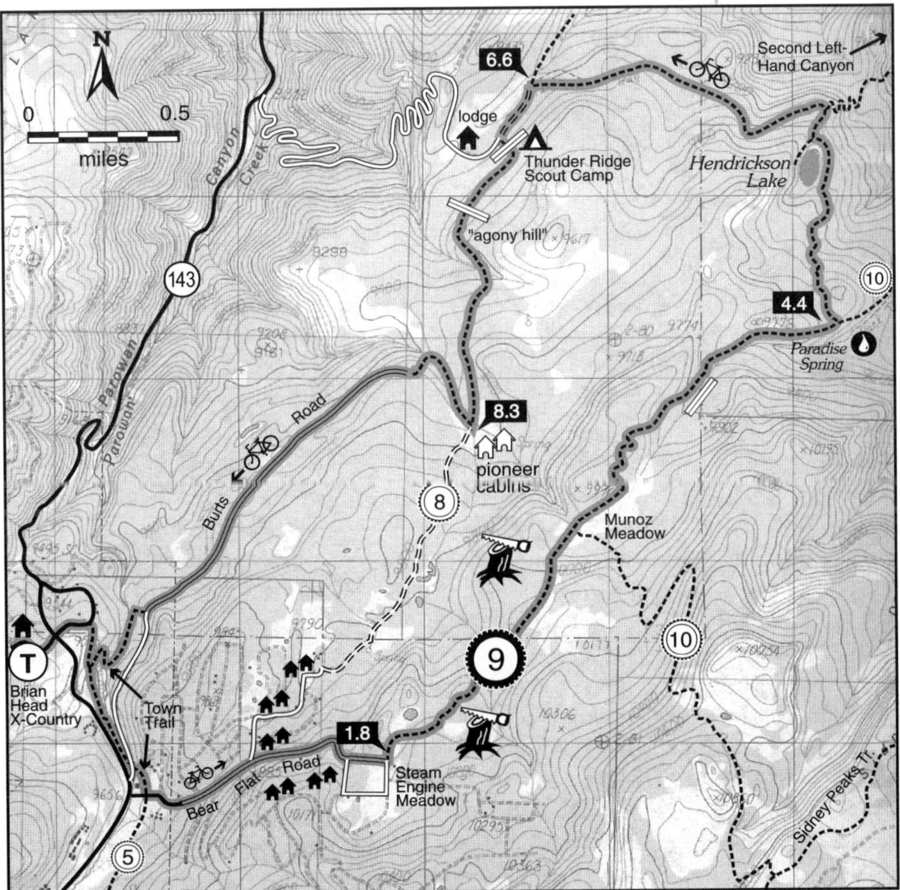

USGS 1:24,000 scale: Brian Head (40 foot contour interval).

Aspens enshround Hendrickson Lake on Scout Camp Loop's "back nine."

mile to a bed of boulders alongside a log fence. Over the next mile, the trail varies from tame and cushy to wild and technical. Fork left at the signed Paradise Spring junction (**m4.4**) toward Scout Camp and Hendrickson Lake. Downshift quickly or you'll stall mid-climb on the "sucker" hill immediately ahead.

More of the same awaits you—exhilarating roller-coaster-style singletrack whipping through aspen glades that flicker like a strobe light in your peripheral vision. Again, watch for hairpin turns, quick drops, and trail obstacles. Exit the aspens at a small clearing above Hendrickson Lake. Zig right on the main trail, passing Hendrickson Lake Trail to the left, and then zag left a couple hundred feet farther, passing a trail that drops to Second Left Hand Canyon. Ahead, the main trail undulates through fir trees that all but eclipse the sun overhead.

Exit the forest at the signed junction for Little Thunder Lake (**m6.6**), and take the doubletrack left/south alongside the meadow (Thunder Ridge Scout Camp). In less than 0.5 mile, fork left at a break in the log fence, signed "Brian Head 3 miles," and climb gently into the aspens. (You missed this turn if you reached the scout camp's headquarters. If you descended a steep dirt road to UT 14 in Parowan Canyon, you've gone *way* too far!) As you rise gently through the aspens, you might think "life is good on a mountain bike." Then you arrive at a steel gate that announces "agony hill," where boulders savagely chomp at your wheels. This little grinder is a test of your bike-handling skills, power output, and pain threshold. Thereafter, you climb gradually once more, and then come to a trail junction on the edge of a spacious meadow, signed "Burts Road (right), Bear Flat (straight)" (**m8.3**). Take a break from all the climbing, and visit a pair of turn-of-the-century pioneer cabins at the top of the meadow. Then take the singletrack downhill, cross a creek, and connect with "Burts Road to Nowhere." (See Pioneer Cabins, also.)

Take Burt's Road (dirt and gravel) about 1 mile, and then fork right on the Town Trail. You'll face a couple of quick climbs, cross a footbridge spanning Parowan Creek, and then pop out behind Timber Brook Village Condominiums to conclude the loop. Once again you might think "life is good."

Notes & Precautions:

Logging activity has forced rerouting of the trail between Steam Engine and Muñoz Meadows. Future logging and residential development may cause temporary trail closures and reroutes. Check with Brian Head Cross Country for updates. Be courteous when passing through Thunder Ridge Scout Camp and parcels of private property. You are a visitor.

Trailhead Access:

Begin at Brian Head Cross Country, located in the Lodge at Brian Head on Hunter Ridge Road.

10 Dark Hollow Trail–Second Left Hand Canyon

Location: Brian Head Peak to Parowan

Length: 14.5 miles

Configuration: Point-to-point

Tread: Singletrack, doubletrack, pavement

Physical Difficulty: Intermediate (all downhill except for two short climbs; strong forearms are required for continual braking)

Technical Difficulty: Moderate (smooth, twisting singletrack interrupted by short, rocky descents; loose surface on doubletrack; one usually rideable creek crossing)

Elevation Changes:
High: 11,307 feet (trailhead: Brian Head Peak)
Low: 5,990 feet (trail end: Parowan)
Gain: 100 feet (give or take)
Loss: 5,317 feet

Maps: USGS 1:24,000 scale: Brian Head and Parowan, Utah (Dark Hollow Trail is not shown)

Land Status: Dixie National Forest (Cedar City Ranger District)

If mountain biking is the frosting of life, then wallow in its sweetness on the Dark Hollow Trail–Second Left Hand Canyon tour. Brakes are your friend and gravity is your accelerator on this classic route. You begin atop Brian Head Peak at 11,307 feet (Utah's highest mountain biking trailhead) and end in Parowan after a 5,000-foot descent. Locals have appropriately dubbed this route the "Vertical Mile." Along the way, you'll drop from crisp alpine tundra through lush forests to toasty Sonoran desert—from Brian Head Peak's barren volcanic cap to Parowan Canyon's glowing redrock—all on blue-ribbon singletrack and raging doubletrack. As they say in the Old Milwaukee beer commercial, "it doesn't get any better than this."

Take in the view of Cedar Breaks National Monument from atop Brian Head peak before embarking on "The Vertical Mile."

Don't be hasty in departing from Brian Head Peak because there is much to see. Your eyes naturally gravitate to Cedar Breaks National Monument—a natural intaglio of cream, pink, and orange limestone carved from the plateau's forested edge. Cedar Breaks' 3.5-mile-wide, 2,000-foot-deep amphitheater is ornately adorned with spires and corrugated ridges, much like Bryce Canyon National Park, nearly 50 miles away, but to an immature degree.

From atop Brian Head Peak, you can survey other biking trails and locales: the resort's mountain bike park below, Lightning Point across the highway, Blowhard Mountain on the distant rim of Cedar Breaks, and Twisted Forest–High Mountain on the western edge of Ashdown Gorge. Sunset Cliffs, the pink ribbon drawn upon the eastern horizon, is the subject of nearly half of this guidebook's trails. The Tushar Mountains to the north, beyond the rolling plateaus, mold the skyline with alpine regalia.

Set out by coasting down the Brian Head Peak Road to the bend; then fork left on Sidney Peaks Trail. Take the ridge-top singletrack over tundra meadows and through patches of fir for 1 mile to the signed junction for Dark Hollow Trail. Turn left and plunge off the rim on a highly technical shot through hairpin turns. The trail mellows as it passes Mace's Run Trail and Cub Lake. (Lake is a generous term.) Dive back into the conifers and hold on tight for the thrilling descent to Muñoz Meadow (**m4.0**). (Had enough? You can bail out by heading left/south to Steam Engine Meadow and then descending Bear Flat Road to town.) In Muñoz Meadow, the trail has been relocated from the wildflower-endowed field to the aspens on the meadow's western perimeter.

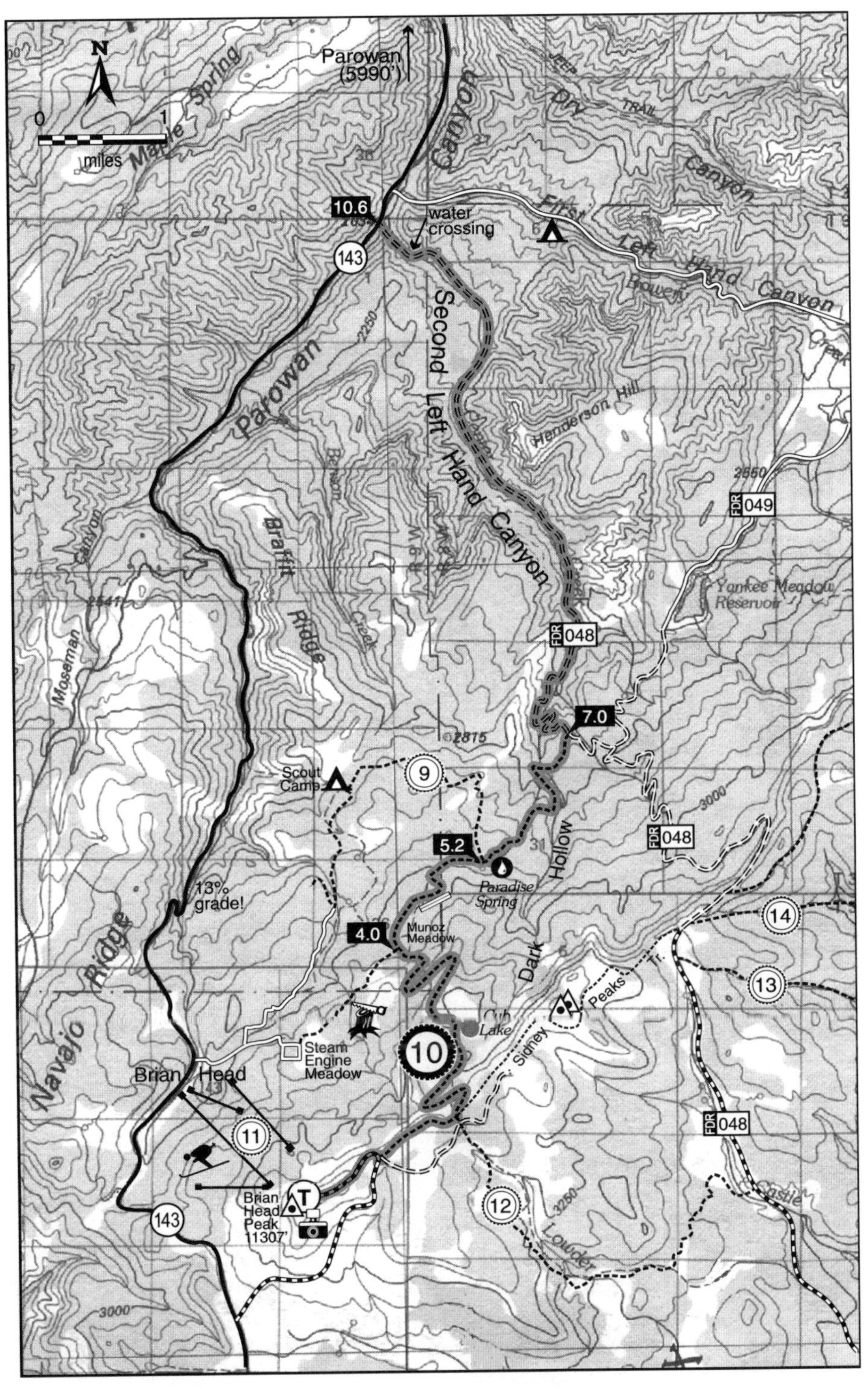

USGS 1:100,000 scale: Panguitch (50 meter contour interval).

Towering aspens engulf lower Dark Hollow (left); Edgar shows no fear crossing Center Creek in lower Second Left Hand Canyon (right).

Descend rapidly on the new trail to a log fence where you must pick your way through volcanic boulders. Ahead, you coast down a sweet trail that tickles your tire treads for the most part. But in places, you're tires will bash patches of rocks. One mile from the log fence, fork right toward Paradise Spring (**m5.2**). (The left fork leads to Hendrickson Lake on the Scout Camp Loop.) Aspens engulf the trail, and during autumn their golden leaves enrich the forest like doubloons. You'll encounter several rattling descents and cross a couple of newly constructed footbridges. Climb two rough hills that awaken your legs and lungs, and then drop to the Second Left Hand Canyon road (**m7.0**). You guessed it; continue descending as fast as you dare. But be wary of pebbly curves and tire-nabbing ruts.

Quickly, the cool alpine forest gives way to ponderosa pines, Douglas fir, juniper, and pinyon, which thrive in warmer climes. The nearby limestone slopes are drenched with orange hues the color of steamed crab. Only Dr. Seuss could conjure up the such peculiar shapes in the eroded limestone. As the canyon widens and the grade lessens, you approach the infamous crossing of Center Creek. A prudent biker will scout the miniature rapids before committing; a kamikaze will plunge headlong, emerging a hero or swimming like a flounder. You'll soak your toes, at the very least, either way. When you reach the highway (**m10.6**), coast down to Parowan for a plunge in the town pool while awaiting your shuttle. As you sit poolside, basking in the sun, glance up toward Brian Head Peak and reflect upon the poignant moto of the Adventure River whitewater company, "This place sucks . . . Let's stay!"

Option: Brian Head Peak Trail–Steam Engine Meadow loop

First let Giant Steps Lift carry you to the top of Brian Head Resort. Take Color Country Trail and then Brian Head Peak Trail around to the Sidney Peaks trailhead on the Brian Head Peak road. Ride Sidney Peaks Trail, and then descend Dark Hollow Trail to Muñoz Meadow, as described above. Take the singletrack left/south to Steam Engine Meadow, turn right on doubletrack, and descend Bear Flat Road to town. (See Brian Head Resort and Scout Camp Loop, also.)

Specs.: 8.3 miles; 400-foot gain

Option: Brian Head Peak Trail–Scout Camp loop

First let Giant Steps Lift carry you to the top of Brian Head Resort. Take Color Country and then Brian Head Peak Trail around to the Sidney Peaks trailhead on the Brian Head Peak road. "Bag" Brian Head Peak for good measure, and then ride out Sidney Peaks Trail, as described above. Descend Dark Hollow Trail to the Hendrickson Lake–Paradise Spring junction. Return to town by following the "back nine" of Scout Camp Loop. (See Scout Camp Loop, also.)

Specs.: 13 miles; 750-foot gain

Option: Parowan Canyon loop, a.k.a., the Brian Head Death March

"We Don't Need No Stinkin' Shuttle!" Skip Giant Steps Lift and pedal from the base of Brian Head Resort to the chair's summit. (See Brian Head Resort.) Take Color Country Trail and then Brian Head Peak Trail around to the Sidney Peaks trailhead on the Brian Head Peak road. No cheating—you must "bag" Brian Head Peak next. Ride Dark Hollow Trail–Second Left Hand Canyon all the way to UT 143, as described above. Now put your nose to the handlebar and hammer up Parowan Canyon to Brian Head, which is 9 miles and 3,000 vertical feet away. Piece of cake, you say? Just wait, the 13-percent grade through the S-turn will grind your quadriceps to hamburger.

Specs.: 25 miles; 4,600-foot gain

Notes & Precautions:

The flow rates of Center Creek at the bottom of the Second Left Hand Canyon road can vary, making the creek crossing either toe quenching or hub submersing. Also, the flow rates can increase both dramatically and instantly during sudden storms.

Trailhead Access:

First, shuttle a vehicle 12.5 miles from Brian Head down UT 143 to Parowan. Park at the town pool (300 North and Center Street) for an après-ride swim. Alternatively, park alongside UT 143 at Center Creek Reservoir near First Left Hand Canyon (between mileposts 6 and 7). Return to Brian Head, and drive 2.5 miles south on UT 143 to the Brian Head Peak road (Vista Point). Travel the all-weather road 3 miles to Brian Head Peak and embark.

11 Brian Head Resort Mountain Bike Park

Location:	Brian Head Resort (Giant Steps center)
Length:	Up to 16 miles
Configuration:	Point-to-point with chairlift access
Tread:	Singletracks
Physical Difficulty:	Intermediate to advanced (downhill trails require good handling skills)
Technical Difficulty:	Low to high (groomed trails range from baby-butt-smooth to rough and gnarly; sweeping curves and hairpin turns; gentle descents to hang-your-butt-off-the-back drops)
Elevation Changes:	High: 10,625 feet (top of Giant Steps Lift) Low: 9,760 feet (bottom of Giant Steps Lift) Loss: 865 feet
Maps:	Brian Head Mountain Bike Park (available at Brian Head Resort)
Land Status:	Private property (Brian Head Resort) and Dixie National Forest (Cedar City Ranger District)

Brian Head is renown for its downhill trails: Dark Hollow, Bunker Creek, and Blowhard Mountain to name a few. Brian Head Resort takes the lure of downhill riding one step further by providing chairlift service to its Mountain Bike Park. Choose from six trails that vary from idle cruises across the mountain's slopes to technical shots requiring exact handling skills. Although each trail has a unique character, they are bound by a common theme. Each offers scenic views across lofty plateaus to deep, colorful canyons and provides two-wheeled interludes with the alpine ecosystem. Ride the whole park, revisit your favorite trail, or use the resort as a stepping stone to explore neighboring trails.

Trail #1: Color Country Trail (3.7 miles, novice to intermediate)

Color Country Trail is the resort's main trail, and as its name implies, Color Country Trail is packed with vistas of the Markagunt Plateau. Since this route is relatively tame, you can enjoy these views while riding, without fear of "stuffing" your front tire.

From the summit of Giant Steps, exit to the right. Color Country Trail begins as doubletrack. Past the junction for Brian Head Peak Trail, the trail narrows to singletrack and then drops into a small fertile gulch. Pause for a minute, or at least slow, as you approach a bend marked with a picnic table. Here, your eyes fall upon a band of strawberry cliffs breaking from Navajo Point and upon Cedar Canyon in the distance. Ride across a small, elevated valley and drop to the Lightning Point Trail junction (left). Stay right and speed down Color Country Trail, but be alert to ruts and ditches in the trail. Pass under Dunes Lift, cross a dirt road, and arrive at Lake Drano—the water source for snow-making operations. Pedal clockwise around the pond on its cinder embankment. Once back in the trees, you'll dodge boulders that nip at your pedals.

Traverse ski runs under Giant Steps Lift and then come to a dirt road. The main route forks left as singletrack, which descends very steeply and crosses under the lift again. Culminate Color Country Trail by banking downhill to the base. (To extend Color Country Trail a bit, take the before-mentioned dirt road toward Roulette Lift

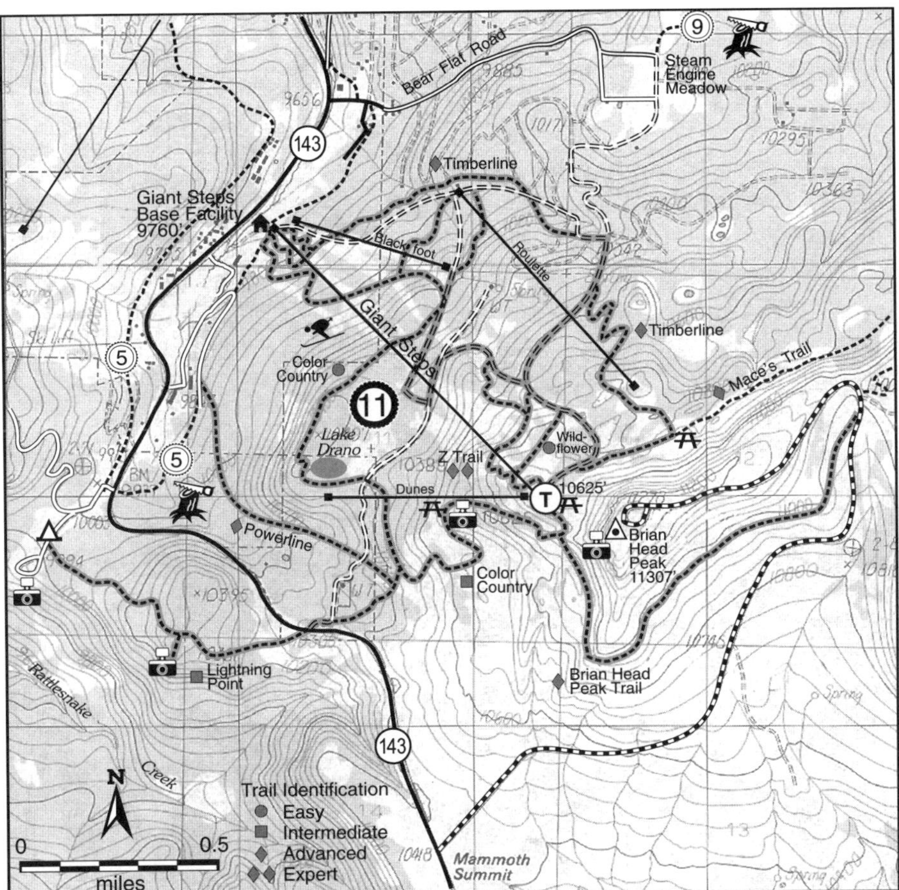

USGS 1:24,000 scale Brian Head (40 foot contour interval).

instead of descending singletrack. Fork right on a trail into the trees that soon drops to the base of Roulette Lift. From the lift's base, follow trail markers downhill past maintenance sheds and dart back into the trees. Cross under Blackfoot and Giant Steps Lifts and bank down a handful of switchbacks to the resort's base.

Trail #2: Timberline Trail (2.3 miles, advanced)

Timberline Trail begins as a moderately challenging trail, weaving through stands of fir and spruce beneath the craggy face of Brian Head Peak. The trail becomes progressively more technical as it nears the resort's base. Timberline Trail is also the main course for downhill races, so it commonly attracts bikers who "feel the need for speed." For a longer ride, you can take Mace's Run Trail out of the resort to Steam Engine Meadow then loop back to the resort (see Options).

Exit Giant Steps Lift to the left; then fork right on Timberline Trail. The trail is mostly level, but the imbedded rocks in the tread create moderately technical condi-

At Brian Head Resort Mountain Bike Park, you can enjoy a peaceful view . . .

tions. Pass a picnic table, and then come to the junction for Mace's Run Trail, Dark Hollow Trail, and Parowan (all to the right). Fork left, descend across hummocky terrain, and cross under Roulette Lift. Intersect and follow a dirt road to a junction, signed "Scout Camp, Exiting Bike Park." (This is where you reenter the resort's trail system if you pursue the optional Mace's Run Trail.) Fork left again to blaze down Timberline Trail, sliding through curves and flying over berms. Cross ski runs and pass under Black Foot Lift. Hang your butt off the back for the double-black-diamond drop to the resort's base.

Trail #3: Wildflower Trail (3 miles, novice to intermediate)

Wildflower offers a mellow alternate to the more treacherous Z Trail nearby. The lower half follows Color Country Trail to the resort's base. Upon exiting Giant Steps Lift, fork left for both Wildflower and Z Trails. Round a pair of biker-friendly turns, and then fork right to continue on Wildflower Trail (Z Trail drops left). Soon, the trail intersects a dirt road; take the road downhill. Although there are no gnashing rocks ripping at your tires, like on Z Trail, descend cautiously just the same because this "novice-level" route is steep and is covered with loose dirt and pebbles. When wet, this section gets real gooey. Curve south around a knobby knoll, and then descend under Giant Steps Lift to a broad, flat area. Continue straight until you reach Lake Drano. Now, follow Color Country Trail around the lake and descend to the base, as described above.

. . . or crash the gates during a downhill race.

Trail #4: Lightning Point Trail (4.5 miles, intermediate)

Lightning Point Trail begins on upper Color Country Trail and culminates on Town Trail. From Lightning Point, you can step out to a viewpoint overlooking forested slopes and orange, white, and pink cliffs of the upper Ashdown Gorge Wilderness.

Upon unloading from Giant Steps Lift, follow Color Country Trail to the right. Descend about 1.3 miles and fork left on Lightning Point Trail, which descends to highway 143. Cross the road, follow trail markers across a small meadow, and then climb the steep doubletrack up the forested knoll. Once on top, take the spur trail left to the cliff-edge viewpoint. During autumn, the deep green color of isolated fir trees interrupts a sea of golden and rust-orange aspens. Return to the junction in the trees and descend left/westward. Exit the woods at a backcountry camping area and take the doubletrack (Sugarloaf Mountain Road) up the meadow to the highway. Cross the highway and hop on Town Trail, which weaves through a logging zone. When you exit the trees, er, what's left of them, take the dirt road down to the condominiums, and then follow trail signs back to the base of Giant Steps Lift.

Trail #5: Z Trail (3.5 miles, advanced to expert)

Upon exiting Giant Steps Lift, fork left for both Wildflower and Z Trails. Stay left again, ignoring the right turn for Wildflower, and get ready to take a plunge down white-knuckle turns beneath the lift. The trail veers right and intersects a dirt road. Follow the road downhill (following Wildflower Trail) to connect with Color Country Trail, or head northward and descend through the Roulette Lift area. If pursuing the latter, take Timberline to the resort's base or peel off left near the base of Roulette Lift and follow singletrack across ski runs to the resort's base.

Uphill Route: (2.5 miles, advanced to expert)

Snub the lift and earn your downhill ride. This route follows lower Color Country Trail (#1) and Wildflower Trail (#3) from the resort's base to its summit. It's granny gear all the way.

From the base of Giant Steps Lift, go right and pedal up Color Country Trail's lower switchbacks. Cross ski runs and pass under Giant Steps Lift. Immediately thereafter, fork right and climb a torturous hill that will pop the blood vessels in your eyeballs. Atop the hill, exit Color Country Trail to the nearby dirt road. (Instead of suffering up this hill, fork left, go into the trees, and pass under Black Foot Lift. When you reach the base of Roulette Lift, curve right and grind up the dirt road for 0.5 mile to the top of the previously mentioned hill.) Catch your breath as you pass under Giant Steps Lift again. Now, fork left twice on doubletracks and climb the dirt road to the resort's summit. Alternatively, take Wildflower Trail (#3), which branches from the doubletrack.

Option: Mace's Run Trail (7-mile loop, advanced)

Mace's Run Trail is dedicated to Brent Mace, a long-time employee of the Cedar City Ranger District, who died after battling cancer. Mace's Run connects Brian Head Resort, with its handy chairlift service, and Dark Hollow Trail. There, options abound, but this loop version guides you back to Timberline Trail in the resort.

Upon unloading from Giant Steps Lift, go left and onto Timberline Trail. One half-mile out, fork right on Mace's Run Trail, which cuts under the blocky cliffs supporting Brian Head Peak. Rocks and roots protruding from the trail create moderately to highly technical conditions. Portage across a bouldery gulch, and then push up the opposing slope. The pedaling is easier after entering the trees, and the loamy trail deadens the sound of your travel, except your deep breaths. Cross a low rise and fork left on Dark Hollow Trail. Pass Cub Lake and descend an exciting stretch of singletrack through thick conifers to Muñoz Meadow. Turn left and ride singletrack to Steam Engine Meadow. (If you go right, you'll follow Dark Hollow Trail to the junction for Scout Camp Loop and Second Left Hand Canyon.)

From the old steam boiler, take the doubletrack due south across the meadow. Curve right and climb gradually into the trees. Near a green-roofed shack, fork left and go uphill. Where the hill levels, fork right and enter the resort near a junction of dirt roads. Head downhill, following trail signs for Timberline Trail. A wild descent on a roller coaster trail takes you around the base of Roulette Lift, into the trees, and to the resort's base.

Notes:

Lift tickets are sold at the resort's Giant Steps center. (Prices below are based on the 1998 season.) Giant Steps Lift operates Friday through Sunday 10 a.m.–5 p.m. Rentals and service are available at the resort.

Single ride: $7.00   All day pass: $15.00

Resort Rules:

- Helmets are required at all times when biking on the resort
- Always ride in control
- Avoid biking alone
- Be aware of hikers on the trails and yield the right-of-way
- Littering will result in loss of ticket
- Downhill riders always have the right-of-way
- Ride on marked and designated trails
- Attach lift ticket to hand brakes or derailleur cables
- Tread lightly; locking brakes erodes trails
- Smoking is not permitted on the lift or on the trails

Tips and advice:

In case of an accident, notify the Patrol at the bottom of Giant Steps. If a storm develops, seek shelter at the resort base. Stay away from ridge tops, lift shacks and towers, power lines, open ski runs, and lone trees. Stay clear of snowmaking equipment (pipes, valves, etc.).

Trailhead Access:

All routes begin atop Giant Steps Lift at Brian Head Resort's main ticket center.

12 Lowder Ponds

Location:	4 miles east of Brian Head
Length:	11.5 miles
Configuration:	Loop
Tread:	Singletrack, all-weather road
Physical Difficulty:	Intermediate to advanced (steady, moderate climb up the Sidney Valley road; several short, steep climbs on Sidney Peaks Trail)
Technical Difficulty:	Moderate (zones of loose rocks and exposed roots on singletracks; some washboards on the Sidney Valley road)
Elevation Changes:	High: 11,000 feet (trailhead: Sidney Valley Trail) Low: 10,000 feet (Sidney Valley road) Gain: 1,440 feet
Maps:	USGS 1:24,000 scale: Brian Head, Utah (Sidney Peaks and Lowder Ponds Trails are not shown)
Land Status:	Dixie National Forest (Cedar City Ranger District)

Siskel and Ebert would give Lowder Ponds Trail "two thumbs up." One thumb up is for the total riding experience: The route follows spirited singletracks, a serpentining ATV track, and a mellow dirt road. The ever-changing scenery includes grass-rimmed ponds, muffled woods, and powerful ridge-top vistas. The second thumb up is for the loop configuration: No shuttle is required.

From the parking area, cross the road and take Sidney Peaks Trail out the windswept ridge through islands of fir trees. Turn right at the Dark Hollow Trail–Lowder

Ponds Trail junction (**m1.0**). (Dark Hollow Trail forks left; Sidney Peaks Trail continues straight. You'll return on the latter, later.) Follow the cairns to a junction with the old Sidney Peaks doubletrack, signed "Dark Hollow Trail," and cross straight over the road. (A sometimes-hidden carsonite post marks the route.) Follow trail markers across the tundra slope, dip through a small gully (usually dry), and head back into the trees.

Descend the south slope of the ever-deepening Lowder Creek gulch, while negotiating roots, trail-side trees, and loose rocks deposited from nearby talus. After a mile of frenzied downhilling, you exit the singletrack onto a doubletrack next to a pond. (There's a trail sign here for Dark Hollow Trail #032.) Take this track a few hundred yards to a T junction and turn left/north. (If you turn right, you'll eventually go through a subdivision and reach UT 143, which is many miles from Brian Head Peak.) After a few hundred feet, you come to another junction where a doubletrack forks right (**m2.8**). Stay straight/north and cross the creek to continue the loop. (Turn right to visit the pioneer cabin ruins and Lowder Ponds. There you can while away the afternoon, fish for trout, or search for elusive beaver. During the early 1900s, the Lowder family grazed cattle among these meadows in the summer and made butter and cheese to sell in Cedar City in the fall.)

Ahead, the doubletrack narrows to an ATV trail; it crosses a broken log fence, bends right, and rises around the northern perimeter of the Lowder Ponds meadow. Over the next 2 miles, the trail rolls through thick woods, traverses several meadows, and passes a placid pond. You'll snap your bike around slalom-like turns, while imitating the sounds of skidding tires like when you were a child. After dropping off a hill, the trail enters spacious Sidney Valley. Follow trail markers north to the middle of the meadow, and then curve south to cross Castle Creek. Scoot up the small knoll to reach the Sidney Valley road (**m5.4**).

Climb steadily up the cindered and sometimes-washboarded road for 2.3 miles to the summit and the Bunker Creek trailheads. Cross the clearing to reach the Parowan

A lone biker skirts a grove of aspens near Lowder Ponds (left); a group crosses a high meadow on route to upper Lowder Ponds Trail (right).

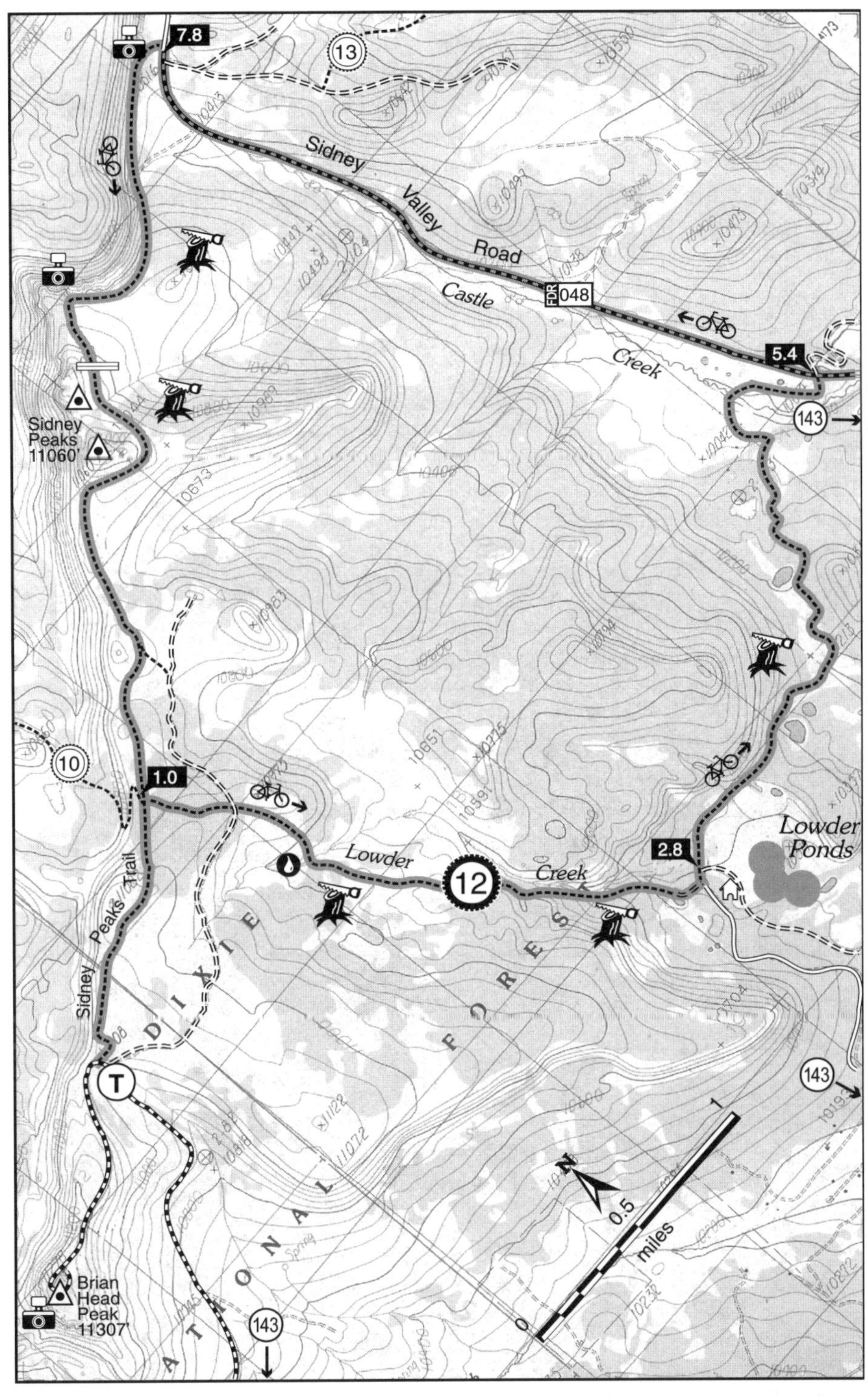

USGS 1:24,000 scale: Brian Head and Panguitch Lake (40 foot contour interval).

Canyon overlook (**m7.8**). Shutterbugs will have a field day positioning friends along the ridge, which is backdropped by endless forests and vermillion cliffs.

To complete the loop, take Sidney Peaks Trail #210 south and conquer a protracted climb laced with tree roots. Your effort is rewarded by a second, equally-impressive overlook of Parowan Canyon. Struggle uphill past timbered slopes that have been nearly wiped out from beetle infestation and from the high winds associated with Hurricane Nora in 1997. After racing across a broad saddle and rising up the opposite side, stay right at a Y junction and continue along the ridge. (The trail forking left also returns to the trailhead but via the old Sidney Peaks doubletrack.) Go straight at the Dark Hollow–Lowder Ponds trail junction to return to the trailhead.

Option: Lowder Ponds–Bunker Creek (point-to-point)

Instead of returning to the trailhead from the Parowan Canyon overlook via Sidney Peaks Trail, digress by following either the Right Fork or Left Fork Bunker Creek to Panguitch Lake. This option offers double the downhill pleasure, provided you don't mind climbing up Sidney Valley Road in between. (See Left Fork and Right Fork Bunker Creek.) A vehicle shuttle between Brian Head Peak and Panguitch Lake is required.

Specs.: 16.0 miles; 1,000-foot gain

Option: Lowder Ponds–Bunker Creek (loop)

Go for broke! Upon reaching the Parowan Canyon overlook at the top of the Sidney Valley road, tack on an extra 6 miles by first descending Left Fork Bunker Creek and then climbing Right Fork Bunker Creek. Ascending Right Fork is surprisingly rideable, albeit granny gear all the way. But it's worth the effort if you relish a little leg burn. You'll double the above elevation gain on this little digression. This route rates as one of the best loop rides in the region.

Specs.: 18.0 miles; 2,800-foot gain

Notes & Precautions:

Logging activity between Lowder Ponds and Sidney Valley Road has altered the trail in years past. But the Cedar City Ranger District is committed to reconstructing the trail when needed. Check with the Cedar Ranger District or local bike shops for logging and trail updates. Use extreme caution if you are near logging activity. Truck traffic may be encountered on the Sidney Valley road.

Trailhead Access:

From Brian Head Mall, drive 2.5 miles south on UT 143; then take the Brian Head Peak road (all-weather road) 1.8 miles to the Sidney Peaks Trail parking area. (Brian Head Peak/Vista Point is 1 mile farther.)

13 Left Fork Bunker Creek

Location:	Brian Head Peak to Panguitch Lake
Length:	12 miles
Configuration:	Point-to-point
Tread:	Singletrack, doubletrack, minor pavement
Physical Difficulty:	Intermediate (mostly downhill; small climbs on Sidney Peaks Trail; one modest climb on doubletrack after Left Fork Bunker Creek)
Technical Difficulty:	Moderate (tree roots, loose rocks, steep slopes, sharp turns on Left Fork; low whoop-te-doos on doubletrack)
Elevation Changes:	High: 11,000 feet (trailhead: Sidney Peaks Trail)
	Low: 8,300 feet (trail end: UT 143 at Panguitch Lake)
	Gain: 360 feet
	Loss: 3,000 feet
Maps:	USGS 1:24,000 scale: Brian Head and Panguitch Lake, Utah (Sidney Peaks and Left Fork Trails are not shown)
Land Status:	Dixie National Forest (Cedar City Ranger District)

Left Fork Bunker Creek showcases Brian Head's rollicking downhill singletrack riding, for which the region is famed. But to reach the Left Fork trail, you must first ride Sidney Peaks Trail, which scrapes the belly of the heavens and offers jaw-dropping views of color-rich cliffs and thick forests. Left Fork Bunker Creek is a bit more technical than Right Fork, its alter ego, because you must negotiate a steady stream of modest challenges. Nothing daunting, just good clean technical fun. The route culminates on an exciting doubletrack punctuated with whoop-te-doos and sweeping curves.

From the parking area, cross the Brian Head Peak road, and take Sidney Peaks Trail out the tundra ridge through islands of fir and spruce trees. Occasionally, the trail is booby trapped with sharp turns, root networks, and boulder zones. All are without consequence; they just keep your riding style honest. Continue straight on Sidney Peaks Trail at the junction for Dark Hollow and Lowder Ponds Trails (**m1.0**). After crossing a broad, treeless saddle, you climb a modest hill around Sidney Peaks. Enter and exit the trees. Then while descending, be alert to a gated wire fence across the trail: it has been the site of many spectacular crashes. Just beyond, bend right at a viewpoint of Parowan Canyon, and drop steeply through the trees while bounding over swarming roots. Follow the ridge 0.5 mile to the second and equally impressive Parowan Canyon overlook, at the head of Sidney Valley Road (**m3.8**). (During 1997, strong winds from remnant Hurricane Nora knocked down a great number of trees. This, coupled with tree harvesting to control beetle infestation, has devastated the forest.)

At the viewpoint, you'll see castle-shaped buttes and fortress walls the color of steamed crab poke up through verdant forests composed of aspen and fir, all beneath a darkened volcanic lineament and ultramarine sky. At your feet, pastel lichens are splashed about the cliffs like pressed wildflowers. And when aspens turn golden during autumn, the color spectrum is as varied as a box of Crayolas.

Go across the clearing to the multi-signed junction on the Sidney Valley road, jog right, and then fork left on the doubletrack signed "Left Fork Bunker Creek #033."

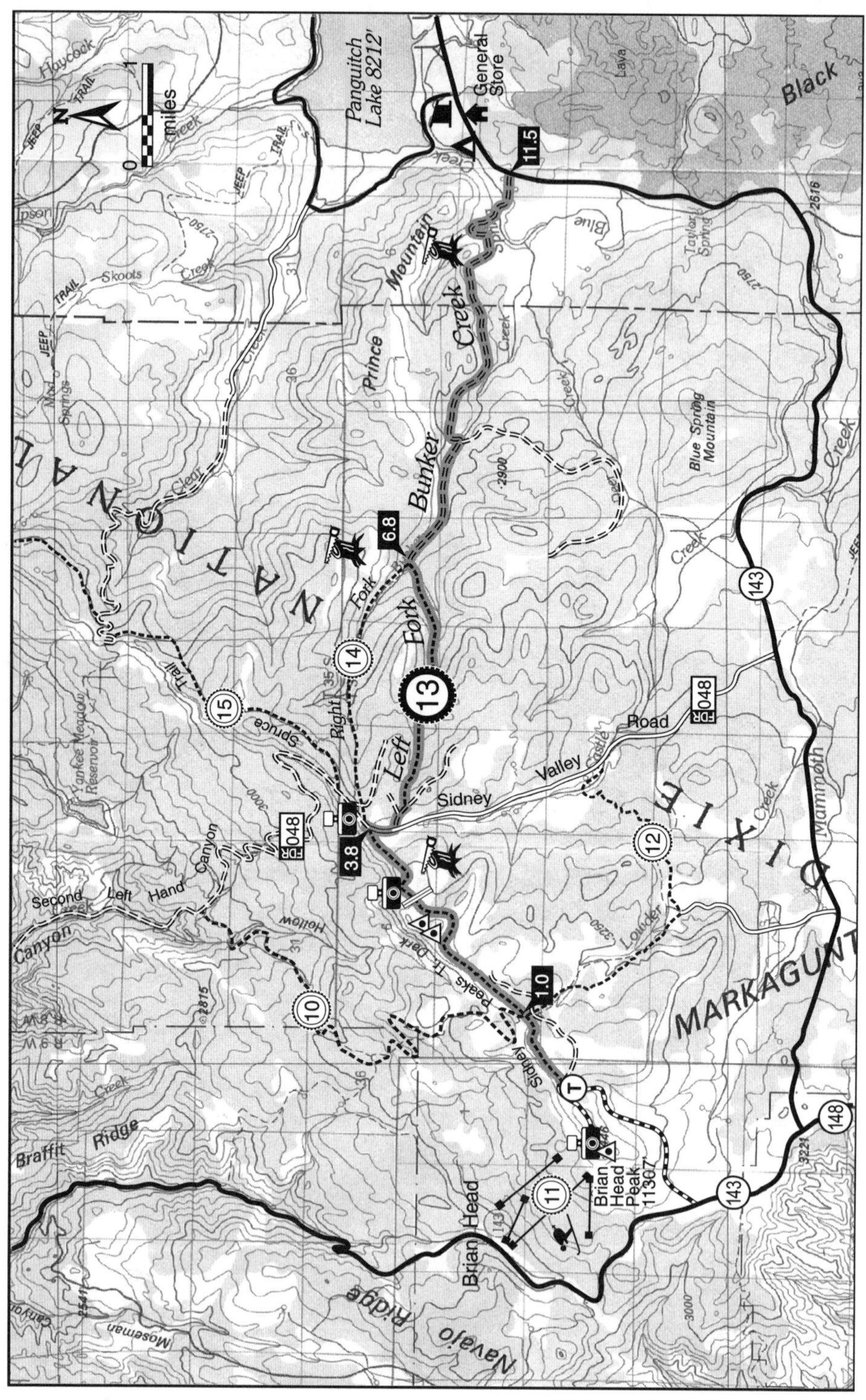

USGS 1:100,000 scale: Panguitch (50 meter contour interval).

Mary and Joel overlook Parowan Canyon from the Sidney Peaks Trail.

Ignore a faint track forking left immediately thereafter. Pedal over a low rise, and then leave the doubletrack to embark on Left Fork Bunker Creek Trail. The descent is fast and furious from the outset. Anticipate log drops, root networks, rock gardens, off-camber slopes, rutted trail, steep descents, side-swiping trees, and, often times, combinations of all. Go with the flow, don't fight it, keep the wheels rolling, and "let the force be with you." After 2.5 miles, the trail veers left, crosses the creek, and joins Right Fork Bunker Creek at a signed and gated fence (**m6.8**). (You may ask, "why is Left Fork to the right and Right Fork to the left?" Because tributaries of waterways are named when viewed upstream, and you just rode downstream.)

Take the doubletrack downhill, but lower your seat a notch. The barrage of low earthen berms ahead will kick up the back wheel of an unsuspecting biker or provide adequate "lift" for gravity-defying test pilots. At a Y junction 1 mile down the track, swing left and climb a modest hill through rustling aspens. Rocket down the remaining doubletrack through sweeping turns and around Blue Spring Valley. Chug up to UT 143 (**m11.5**), and then glide 0.5 mile to the Panguitch Lake General Store. Pop a cold beverage of your choice, wolf down a mustard-smeared wiener from the Doggy Delight next door, and reminisce the day's adventure.

Option: Left Fork–Right Fork Bunker Creek (loop)

All play and no work make Jack (and Jill) doughy around the midsection. Toss some climbing into this freebie ride by looping back to the Parowan Canyon overlook on Right Fork Bunker Creek. Then backtrack on Sidney Peaks Trail to the trailhead. Be forewarned. The 1,300-foot climb up Right Fork is no spin through the

Joel emerges from the trees in Left Fork Bunker Creek.

park—it's granny gear all the way. But it's also surprisingly rideable and much less technical than Left Fork. You may be forced to dismount a couple of times, once where the trail has sloughed and again at a rock garden past the upper creek crossing. Keep in mind that riding Sidney Peaks Trail back to the trailhead requires solid effort, too. Still, this is a great intermediate–advanced loop ride.

Specs.: 14 miles; 2,280-foot gain

Notes & Precautions:

Be alert to logging activity in the area; trails are subject to closure as a result. The Cedar City Ranger District keeps Brian Head bike shops abreast of the current logging schedule.

Trailhead Access:

Shuttle a vehicle to Panguitch Lake by first driving 4 miles south on UT 143 from Brian Head Mall to the junction with UT 148 (Cedar Breaks National Monument). Turn left and continue on UT 143 for 12.5 miles to the Blue Spring Valley road/FDR

081. Park near the intersection (at your discretion) or 1 mile farther near Panguitch Lake General Store. (Ask for permission to park at the store; they may charge a fee.) Return to Brian Head, and drive 1.8 miles up the Brian Head Peak road to the Sidney Peaks Trail parking area. (Brian Head Peak/Vista Point is 1 mile farther.)

14 Right Fork Bunker Creek

Location:	Brian Head Peak to Panguitch Lake
Length:	12 miles
Configuration:	Point-to-point
Tread:	Singletrack, doubletrack, some pavement
Physical Difficulty:	Intermediate (mostly downhill; small climbs on Sidney Peaks Trail; one modest climb on doubletrack after descending Right Fork Bunker Creek)
Technical Difficulty:	Low to moderate (short, rocky section on Right Fork Trail; low whoop-te-doos on doubletrack)
Elevation Changes:	High: 11,000 feet (trailhead: Sidney Peaks Trail) Low: 8,300 feet (trail end: UT 143 at Panguitch Lake) Gain: 360 feet Loss: 3,000 feet
Maps:	USGS 1:24,000 scale: Brian Head and Panguitch Lake, Utah (Sidney Peaks Trail is not shown)
Land Status:	Dixie National Forest (Cedar City Ranger District)

The Right and Left Forks of Bunker Creek are like Dr. Jekyll and Mr. Hyde. Both are superlative downhill singletracks, but Right Fork, Dr. Jekyll, is less threatening, and it's ideal for strong novice and intermediate bikers. Still, on Right Fork you will face a handful of moderately technical challenges, but overall you'll be as giddy as a kid in a candy shop. As Jackie Gleason would say, "How sweet it is!"

From the parking area, cross the road and take Sidney Peaks Trail out the tundra ridge through stands of fir and spruce trees. The riding is easy—well, as easy as riding at 11,000 feet above sea level can be. Watch out for a few quick turns, a boulder or two plopped in the trail's tread, and some tree roots poking up here and there. Continue straight on Sidney Peaks Trail at the junction for Dark Hollow and Lowder Ponds Trails (**m1.0**). After crossing a broad, treeless saddle, you climb around Sidney Peaks. This hill is trivial on an absolute scale, but at these elevations you'll find yourself milking your easiest gears. Enter and exit the trees, and then, while descending, watch for a gated wire fence across the trail: it has been the site of many spectacular crashes. Bend right at a photo-worthy overlook of Parowan Canyon, and drop down a technical stretch through the trees. Follow the ridge a bit farther to the second and equally impressive Parowan Canyon overlook at the top of the Sidney Valley road (**m3.8**). (If you are wondering why the forest has been devastated, it's from a combination of tree harvesting to control beetle infestation and the high winds from remnant Hurricane Nora during 1997.)

First and Second Left Hand Canyons crease the forested valley far below. The Grand Castle and Noah's Arc are built of the same luminescent rocks that form Cedar Breaks National Monument. The peaks to the north are the Tushar Mountains

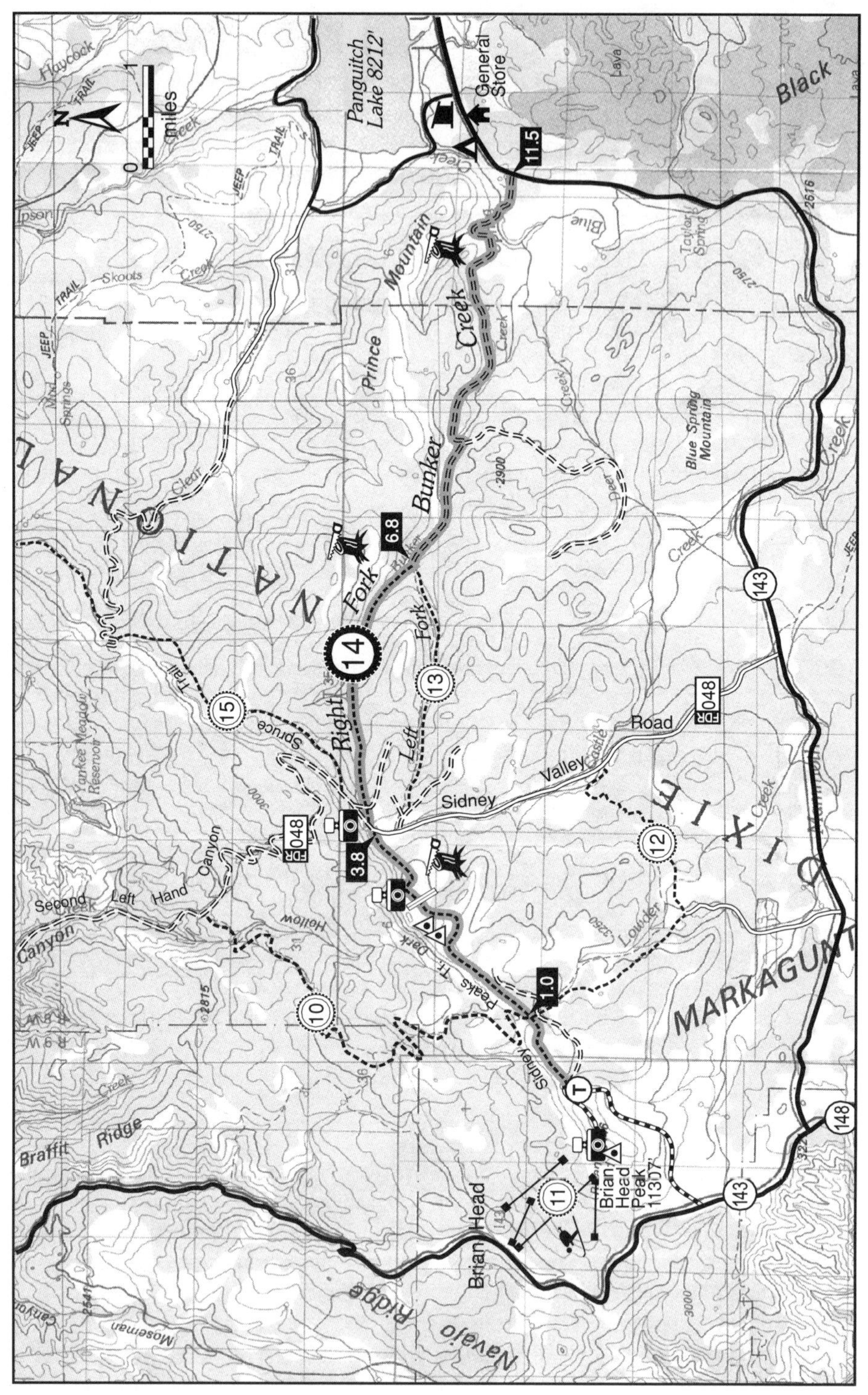

USGS 1:100,000 scale: Panguitch (50 meter contour interval).

Racing down the doubletrack below Right Fork Bunker Trail Creek (left).
"Flight tower . . . requesting permission to land" (right).

near Beaver; the Little Salt Lake Valley sprawls away from Parowan; and Nevada sits on the horizon. Photo opportunities abound.

Cross the clearing to the multi-signed junction on the Sidney Valley road. Go left/north, and then fork right on Right Fork Bunker Creek Trail (#040). Be sure to cross a doubletrack, after descending one-quarter mile, to continue on the trail. This upper stretch is steep in spots, and you may have to dismount for a bouldery stretch preceding the creek crossing. Thereafter, Right Fork is a ribbon of smooth dirt unraveling through the trees that makes you giggle with excitement the entire way. Use your left foot as an outrigger where the trail has sloughed. Singletrack turns to doubletrack at the steel gate where Left Fork Bunker Creek joins from the right (**m6.8**).

Descend on the doubletrack, bounding over a succession of low earthen berms. How much air do you dare let filter between your tires and the trail? At a Y junction 1.5 miles down the track, fork left, and climb a modest hill through the aspens. Rocket down the remaining track through sweeping turns and around Blue Spring Valley. Chug up to the highway (**m11.5**), turn left, and glide downhill to the Panguitch Lake General Store for après-ride munchies.

Notes & Precautions:

Be alert to logging activity in the area; trails are subject to closure as a result. The Cedar City Ranger District keeps Brian Head bike shops abreast of the current logging schedule.

Trailhead Access:

Shuttle a vehicle to Panguitch Lake by first driving 4 miles south on UT 143 from Brian Head Mall to the junction with UT 148 (Cedar Breaks National Monument). Turn left and continue on UT 143 for 12.5 miles to the Blue Spring Valley road/FDR 081. Park near the intersection (at your discretion) or 1 mile farther near Panguitch Lake General Store. (Ask for permission to park at the store; they may charge a fee.) Return to Brian Head, and drive 1.8 miles up the Brian Head Peak road to the Sidney Peaks Trail parking area. (Brian Head Peak/Vista Point is 1 mile farther.)

15 Brian Head to Panguitch

Location:	Between Brian Head Peak and Panguitch
Length:	37 miles
Configuration:	Point-to-point
Tread:	All-weather roads, doubletracks, maintained and primitive singletracks
Physical Difficulty:	Expert (long distance, large elevation gain, periodic dismounting and portaging, technical conditions, route finding)
Technical Difficulty:	Low to extreme (Spruce and Delong Trails are infrequently maintained; both may have deadfall, exposed roots, boulders, and eroded conditions)
Elevation Changes:	High: 11,000 feet (trailhead: Sidney Peak Trail) Low: 6,600 feet (trail end: Panguitch) Gain: 3,450 feet Loss: 7,000 feet
Maps:	USGS 1:24,000 scale: Brian Head, Fivemile Ridge, Panguitch, Panguitch Lake, and Red Creek Reservoir, Utah (route is mostly accurate)
Land Status:	Dixie National Forest (Cedar City Ranger District)

If there's a will, there's a way to pedal from Brian Head to Panguitch without letting your tires touch pavement. Don't let the whopping elevation loss mislead you because this route is a far cry from a downhiller's dream ride. This is an adventurer's ride—a ride that revives the fundamentals of mountain biking by crossing huge chunks of terrain largely inaccessible to combustible means of travel but with greater efficiency than foot travel.

Navigation is nearly as challenging as the seldom-used singletracks traveled midroute. And many of the descents encountered are all-out technical assaults that sap nearly as much energy and require as much adeptness as the taxing hills they follow. But Brian Head to Panguitch is more than a ride of attrition; you'll obtain sweeping panoramas of the High Plateaus from several vantage points, and you'll mingle with peaceful forests in between.

For the full effect, first pedal the extra mile from the trailhead to the very summit of Brian Head Peak. Return to the trailhead and take Sidney Peaks Trail (singletrack) out the tundra ridge through patches of fir and spruce trees. One mile out, pass the signed junction for Dark Hollow and Lowder Ponds Trails; take Sidney Peaks Trail all the way to the Parowan Canyon overlook at the top of Sidney Valley Road (**m3.7**).

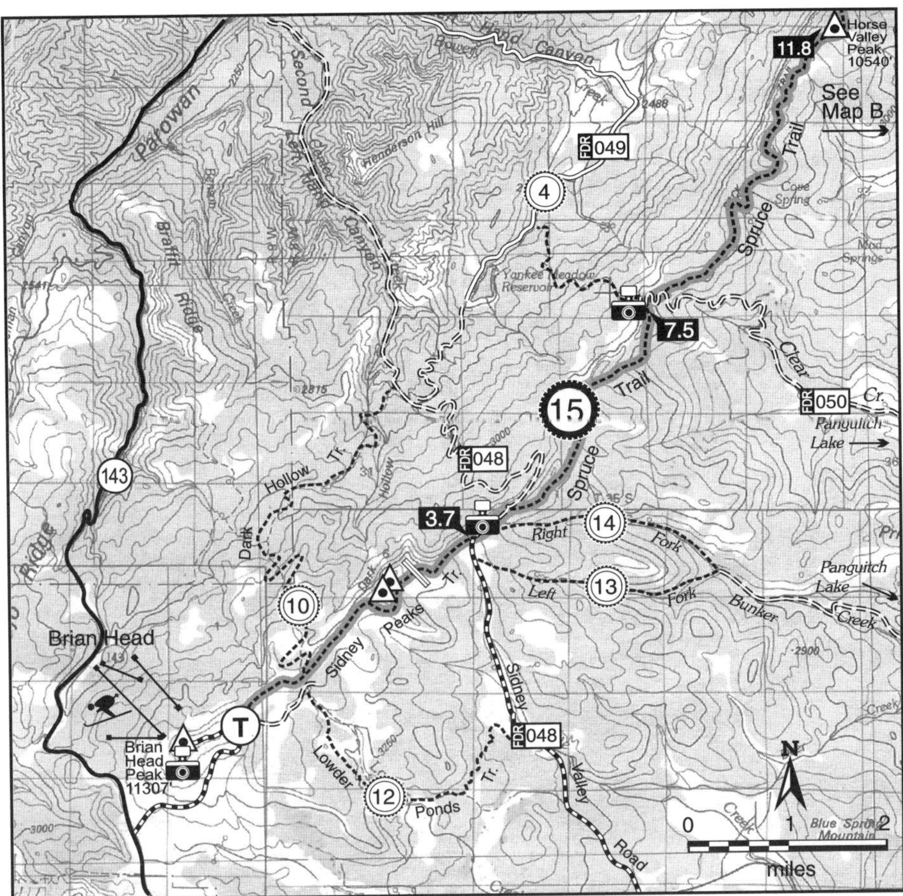

Brian Head to Panguitch–Map A. USGS 1:100,000 scale: Panguitch (50 meter contour interval).

The views of bounteous forests, colorful cliffs, and distance valleys warrant photos. But don't dally; there's a lot of ground to cover.

Go to the nearby junction for Sidney Valley Road/FDR 048, head north/left, and then fork right on Spruce Trail #043. (Important: If you miss this turn and continue straight on FDR 048, you'll descend westward off the ridge into Parowan Canyon and end up on the wrong side of the mountain!)

Spruce Trail generally contours around the east side of the ridge for 1.5 miles; then it descends steeply for another mile through thick woods where conditions are highly technical. At times, the trail can be faint and elusive. Push and pedal your bike 0.5 mile to join the Clear Creek road at its summit (**m7.5**). Here you can look back over the route you've traveled and peer down into Parowan Canyon.

Descend the Clear Creek road to the right/east, about one-half mile, to the second right-hand turn; then hop onto the continued Spruce Trail, signed "Forks Valley 5 miles." (If you've had enough all ready, bail out by descending the Clear Creek road

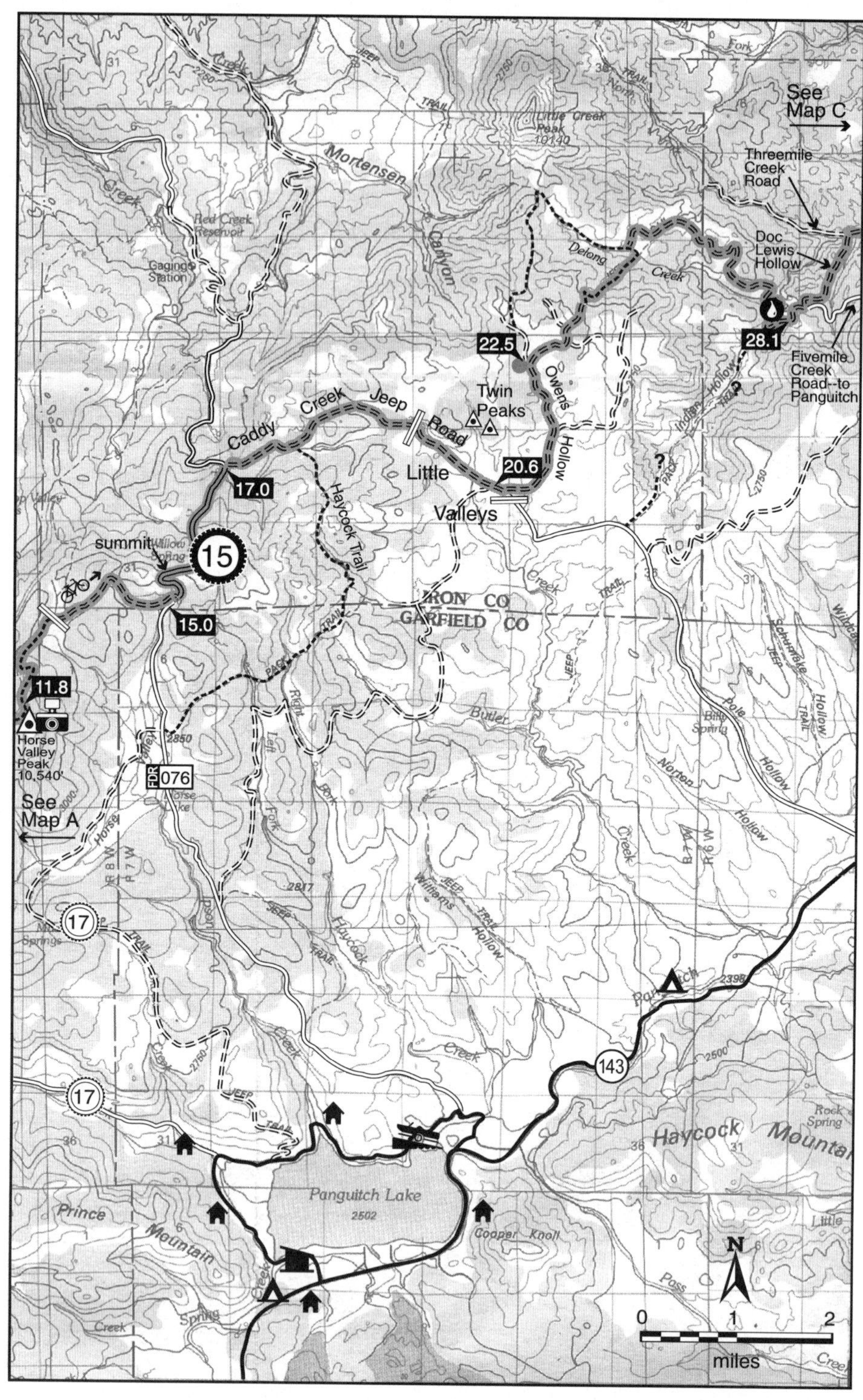

Brian Head to Panguitch–Map B. USGS 1:100,000 scale: Panguitch (50 meter contour interval).

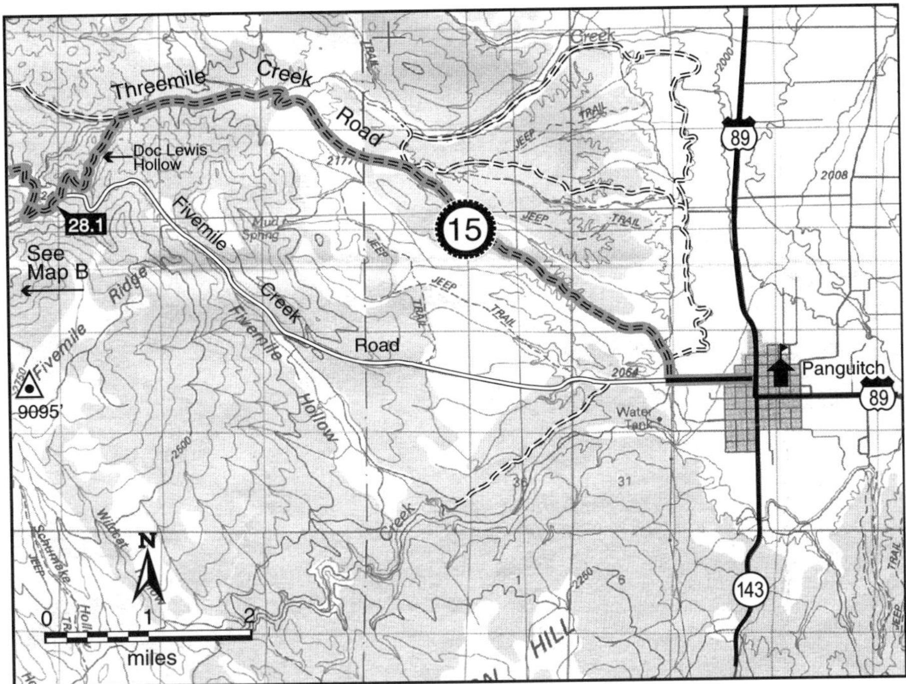

Brian Head to Panguitch–Map C. USGS 1:100,000 scale: Panguitch (50 meter contour interval).

to Panguitch Lake and hitching a ride back to Brian Head.) Dart into the woods on a serendipitous path, cross open slopes offering grand views of Panguitch Lake miles below, and then enter aspens again. Drop down and then portage up a technical stretch filled with boulders. (Trail may be rerouted in the future.)

Two miles from the Clear Creek road, the trail enters a sloping sage-covered field bordered by aspens on the trail's downhill side. In years past, this section was dreadfully confusing. Do not contour around the peak; this is a false trail. Instead, ride across the field a few hundred feet, no more. Then place your bike on your shoulder and hoof it uphill through the sagebrush and rocks. Angle roughly 45 degrees up the slope toward the distant interface of aspen and fir, keeping an eye out for cairns marking the line. Once you are up the hill and in the trees, the trail is evident. (This section may be rerouted and/or resigned in the future.)

Traverse the volcanic rubble sloping down from the ridge and cross a pair of meadows encircled by aspens. (The trail can be faint in the meadows. Cut straight across, heading due north. The trail is evident when in the trees.) Now portage up the flank of Horse Valley Peak (**m11.8**). Heavy sigh! Eat, drink, take a snooze if you must, and soak up the unencumbered view of southern Utah's High Plateaus from the summit.

The initial descent off Horse Valley Peak sends adrenaline surging through your veins as you negotiate rough trail and hairpin turns. The remainder, although primitive and subject to deadfall, sparks a beaming grin because you float on a mat of

Parowan Canyon overlook (left); exiting Delong Creek Trail (right).

grass and pine needles. Pass a log fence, and then break out to a sage meadow at a trail sign and onto a doubletrack. Cross the saddle between two low hills, and descend Forks Valley to the junction with the Horse Valley road/(FDR 076), which is marked with a Dixie National Forest sign (**15.0**). (Had enough? Bail out by descending the Horse Valley road to Panguitch Lake and hitching a ride back to Brian Head or ahead to Panguitch.)

A quick climb takes you to the summit of the Horse Valley road. Descend the other side about 1.5 miles, and then turn right on a doubletrack, signed "Caddy Creek Jeep Road, Little Valleys" (**m17.0**). If you face a short hill of jumbled rocks, you're on the right track. (If you miss this turn, you'll descend toward Red Creek Reservoir on the Parowan side of the mountain—a day's effort from Panguitch.)

One-half mile past the trailhead for Haycock Trail, the road bends right and heads down Little Valleys where pedaling is easy. Cross a cattle guard, pass Twin Peaks on the left, and then come to a Y junction signed (in reverse) for Caddy Creek Jeep Road. (Here you'll find a lush meadow to the right where cattle commonly graze.) Immediately ahead, fork left/northeast on a faint doubletrack paralleling a wire fence (**m20.6**).

Now turn on your Global Positioning Satellite (GPS) receiver because directions to the Delong Creek trailhead are sketchy at best: One-half mile from Caddy Creek Jeep Road, fork left/north away from the fence and up grassy Owens Hollow. Descend slightly, ignore a prominent doubletrack forking right and leading up to Horse Bench, and dip through an arroyo. One mile farther, you reach "Prestone Pond"—a cattle wallow often the putrid color of antifreeze (**m22.5**). Now fork right! One-half mile up, fork left followed by a right turn (before crossing another arroyo), and climb to a log fence at the divide, signed "Delong Creek Trail." Whew!

Delong Creek Trail is not a Forest Service "priority trail," so expect technical conditions and deadfall on this mile-long descent. In between technical stunts, you'll be overwhelmed by the decaying scent of fallen trees and fresh fragrance of new growth. Step across Delong Creek, but do not follow the distant wooden northward up the hill. Instead, angle left (10 o'clock or so), and bushwhack uphill several hundred yards, across cinders and through prickly sage, to a faint doubletrack. Take the doubletrack up to the low divide. Descend a bit while heading east, tackle a steep pitch, ignore the doubletrack forking left at the top, and drop nearly 2 miles to Delong Creek again and to the Panguitch municipal water pipeline. Scoot up to the Fivemile Creek road, and climb left to the Doc Lewis Hollow trailhead (**m28.1**).

Had enough? If so, make an 8-mile beeline for Panguitch on the Fivemile Creek road (washboards). Otherwise, descend Doc Lewis Hollow (rocky) to the Threemile Creek road (mostly smooth). There you'll find easy pedaling for nearly 2 miles before the road rises up a set of rocky switchbacks—easy work on an absolute scale but brutal after 30 miles. Culminate the day by cruising 5 miles to Panguitch, forking right at a prominent junction amidst juniper and pinyon. The Sunset Cliffs, which line the far edge of the Sevier River Valley, guide you to town.

Notes & Precautions:

Good route-finding skills are required along this route, especially on Spruce Trail, when seeking the Delong Creek Trail, and upon exiting Delong Creek Trail. Carry appropriate maps, watch for trail markers, and allow extra riding time in the event you get off track and have to reconnoiter. Got a GPS receiver? Bring it. Check forecasted weather, and avoid afternoon storms by starting early. Carry ample water and food, emergency rain wear, and a complete repair kit. Rescue can be difficult and time consuming. Water can be purified from Delong and Threemile Creeks.

Trailhead Access:

Shuttle a vehicle to Panguitch by first driving 4 miles south of Brian Head Mall on UT 143 to the junction with UT 148 (Cedar Breaks National Monument). Continue on UT 143 (left) for 32 miles to Panguitch. Park at your discretion in town. Return to Brian Head, and drive 1.8 miles up the Brian Head Peak road (all-weather road) to the Sidney Peaks Trail parking area. (Brian Head Peak is 1 mile farther.)

16 Tour de Frog (Brian Head to Bullfrog)

Location:	Brian Head Peak to Bullfrog Resort on Lake Powell
Length:	250 miles (approximate)
Configuration:	Point-to-point
Tread:	Everything but slickrock
Physical Difficulty:	Easy if you're driving the support vehicle, "off-the-meter" if you pedal the whole way, somewhere in between if you share driving duties.
Technical Difficulty:	Cushy all-weather roads to eyeball-rattling, washboarded doubletracks; silky singletrack to exacting pack trails; freewheeling downhills to jackhammer descents; easy climbs, tough climbs, insane climbs; and more . . .)
Elevation Changes:	High: 11,307 feet (trailhead: Brian Head Peak) Low: 3,700 feet (trail end: Bull Frog Resort) Gain: 15,000 feet (perhaps more)
Maps:	USGS 1:100,000 scale metric: Panguitch, Escalante, and Hite Crossing, Utah
Land Status:	Dixie National Forest (Cedar City, Powell, and Escalante Ranger Districts) and Bureau of Land Management (Beaver River Resource Area and Escalante Resource Area)

The following account, written by Gregg Bromka and Linda Carlson, appeared in *Sports Guide*, May 1991:

Of all the multi-day mountain bike tours in Utah, only a few top the list: White Rim Trail, Kokopelli's Trail, and Skyline Drive. During the fall of 1990, a new contender was introduced—the Brian Head to Bullfrog Mountain Bike Tour, dubbed by its lucky scouting crew "The Tour de Frog."

The goal of the tour, as described by Garfield County promoter Jean Seiler, was to bicycle from the very crest of 11,307-foot Brian Head Peak across three lofty plateaus (Markagunt, Paunsagunt, and Aquarius), and then to descend through southeastern Utah's canyon country to the sandstone shoreline of Lake Powell—250 miles, in five days, through remote backcountry, all on dirt roads and trails.

Hesitancy turned to optimism when Jean further explained that the adventure was not an ultra-marathon race nor a short course in wilderness survival but a fully supported familiarization (FAM) tour sponsored by Garfield County, Dixie National Forest, Bureau of Land Management, and local businesses, all of whom recognized the mountain bike potential of the region. All we had to do was pedal and eat!

The group's core participants gathered at the Brian Head Hotel (now the Cedar Breaks Lodge)—an unlikely mix of journalists and freelancers from Colorado, Utah, and Nevada (Andrew, Linda, Gregg, and Richard); one tourism promoter (Ken); a bike shop owner (Murph); and a local Panguitch biker familiar with the terrain (Dennis). More would join and drop in the upcoming days. Ability levels ranged from first-time rank beginner to the well-seasoned sprocket head, and everyone gleamed with enthusiasm, at least at the outset.

Brian Head to Panguitch (41 miles)

Atop Brian Head Peak we huddled and shivered on a crisp October afternoon, awe-struck by southern Utah's sublime panorama. The 12,000-foot Tushar Mountains pierced the northern skyline while Zion National Park's divine temples capped the south. Beneath our feet laid the yawning negative space of Cedar Breaks National Monument, a Bryce Canyon National Park one million years immature.

One by one we pedaled north along the Sidney Peaks ridge, slipping into the silent cover of fir and spruce at a steady conservative pace—except for Dennis, the group's strongest rider and tour guide, who twitched and pitched in the first mile, making the required initial tour sacrifice. Atop the ridge we enjoyed long vistas westward of conifer and aspen-clad Second Left Hand Canyon, of Yankee Meadow Reservoir, and of strawberry-colored slopes descending to the alkaline desert floor of Parowan.

On Right Fork of Bunker Creek, our route dropped east toward Panguitch Lake, whose name is derived from a Piute phrase for "Big or Many Fish." The unsigned [then-primitive] trail rolled 5 miles downhill through dense aspens sprinkled with sun bursts, banking playfully on occasion, testing our

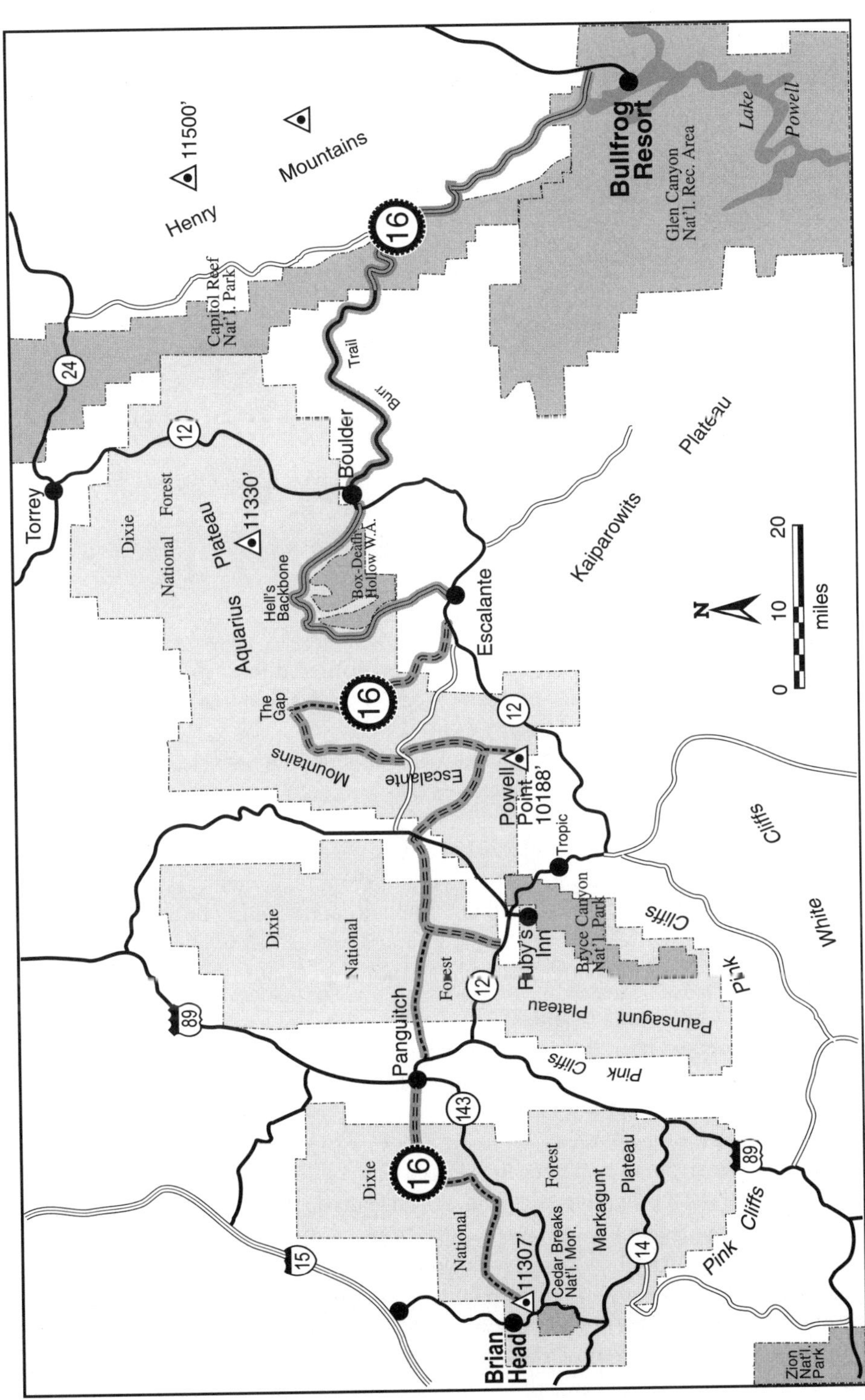
Torrey
24
12
Capitol Reef Nat'l. Park
Henry Mountains
11500'
16
Bullfrog Resort
Glen Canyon Nat'l. Rec. Area
Lake Powell
Dixie National Forest
Aquarius Plateau
11330'
Boulder
Burr Trail
Hell's Backbone
Box-Death Hollow W.A.
Escalante
Kaiparowits Plateau
N
0 10 20
miles
The Gap
16
Escalante Mountains
Powell Point 10188'
12
Tropic
Cliffs
White
Dixie National Forest
Ruby's Inn
Bryce Canyon Nat'l. Park
Cliffs
Pink
Panguitch
12
Paunsagunt Plateau
Pink Cliffs
89
143
16
Dixie National Forest
Markagunt Plateau
11307'
Cedar Breaks Nat'l. Mon.
14
15
89
Pink Cliffs
Brian Head
Zion Nat'l. Park

The core group of "Froggers:" Murph, Steve, Ken, Andrew, and Linda.

skills with challenging maneuvers elsewhere. A musky deep forest aroma of crushed pine needles and fallen aspen leaves filtered through the mountain air. Singletrack graded to jeep road laced with deadfall and whoop-te-doo berms, and we descended briskly to UT 143.

A late lunch awaited at Panguitch Lake General Store, where we reviewed the morning's adventure and surmised that we could handle this for a week. Afterward, we wrapped around the lake and ascended to the Indian Hollow Trail—a long strenuous singletrack—and descended murderous paint-shaking jeep roads to Panguitch. Ambition clouded our judgement, for the sun had arced low in the western sky and nightfall was approaching rapidly. We had long since parted ways with the support van and so had little choice but to accept our fate of a moonlit arrival in town.

Panguitch to Bryce (34 miles)

We emerged from the tour's first day slightly bruised, like ripe fruit from a fanny pack. But after carbo loading on the Flying M Cafe's buckwheat hotcakes and gulping bottomless pots of coffee sweetened with aspirin, we were eager for the next leg.

The classic thin-tire approach to Bryce Canyon National Park is via blacktopped UT 12 through the fairyland of Red Canyon, but our exploratory off-road mission led up Casto Canyon, located just 2 miles north.

Casto is every bit national-park caliber but devoid of the seasonal crowds. Walls lined with bulbous columns and magnificent towers, crumbling balconies and collapsing pinnacles engulfed and charmed us with vibrant shades of ivory and orange—a child's fantasy of dripping creamsicles.

There was no road through the canyon; our path simply meandered up the technical, rock-filled, dry stream bed. After a short distance, we intersected a narrow, smooth cattle trail draped with pine boughs that often forced hasty dismounts. Butch Cassidy sought harborage among Casto's twisted maze, and the foundation of one of his hideouts is tucked out of sight near the top of the canyon.

From the top of Casto Canyon we worked our way via rutted dirt roads up to the base of wind-swept Casto Bluff. We then dropped eastward off the Paunsagunt Plateau on the Flake Swale road—a fast and furious shot through waving fields of grass, backdropped by the gigantic movie set of the Aquarius Plateau.

The history of this barren country deepened a few miles later when we encountered a ghostly weather-beaten ranch and the lonesome Widtsoe cemetery—a silent monument to the turn-of-the-century pioneer homesteaders. Headstones chronicled lives of entire families who battled scarcity of water and the lack of medical attention. Such hardships crept deeper into our thoughts as we opted for the southern Utah hospitality of Ruby's Inn at the entrance to Bryce Canyon National Park.

Bryce to Escalante (45 miles)

Awakened by "75-mile hangovers" we hobbled to our van, which ironically was lent to us by the Garfield Golden Agers, their logo proudly displayed on the side.

From Ruby's we eyed our morning's destination, Powell Point, an imposing but colorful escarpment terminating the Table Cliff Plateau. Much to our delight, our escorts suggested shuttling 25 miles to the 10,000-foot trailhead at the head of Pine Canyon. For 3 miles, the Point's undulating jeep road rolled through subalpine fir and Engelmann spruce, which periodically thinned to reveal edge-of-the-world vistas in every direction. Yet the route's highlight was the last mile, where the narrow crest, populated with Bristlecone pines, terminated abruptly at a powerful viewpoint. Brian Head Peak faded in the distant haze, Lake Powell hid beyond Escalante's deeply incised canyon country, and Bryce Canyon's vermillion ramparts overlooked the tangled Paria River gorge.

It was here atop the 10,000-foot plateau that Richard, a fat-tire neophyte straight from Las Vegas and dressed in blue jeans, heavy hiking boots, and motorcycle leathers, made his mountain biking debut. The gang now a dozen strong had long-since returned from Powell Point, glowing with excitement and eager to indulge in another extravagant buffet lunch, when we realized Richard was MIA. Miles back along the trail—his chest heaving, face flushed, and drenched in a waterfall of perspiration—Richard no doubt longed for his Harley and the neon lights of home. Henceforth, Richard was the conscientious commander of our support vehicle.

For three days now our local guides had boasted of "The Gap," a reputedly outrageous and elusive singletrack hidden on the Griffin Top Plateau.

First, however, we had to cross the Barney Top and 10 miles of tough jeep roads ending with a wicked descent through a field of volcanic scree: wicked (***wik'***-*id*) *adj. 1. exceeding the limits of what is normal or tolerable. 2. involving the possibility of injury, pain, or loss.* Enough said.

Riding the Gap was a short course in observed trials riding—a 3-mile obstacle course laden with volcanic boulders, deadfall, steep off-angle slopes, and hairpin turns. Spontaneous bursts of whooping and hollering pierced the calm forest, as did the evening's blinding sunbeams. Barker Reservoirs marked the end of singletrack and the beginning of a full-throttle, 17-mile downhill to Escalante, punctuated with sweeping turns and two soak-me-to-the-bones water crossings.

Escalante to Boulder (45 miles)

We poured slowly out of the Moqui Motel for a late breakfast and casual discussions with the Forest Service and Bureau of Land Management representatives about biking opportunities in the Escalante area. Despite these alluring biking prospects, our thoughts were tightly focused on the 3,000-foot wake-up climb to the summit of Hell's Backbone atop the Aquarius. But not wanting the Golden Agers van to be deemed a poor investment, we frantically piled in. As elevation rose so did our spirits, and before long we marveled at the scenic oddity of pedaling through sun-drenched aspen groves and viewing deeply incised slickrock canyons.

At the turn of the century, Escalante was difficult to reach because of the rugged and broken terrain. Boulder, on the other hand, was near the edge of the world. During the 1930s, the Civilian Conservation Corps built the daring Hell's Backbone road across the flank of the Aquarius Plateau, linking the two towns. The road was coined the "poison road, one drop sudden death." At the road's apex, the Hell's Backbone Bridge still spans the deep cleft along a ridge no wider than the single-lane bridge itself. Sheer canyon walls hundreds of feet tall drop to the bottom of Death Hollow and Sand Canyon, the headwaters of the Escalante River.

We spent a lot of time at the bridge gazing across the wondrous and foreboding terrain. Geologist Clarence Dutton, in the 1880s, described the region in vivid prose unlike a scholar of science: ". . . crumbling buttes, red and white domes, rock platforms gashed with profound canyons . . . burning with bright color and flooded with blazing sunlight." The upper Escalante River's tributaries flow through a designated Wilderness Area but still face challenges from carbon dioxide drilling and logging proposals to harvest the Aquarius Plateau's timber.

Once off the Backbone, we savored a few miles of UT 12, one of America's most scenic highways, which winds into Boulder. After a quick lunch we were off pedaling again. Alpine forests and rim-edge panoramas became memories as we dropped into the fiery canyon country along the Burr Trail. At Deer Creek Campground, Anasazi State Park curator Larry Davis and his family greeted us with a fine Dutch oven banquet of barbecued pork and chicken, accented with western potatoes and well-seasoned with pepper and onions. As we huddled around a roaring campfire late into the night beneath the star-speckled October sky, Larry told enchanting tales of the "Ancient Ones" to the background music of taped Indian flute songs and Craig's harmonica.

Boulder to Bullfrog: The Burr Trail (50 miles)

Daybreak arrived with the tranquility expected of the desert, and heads poked one-by-one from nylon cocoons. Overhead, clear skies prevailed once again, but a faint rumble from afar grew increasingly louder. Seconds later the ground trembled, not from Nature unleashing her fury from cumulus clouds but from the thundering rounds of downshifting diesels as heavy machinery rolled to work sites along the Burr Trail. "Hayduke Lives," we thought, but we laid low.

Throughout mystical Long Canyon, we observed proper trail etiquette by "yielding the trail" and testing the truck drivers' reactions with a friendly wave and a tip of the helmet. In a region of heated environmental controversy, their return greetings ranged from friendly-but-surprised nods to the proverbial outstretched middle finger.

But it was Ken who, resplendent in flaming-red bike shorts and jersey and donning a Ralph Loren lariat-and-cowboy-patterned designer bandanna, went in for a closer cultural exchange. Overcome with amiability, he approached a group of weather-torn workers resting in the blade of their monstrous D–8 dozer and asked if anyone would like to take his trusty steed for a whirl. "Sheeit," one salty dog barked, "you won't catch me on one o' them sumbitch crotch rockets." End of the cultural interlude.

The "improved" Burr Trail wound silently past the Circle Cliffs and through reclusive country no doubt crossed by many but visited intimately by few. As the group spread out, many of us rode alone. Hours of steady pedaling on the newly paved road (it's not asphalt but "chip-seal" proponents argue) allowed time for contemplation and reflection, both of the tour's past days and of Utah's treasured public lands.

Smooth cycling graded back to dirt when the Burr plummeted through Muley Twist Canyon in the southern tip of Capitol Reef National Park. Although descending the serpentine switchbacks was riotous, we kept our speeds at bay, the more safely to marvel at this gloriously rugged piece of the world.

Here, at Muley Twist Canyon, the Water Pocket Fold has thrust up a seemingly impenetrable rock barrier or "reef." Late afternoon sunlight illuminated the sheer Wingate sandstone walls and steeply inclined strata, while the Henry Mountains' volcanic peaks loomed overhead—yet another sublime medley of desert redrock and alpine splendor. Andrew, a California inductee to Utah's stunning diversity, summed it up, "This is nuts!"

Alas, after countless miles of the Burr's bone-jarring washboards south of Capitol Reef, we reached our destination—the Defiance House Lodge perched atop the Bullfrog shoreline on Lake Powell. At dinner we feasted. Each tallied the miles he or she accomplished and recapped the tour's highlights. But of all the tour's participants, only one had successfully completed the entire ride from Brian Head to Bullfrog: "Murph," the proprietor of Brian Head Cross Country and Bike Shop—a quiet man of robust stature, many pounds overweight, and who had contracted asthma from years of fighting forest fires. Our first impressions were misleading, for Murph has ski toured and mountain biked many of the most remote and exotic destinations in southern Utah. Few hardcore adventurers have telemarked off Hell's Backbone and Navajo Mountain. Murph's unyielding stamina warranted tremendous respect. His secret? "Those cinnamon Atomic Fireball candies. I get maybe 10 to 15 miles per ball—a half dozen last me all day." So much for PowerBars®.

Author's closing notes:

Duplicating the Tour de Frog is a logistic nightmare. Instead, use the segments above as stepping stones for personal explorations of Utah's southern plateaus and canyon country. Each leg hosts numerous peripheral routes, some well known, many serendipitous treasures. This relatively secluded portion of Utah is a mountain biker's paradise. You'll often discover that the bike tracks you find are simply your own.

17 Spruce Trail (Horse Valley Peak)

Location:	Panguitch Lake (14 miles east of Brian Head, 19 miles southwest of Panguitch)
Length:	23.5 miles
Configuration:	Loop (clockwise)
Tread:	Doubletrack, singletrack
Physical Difficulty:	Advanced to expert (large elevation gain, primitive singletrack, highly technical descent to Panguitch Lake, portaging required)
Technical Difficulty:	Low to high (Clear Creek road is packed dirt but is rocky near summit; Spruce Trail is sometimes highly technical and has several hike-a-bike sections; a good doubletrack through Horse Valley is followed by an uphill hike-a-bike; bouldery descent to Panguitch Lake may require dismounting)
Elevation Changes:	High: 10,540 feet (Horse Valley Peak) Low: 8,240 feet (Panguitch Lake) Gain: 3,600 feet
Maps:	USGS 1:24,000 scale: Panguitch Lake and Red Creek Reservoir, Utah (Spruce Trail is mostly accurate)
Land Status:	Dixie National Forest (Cedar Ranger District) and private property

If you love to climb, crave technical conditions, scoff at portaging your bike a bit, and are keen on backcountry adventures to remote areas on seldom traveled trails, then this is your kind of ride. This loop ride is also the perfect alternative to the Brian Head to Panguitch trek, especially if you curse the required, time-consuming shuttle.

This route begins at Panguitch Lake with initially easy pedaling up the Clear Creek road. But you'll encounter steep, rocky conditions near its summit. Spruce Trail is bittersweet: it crosses pristine terrain where views extend to the earth's cur-

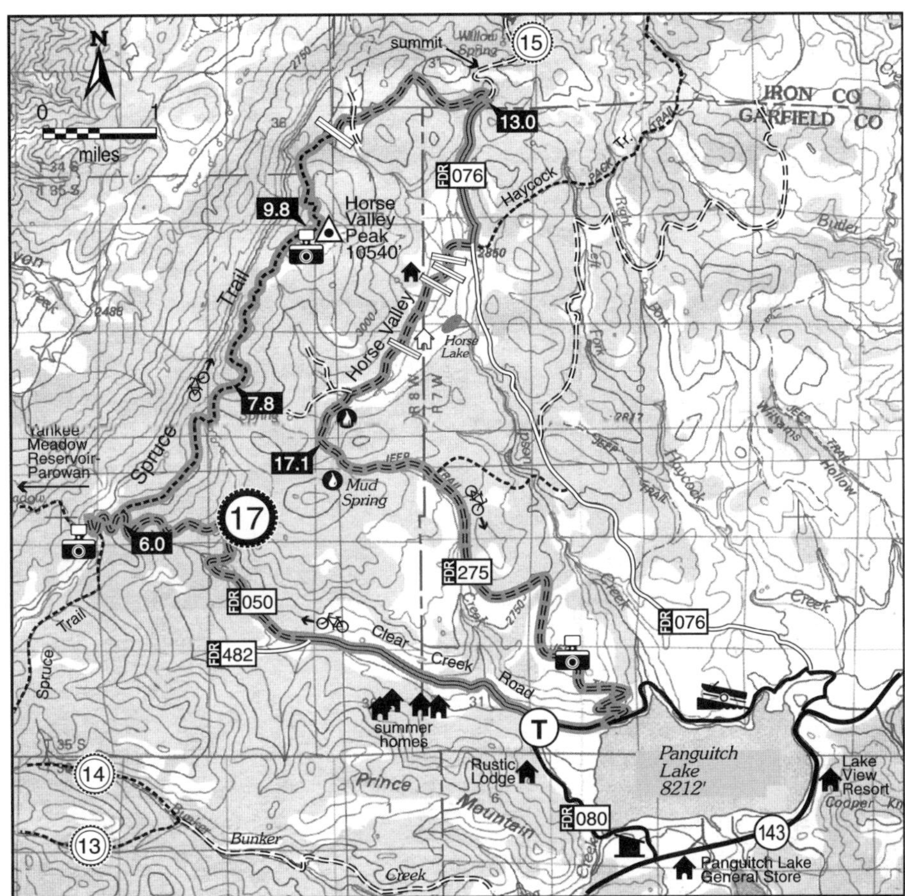

USGS 1:100,000 scale: Panguitch (50 meter contour interval).

vature, but it is fraught with both highly technical sections and slopes that are unbearably steep. Upbeat doubletracks circle back through luscious meadows and peaceful forests. The finale is a tire-bashing descent back to Panguitch Lake.

Regardless of where you park, pedal around Panguitch Lake's marshy shore on the paved west lake road (FDR 080) to the Clear Creek road/FDR 050 (mileage begins here). The all-weather road rises moderately for several miles along the quiescent Clear Creek valley, which is wedged between wooded volcanic knolls. Private homes dot the airy meadows or are tucked exclusively amidst the trees.

The Clear Creek road steepens, becomes increasingly rocky, and begins switchbacking about 1 mile past the junction with FDR 482 (to the left), signed "Dead End, Private Property." You'll exhaust your granny gears quickly. Spruce Trail cuts off to the right on a sharp left-hand turn in the road (**m6.0**), but tack on the extra half-mile climb to Clear Creek's summit for a grand view of the Sidney Peaks

Crossing Horse Valley.

ridge hovering over Parowan Canyon. (Upon descending from the summit, Spruce Trail branches left from the road's second right-hand curve.)

Initially, Spruce Trail is utterly blissful and easily justifies the effort to reach it. But 1 mile out, the path is transformed from a beauty to a beast as it plunges into and then claws out of a bouldery, wooded ravine. Drag your bike up the slope for several hundred feet; then, legs willing, hop in the saddle and inch your way uphill through the aspens. Finally, the trail levels and enters a sloping sage-covered field bordered by aspens on the trail's downhill side (**m7.8**). In years past, this section was dreadfully confusing. Do not contour around the peak; this is a false trail. Instead, cross the slope a couple hundred feet, and then portage uphill through the sage and rocks. Angle uphill, roughly 45 degrees, toward the distant interface of aspen and fir, keeping an eye out for cairns marking the line. The trail is evident after you have made the climb and are back in the trees. (This section may be redesigned in the future.)

The primitive trail stays to the rounded ridge, from which views extend across southwestern Utah. The trail can be indistinct where it leaves the aspens and crosses the grassy meadows. Go straight/north across the meadows; the trail is evident when it reenters the trees. Look for tree blazes, horse hoof marks, sawed logs, and other telltale signs of the path. Horse Valley Peak, looming to the north, is a menacing obstacle that also requires a hike-a-bike to surmount (**m9.8**). Refresh your legs at the peak, and enjoy the circumambient vista across the Brian Head–Bryce countryside.

Duck back into the trees and hunker down for a precipitous descent on a gouged section of trail. Thereafter, scream down the grassy track through musky woods (bunny-hopping deadfall along the way) and exit the trees to a jeep road. Cross the meadow, ignoring doubletracks forking left and right, and ride uphill between two low knolls. Descend through Forks Valley and intersect the Horse Valley road at a Dixie National Forest sign (**m13.0**).

Now cruise down the all-weather road 1.5 miles. Turn right on a doubletrack marked by a solitary post opposite Haycock Trail, and cross Horse Valley. Go through two gates, ignore the third gate that blocks a private drive, and pass through a fourth gate to continue up the wide valley. As the valley narrows, fork left on FDR 275, and make your way up the field to the forest's edge. This section is typically laced with gopher burrows. And since it is seldom traveled, these burrows will keep your suspension active. Water emanating from nearby springs may coat the meadow with a thin veneer, especially during spring.) Dodge left after entering the trees, and then succumb to a widow-maker climb marred with boulders (**17.1**). Once surmounted, the route is virtually all downhill. Over the next 4 miles, the doubletrack varies from rough and rattling to smooth and soothing. After passing Mud Springs, you can spy Sunset Cliffs and Powell Point on the eastern horizon.

Finally, the road affords a view of Panguitch Lake far below, which glistens in the midday sun. But to reach the lake, you must endure a savage descent down a bouldery doubletrack that requires precise handling or prudent dismounts. Cool down while pedaling the lakeside road to the Clear Creek road junction and back to your vehicle.

Notes & Precautions:

This ride requires good route-finding skills; carry appropriate maps. Portions of this route are remote, so plan accordingly by carrying ample water and food, emergency rain wear, and appropriate tools. Horse Valley is private property, but the main road is a public right of way.

Trailhead Access:

From Brian Head, drive 4.0 miles south on UT 143 to the junction with UT 148 (Cedar Breaks National Monument). Turn left and continue on UT 143 for 14 miles to the south shore of Panguitch Lake. Park near the Panguitch Lake General Store or drive FDR 080 to the Rustic Lodge or farther to the Clear Creek road. (Ask permission to park at either the store or the lodge. A fee may be charged.) From Panguitch, drive 19 miles on UT 143 to the south shore of Panguitch Lake and FDR 080.

18 Birch Spring Knoll

Location:	2.2 miles south of Panguitch Lake		
Length:	18.5 miles		
Configuration:	Loop (clockwise)		
Tread:	Doubletrack		
Physical Difficulty:	Intermediate (moderate climb out of Black Rock Valley; route finding near Lake Hollow)		
Technical Difficulty:	Low (packed dirt, scattered rocks and cinder gravels, a few ruts)		
Elevation Changes:	High:	8,650	feet (between Miller Knoll and Birch Spring Knoll)
	Low:	7,675	feet (Black Rock Valley)
	Gain:	1,300	feet
Maps:	USGS 1:24,000 scale: Haycock Mountain and Panguitch Lake, Utah		
Land Status:	Dixie National Forest (Cedar Ranger District) and private property		

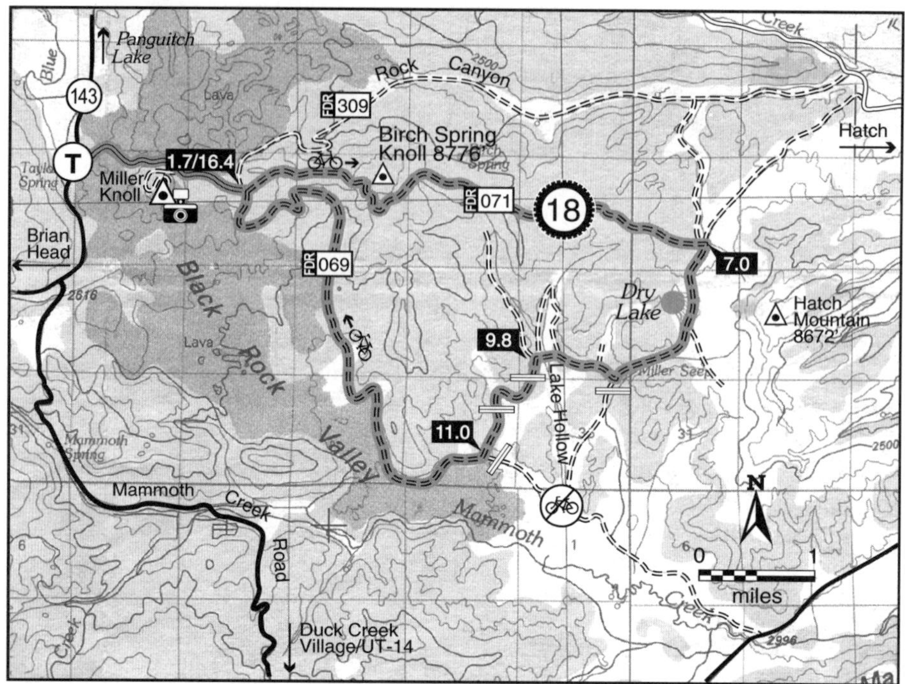

USGS 1:100,000 scale Panguitch (50 meter contour interval).

The Birch Spring Knoll loop is a crash course in volcanic geology. As recently as 1,000 years ago (a snap of the fingers in geologic time), small volcanic centers spewed forth fiery lava and belched glowing embers across these high plateaus. Today you'll recognize these odd features as bleak tongues of black basalt interrupting the plateau's lush forests; as pyramid-shaped cinder cones popping up like huge ant hills above the land's general levelness; and as sink holes, caves, and lava tubes, which are remnant magmatic conduits.

In addition to studying these volcanic features, you'll ride across gentle highlands, wind through small valleys, and amble past mixed forests populated with wildlife. And tranquility abounds since this route is infrequently traveled.

From the outset, the terrain is conspicuously volcanic in origin because the road dissects an ancient lava flow. Once molten rock, these fiery rivers flowed sluggishly and devoured everything in their paths. The lava's surface and leading edge cooled rapidly breaking into bouldery chunks. Upon closer inspection, you'll find that the rock's texture varies from dense and solid to rough and vesicular depending upon how quickly gases, once trapped in the rock, were released. Patches of pastel lichens, as showy as summertime wildflowers, aid the weathering process by gradually decomposing the rock. The smallest amount of newly formed soil wedged into the rocks' cracks can support the tenacious root systems of plants, brush, and trees.

The edge of a conspicuous lava flow.

Miller Knoll, on your right, is a textbook cinder cone. Gaseous explosions once ejected ash, pumice, and cinders that piled around the vent, building its symmetrical shape. You can take a mile-long side trip to the knoll's summit to survey the foreboding terrain you are about to cross. Look at the crudely crossbedded ash and pumice in the small excavation. Geologists argue, mostly in jest, about how to classify such deposits because they are frothy magma when ejected into the air (volcanic) but cooled crystals when deposited by the wind (sedimentary).

Stay straight on the main road at a four-way junction 0.5 mile past Miller Knoll (**m1.7/m16.4**). You'll return on the right fork from Lake Hollow later on. As you pedal out the low ridge toward Birch Spring Knoll, you will gaze upon desolate terrain composed of overlapping lava flows. At a cattle guard on the knoll's east side, the road turns to doubletrack laced with ruts, cinders, and rocks and descends gradually for 3 miles to the base of Hatch Mountain.

Ignore a doubletrack forking left/north. Then at a T junction (**m7.0**), fork right toward Lake Hollow and pedal south for 1 mile. On the far side of Dry Lake (sometimes so dry it's merely a grassy field), fork right at a Y junction on a doubletrack of red cinders, and descend a pine-filled hollow between two knolls. Ignore a road to the left leading to a gate (private property), pass two tracks to the right, and enter the small brush-filled valley of Lake Hollow. Sunlight penetrating the pines spotlights low cliffs of orange-cream limestone. At a four-way junction on the hollow's west side (**m9.8**), fork left/south on a faint doubletrack running along the interface between the pink limestone knolls to the west and Lake Hollow to the east. Do not follow the main road, which bends right/north and rises up Lake Hollow. You'll swear you're lost, but press on.

Pass through a wire gate and then a steel gate over the next mile; both mark the boundary between private property and national forest. (Close both gates behind you, naturally.) One-half mile farther, stay right where an unsigned jeep road forks left and crosses the valley (**m11.0**). The main road then curves west around the southern base of Mahogany Hill and along the edge of the lava beds filling Black Rock Valley. The 4 miles of gentle to moderate climbing through ponderosa pines, aspen, and fir return you to the Birch Spring Knoll road (**m16.4**). Coast past Miller Knoll back to the trailhead.

Notes & Precautions:

This route crosses parcels of private property in Lake Hollow. Cedar City Ranger District affirms the main route is a public right-of-way. Camping, lodging, food, limited supplies, and gasoline are available at Panguitch Lake.

Trailhead Access:

From Brian Head, drive 4.0 miles south on UT 143 to the junction with UT 148 (Cedar Breaks National Monument). Turn left and continue on UT 143 for 11 miles to FDR 069, signed "Birch Spring Knoll." From Panguitch, drive 19 miles on UT 143 to Panguitch Lake Campground and then 2.2 miles farther to FDR 069, signed "Birch Spring Knoll." Park at your discretion alongside the dirt road.

19 Dead Lake

Location:	9 miles east of Brian Head
Length:	7.2 miles
Configuration:	Out-and-back
Tread:	All-weather road, doubletrack
Physical Difficulty:	Novice to intermediate (steady but gentle climb on the return leg)
Technical Difficulty:	Low to moderate (minor washboards; bouldery doubletrack)
Elevation Changes:	High: 9,630 feet (trailhead: UT 143)
	Low: 9,060 feet (Dead Lake)
	Gain: 570 feet
Maps:	USGS 1:24,000 scale: Panguitch Lake, Utah
Land Status:	Dixie National Forest (Cedar City Ranger District)

This is an easy ride geared for first-time bikers and those interested in pioneer history because it follows part of the Historic Old Sorrel Log Road of 1898. The first half of the route follows an all-weather road across sage meadows and through groves of mixed timber. The second half is a bouldery doubletrack penetrating richly scented woods. Contrary to its name, secluded Dead Lake harbors rainbow trout and is a popular destination for anglers. So pack your rod and reel, and spend the afternoon casting a baited hook.

Few educational institutions have a more dramatic founding than Southern Utah University in Cedar City. In 1897, the Utah Legislature selected Cedar City to host a teachers training or "normal" school. The Legislature declared that a new building must house the school rather than the Cedar City Ward Hall, which was initially used. But that decision came in the middle of winter when supplies were scarce, and the

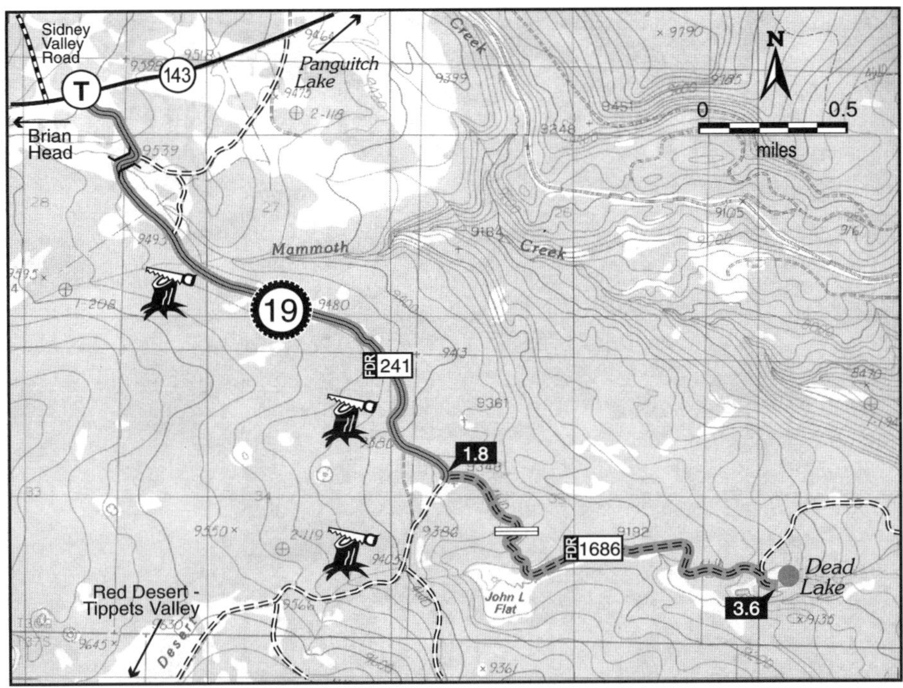

USGS 1:24,000 scale: Panguitch Lake (40 foot contour interval).

The "Old Sorrel" monument on the campus of Southern Utah University.

new building had to be completed by fall of the upcoming year. Rather than lose the institution, the residents of Cedar City, many of whom were uneducated laborers and would never benefit from the higher education training center, donated supplies, food, equipment, and other materials toward the school's construction. But lumber remained insufficient, so an expedition was organized and set out for the Jensen Sawmill near Mammoth Creek.

Loggers, sawyers, and haulers battled blizzard conditions to collect and transport the timber from the frigid mountain to the valley below, with each trip taking over two days. But drifting snow from a two-day storm erased the log road, dashing all hope of completing the journey and of accomplishing the incredible task of building the school. The heroic efforts of an old sorrel horse saved the mission and the men's lives. A strong, quiet work horse of massive stature, "Old Sorrel" would through himself into the snow drifts, rear up, and lunge forward again, breaking down the icy mounds and clearing the route.

Against seemingly unsurmountable odds, "Old Main" was constructed on time to house the Branch Normal School. It later became the first building of Southern Utah University and stands today as a monument to the selfless service and hard work of the 1,500 citizens of Cedar City at the end of the nineteenth century. As you ride this route, reflect upon those who passed this way 100 years earlier, and upon the sacrifices and hardships that were a daily part of pioneer life.

From UT 143, follow the Red Desert road south past markers tagged "Old Main." Washboards may develop during prolonged dry spells, but they are never consequential. After about one-half mile, bend right and cross the small bridge over Mammoth Creek. Ignore all spur roads; these lead to logging areas for fuel wood. Stay on the main road for a total of **1.8** miles from UT 143.

Amidst commingling fir and aspen trees and where the road bends conspicuously right, fork left on a doubletrack posted "FDR 1686, Old Main 25 mi." Now the riding becomes more challenging because the doubletrack is swarmed with volcanic boulders. Dodging the rocks, or simply bouncing over them, may be a novelty for some bikers or a nuisance for others.

Drop down a short hill to John L. Flat, bear left, and follow the narrow creek-fed hollow. Within 0.5 mile, fork right at a T junction. Dead Lake is a few hundred yards farther (**m3.6**). Choose the sunny north shore or shaded south shore from which to cast your line. Return to the trailhead by backtracking.

Although little remains, you can visit the old Jensen Sawmill site by first returning to the T junction, which you encountered prior to arriving at Dead Lake. Follow the doubletrack north and then east for about 1.5 miles. The site is on the downhill side of the jeep road after it bends south and crosses a low ridge. (On a map, it's very near the county line.) Look for an interpretive sign placed by a scout troop. If you continue on this jeep road, you'll eventually descend to summer homes in the Mammoth Creek area.

Notes & Precautions:

Truck traffic may be encountered on the Red Desert road.

Trailhead Access:

From Brian Head Mall, drive 4 miles south on UT 143 to the junction with UT 148 for Cedar Breaks National Monument. Turn left on UT 143 toward Panguitch, and drive 4.9 miles to a dirt and cinder road signed "Red Desert," located immediately east of the Sidney Valley road (FDR 048) and just west of milepost 24. Park alongside the road at the junction.

20 Red Desert–Tippets Valley

Location:	UT 143 (9 miles east of Brian Head) to Duck Creek Village
Length:	15.5 miles
Configuration:	Point-to-point
Tread:	All-weather roads, doubletracks, ATV trail
Physical Difficulty:	Intermediate (rolling terrain throughout but a rocky, 0.5 mile climb in Red Desert; numerous logging roads necessitate some route-finding skills)
Technical Difficulty:	Low to high (easy cruising on good dirt roads; rocky, 0.5-mile climb in Red Desert; some rock hopping across lava boulders in Tippets Valley; steep descent over 100 water bars on Lost Hunter Trail)
Elevation Changes:	High: 9,600 feet (trailhead at UT 143 and in Red Desert) Low: 8,430 feet (trail end at Duck Creek Village) Gain: 700 feet
Maps:	USGS 1:24,000 scale: Henrie Knolls and Panguitch Lake, Utah (Lost Hunter and Duck Creek ATV Trails are not shown)
Land Status:	Dixie National Forest (Cedar City Ranger District)

After you've explored Brian Head's wonderful downhill singletracks, venture on this backcountry tour to Red Desert and Tippets Valley. You'll wander across vast meadows and pass volcanic features that embellish these alpine highlands. For the most part, the riding is relatively easy. However, you will have to tackle a half-mile rock-splattered hill in Red Desert, dismount briefly where the trail clips a lava field in Tippets Valley, and descend countless log water bars on Lost Hunter Trail to Duck Creek Campground. Watch for wildlife on this route; porcupines have been spotted scampering across the meadows and hiding in the trees.

The Red Desert road begins as an all-weather road coated with fine volcanic cinders. Cross Mammoth Creek and pedal across sage meadows separated by stands of fir and aspen. Along this initial section, you'll pass numerous posts tagged "Old Main" that mark the Historic Old Sorrel Log Road of 1898. Ignore spur roads labeled with letters; these roads lead to fuel wood cutting areas. Pass FDR 1686, which forks left at about 1.8 miles from UT 143 and leads to Dead Lake. Instead, round the curve and continue south. Here, the route can be confusing because many logging roads branch from the main road. About 0.25 mile past FDR 1686, the main road bends right and begins rising gently. Thereafter, stay left at an unsigned junction (the right fork is a dead end); then, at the next junction, fork right (**m2.9**). (FDR 2051 forks left.) You navigated these turns correctly if you can view cone-shaped Hancock Peak straight ahead to the west. The Red Desert road curves south and becomes a rock-studded doubletrack following the east edge of Red Desert.

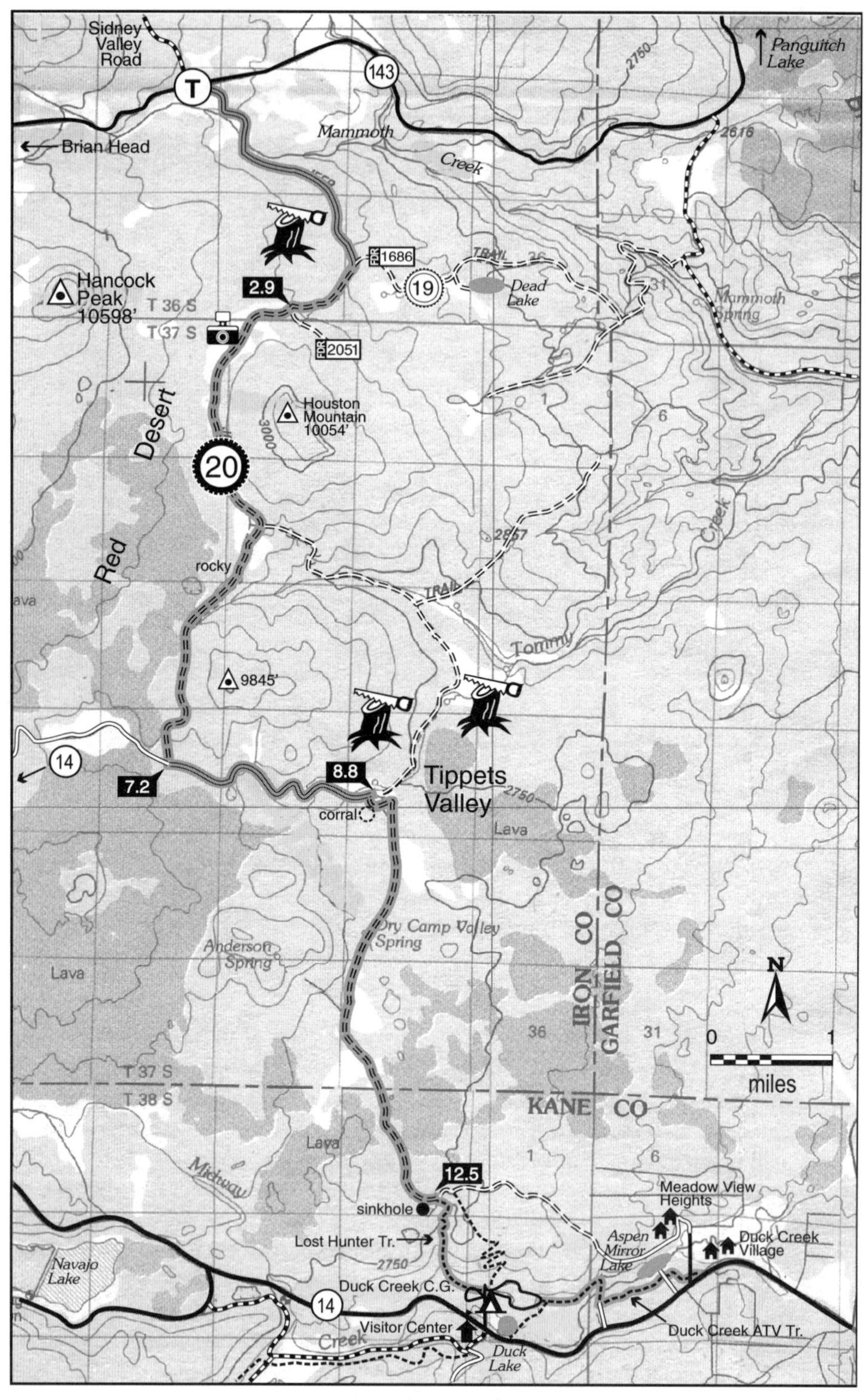

USGS 1:100,000 scale: Panguitch (50 meter contour interval).

Hancock Peak in the Red Desert.

Over the next few miles, you'll pass numerous features that reflect the volcanic activity that occurred 1,000–5,000 years ago. Hancock Peak and other nearby "cinder cones" were relatively small vents from which lava oozed or molten debris was explosively ejected. Geologist use the Hawaiian term "aa" (pronounced ah-ah) to describe the blocky and broken structure of these lava flows. A "lava tube" forms when the surface of a flow cools to a hard crust, but the subsurface molten rock remains liquid and keeps flowing, leaving behind a vacant space. If the roof of a tube collapses a small depression in the ground is created, called a "sink hole." If the lava tube does not collapse, the subsurface tunnel may extend for hundreds of yards or even miles. The Mammoth Creek area northeast of Duck Creek Village is noted for its lava tubes.

Half way across Red Desert, the road descends slightly, cuts across the top of a deepening valley, and then rises up a moderately steep hill scattered with boulders. This is the route's toughest section. Thereafter, the riding is easy and fast paced. At a T junction (**m7.2**), signed "Tippets Valley (left), Sage Valley (right)," take the Tippets Valley road left and swoop through wide turns for 1.6 miles. As soon as the downhill begins to level and the road follows the edge of a grassy field, fork right on a less-than-obvious doubletrack (junction may be signed "Duck Creek, Aspen Mirror Lake, 4x4 only"). A broken log corral tucked amidst the trees is a landmark (**m8.8**).

Take the faded doubletrack past the corral, veer east up the meadow, and then curve south. Orange diamonds tacked to trees mark the track as a winter snowmobile route. Wander across sunny meadows separated by groves of aspen, fir, and spruce, and pass a cattle pond. Hop over volcanic boulders at the edge of a lava bed, tip-toe around a boggy area, and race through the aspens. One-half mile farther, the road bends left along the edge of a clearing defined by a small sink hole. Immediately thereafter, fork right on Lost Hunter Trail (**12.5**), and follow the faint path to "the giant's staircase" where the path descends steeply and is crossed by 100 mostly rideable log water bars. (How many did you count?) Exit the trail to the amphitheater parking area in Duck Creek Campground. (If you miss the turnoff for Lost Hunter Trail, you have another chance a few hundred feet farther on the doubletrack. If you miss the second turnoff, stay on the doubletrack to the Meadow View Heights subdivision. Take Rim Road to Whispering Pines Road to Spring Road and descend "the Cut" to Duck Creek Village.)

Wind through the campground to site 90 on D loop and hop on the Duck Creek ATV Trail (boulders prevent ATVs from entering the campground). Freewheel alongside Duck Creek, cross the metal footbridge, follow the dirt road south a bit, and then fork left on the continued trail. Cross the paved access road to Aspen Mirror Lake, and culminate the tour by dodging ponderosa pines and scattered boulders to Duck Creek Village. Pizza and drinks await at Cedar Mountain Pizza and Subs.

Notes & Precautions:

This route requires some route-finding skills because of the many spur roads that lead to logging areas. This route should be avoided when wet because sections of the Red Desert and Tippets Valley roads are clay based and will turn to tire-clogging glop. Be cautious of truck traffic accessing logging areas.

Trailhead Access:

Duck Creek Village: From Brian Head Mall, drive 4 miles south on UT 143 and then 7.5 miles south on UT 148 through Cedar Breaks National Monument to UT 14. Turn left/east on UT 14, and travel 12 miles to Duck Creek Village. (From Cedar City, travel 30 miles east on UT 14/Center Street to Duck Creek Village.) To reach the trailhead, return through Cedar Breaks, and turn right/east on UT 143 toward Panguitch. Drive 4.9 miles to an all-weather road signed "Red Desert." It's located just east of the Sidney Valley road/FDR 048 and just west of milepost 24. Park at the junction.

21 Virgin River Rim Trail

Location:	Along the Pink Cliffs, centered about Navajo Lake (21 miles southeast of Brian Head, 28 miles east of Cedar City)
Length:	33 miles
Configuration:	Point-to-point (see Options for loop rides)
Tread:	Singletrack, doubletrack
Physical Difficulty:	Advanced to expert (countless intermittent climbs—many are steep and rough; see Options for easier routes; some route finding required)
Technical Difficulty:	Moderate (a gamut of singletrack challenges on the constantly undulating trail; many steep, angular, switchbacks require dismounting)

Elevation Changes: (east to west)	High:	9,000 feet (Strawberry Point)
	Low:	8,250 feet (Strawberry Road)
	High:	9,380 feet (Lars Fork)
	Low:	8,900 feet (Cascade Falls trailhead)
	High:	9,800 feet (near Navajo Peak)
	Low:	9,000 feet (Te-ah Campground)
	High:	9,450 feet (Webster Flat)
	Low:	8,200 feet (Woods Ranch)
	Gain:	4,100 feet
Maps:	USGS 1:24,000 scale: Navajo Lake, Straight Canyon, Strawberry Point, and Webster Flat, Utah (trail is not shown)	
Land Status:	Dixie National Forest (Cedar City Ranger District)	

Built between 1993–1995 by the Dixie National Forest, the Virgin River Rim Trail (VRRT) instantly became a newfound "classic" thus joining Utah's many other world-renown routes. This 33-mile trek overloads your senses by combining a variety of trail-riding conditions and forest nuances with postcard-quality scenery from atop the Grand Staircase. The VRRT traces the rim of the Pink Cliffs, where the edge of the Markagunt Plateau has been clawed by erosion to reveal the colorful Claron Formation—the famed strata of Cedar Breaks National Monument and Bryce Canyon National Park. As your eyes wander away from the rim, they fall upon the timbered headwaters of the North Fork Virgin River, which cuts deep into the White Cliffs and shapes Zion National Park miles away.

The VRRT is no spin through the park; it demands acclimated lungs for high elevations, solid legs to surmount many arduous climbs, and good handling skills to navigate sections stippled with rocks. However, an array of peripheral routes creates limitless options catering to all abilities.

The VRRT was constructed for non-motorized use with help from the Sierra Club and the Alternative Behavior Learning Environment crews (ABLE), and with funding assistance from the Utah Division of Parks and Recreation. Hats off, rather, helmets off, to these groups for their hard work and financial backing and to the Cedar City Ranger District for its visionary mission.

The Virgin River Rim Trail could be a small guidebook in itself, but here's the scoop on the complete point-to-point trek from Strawberry Point to Woods Ranch:

Hold your horses! Before you saddle up and depart from the Strawberry Point parking area, take the short path to the point itself. Straddle the point's brass Geodesic survey cap, and gaze from the quizzically carved cliffs across bountiful forests to the sandstone temples of Zion National Park. An unearthly energy electrifies the air and fills your soul with reverence and awe.

Now begin the VRRT by pedaling down Strawberry Road 0.5 mile and forking right on the signed trail. The 2-mile raveled ribbon of dirt showcases the efforts of those who dedicated time and energy into building the VRRT, for this is arguably one of the finest trails in the region. But if you're not attentive or you carry too much speed into any given curve, you might take a trail-side aspen right in the kisser. Splat!

Cross Strawberry Road (**m1.8**) and zero your altimeter watch; at this point you officially begin climbing. The trail rises at Forest Service regulated six to eight percent grades through five tight switchbacks before exiting onto a doubletrack. Take

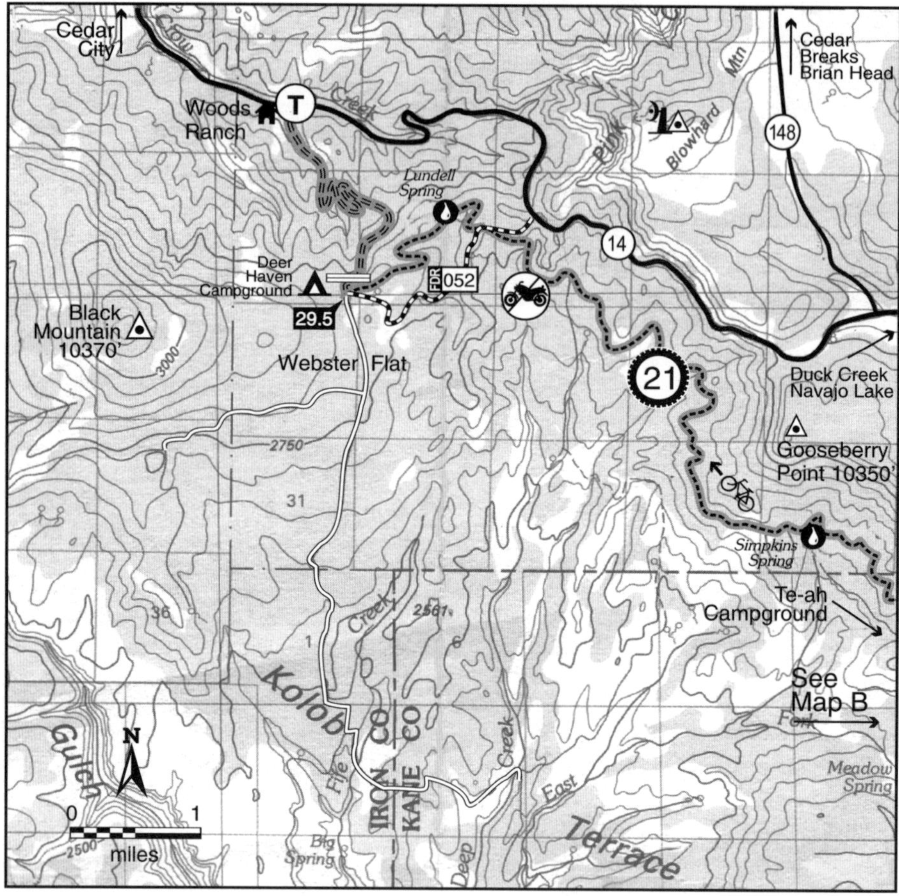

Western section of VRRT—Map A. USGS 1:100,000 scale: Panguitch and Kanab (50 meter contour interval).

the track uphill 0.3 mile, and then fork left on the continued trail. Descend four angular turns to a hollow and cross the doubletrack (closed to vehicles). Cross a lightly flowing creek, and then climb the snaking trail through a darkened tangle of aspen and fir up to a doubletrack. Keep climbing on alternating segments of trail and doubletrack (watch for trail signs) to a stellar viewpoint where you can gaze back toward Strawberry Point. (Peregrine falcons nest in the area, so portions of the trail from Strawberry Road to the Pink Cliffs may be rerouted in the future.)

Take the rim trail along the plateau's edge and past spectacular overlooks to the Lars Fork road (**m7.1**). Then inch up agonizing turns. (Had enough? If so, bail out by descending Lars Fork to Strawberry Road and then circling back to the Point.)

Beyond Lars Fork, the trail follows a more mellow undulating course through the forest, brushing the rim periodically. Short climbs are always offset by exciting downhills. After the trail bends past a knobby point extending from the rim, it descends through sharp turns linked by long straightaways to the parking area for Cascade

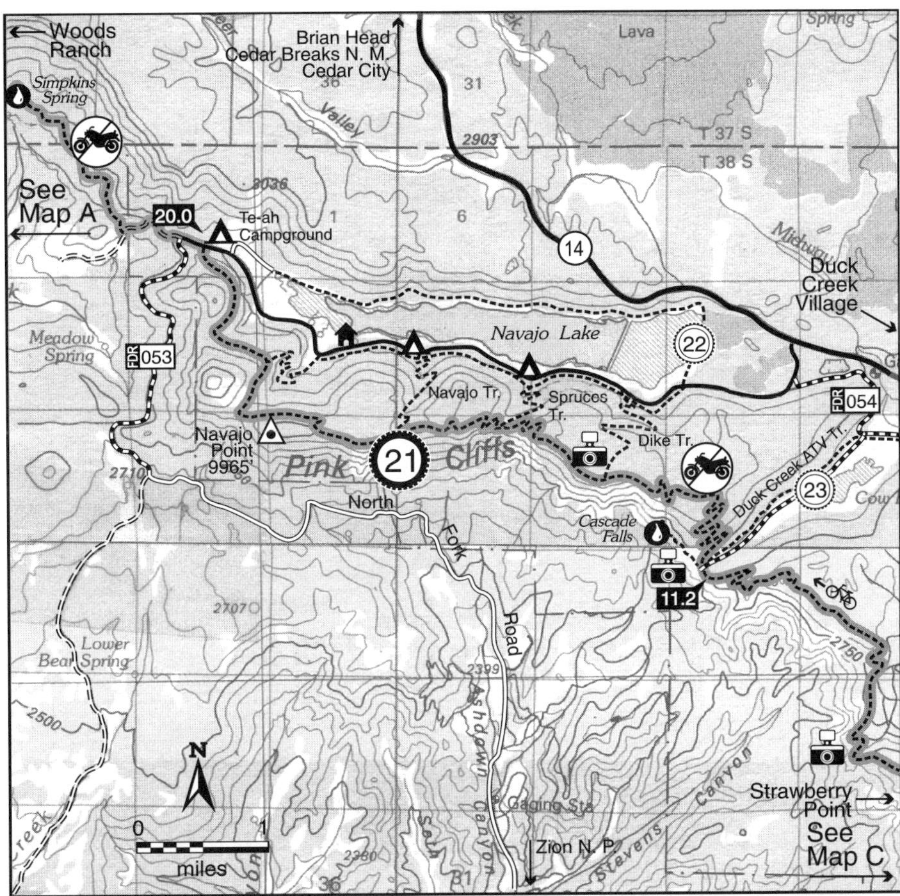

Central section of VRRT—Map B. USGS 1:100,000 scale: Panguitch and Kanab (50 meter contour interval).

Falls National Recreation Trail (**m11.2**). Tether your bike and make the 1-mile round-trip hike to Cascade Falls, which serves as both the subterranean "drain pipe" of Navajo Lake and the headwater of North Fork Virgin River. Absorb as much of the Pink Cliffs' scenery as possible because you'll have fewer opportunities farther along the VRRT.

The next mile is a difficult, 500-foot grind through six angular turns. Milk your granny gear to conserve energy for additional climbs ahead. After a short respite, climb again to the junction with Dike Trail. Zig then zag down to the Saddle to the Spruces Trail junction, and then muscle up to the rim once more, passing Navajo Trail. Curve around the north side of Navajo Point and drop to a pass where the trail bends north. You've paid your dues—for the time being. Give your weary legs a deserved rest on the rampaging, 2-mile descent to Te-ah Campground (**m20.0**), but be alert to trail users ascending the trail from the campground. (Pass Lodge Trail along the way.)

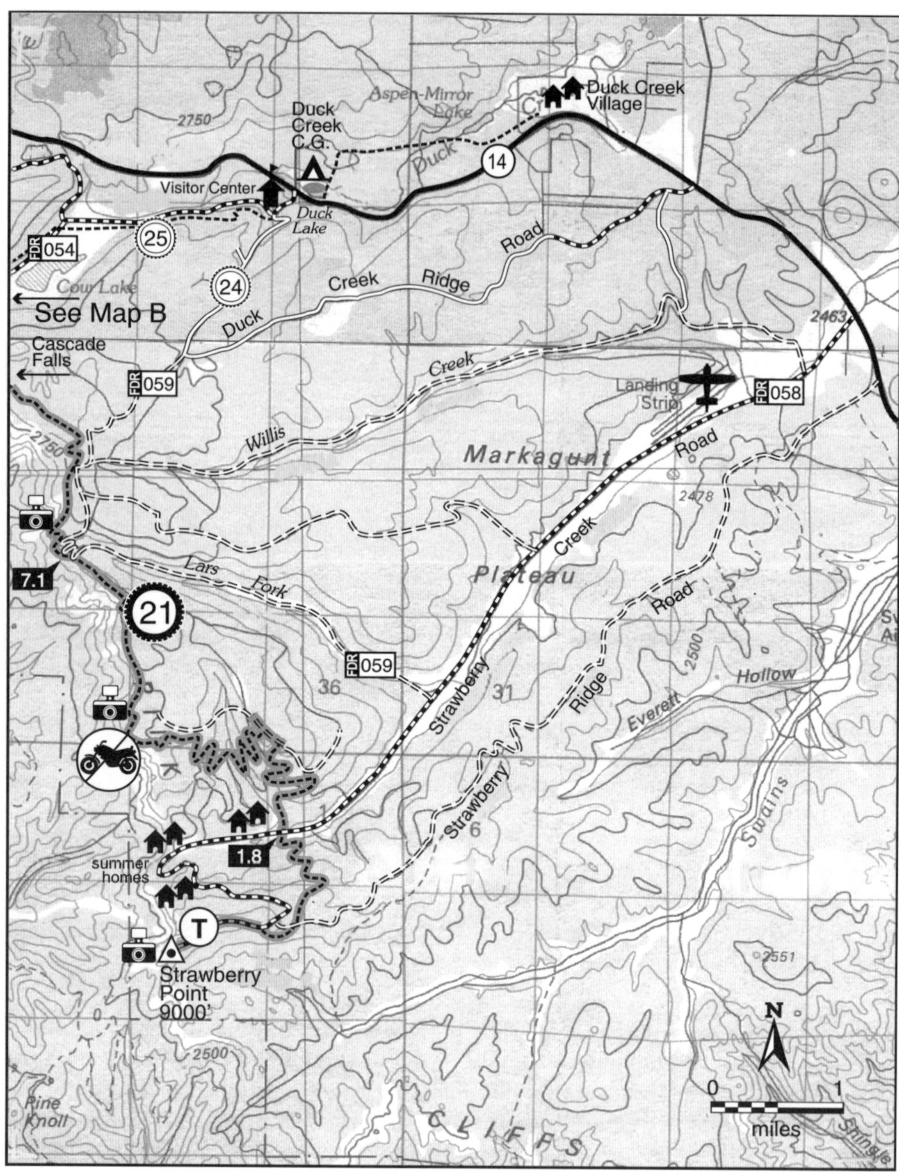

Eastern section of VRRT—Map C. USGS 1:100,000 scale: Panguitch and Kanab (50 meter contour interval).

Now embark on the last leg. Just west of the campground and near the dumpsters, fork right on a doubletrack, descend around a left-hand bend, and fork right 0.25 mile farther on the VRRT signed "Deep Creek, Webster Flat, Woods Ranch." (It's easy to miss this turn, so be looking for it.)

Jim surveys the Virgin River Rim Trail from Strawberry Point (left) then toes the edge of the Pink Cliffs from midroute (right).

Over the next several miles, the VRRT gains a net elevation of only a few hundred feet. Along the way, though, you'll work your gears constantly, as you descend into and then climb out of countless hollows creasing the mountain's side. Although the individual climbs are trivial in of themselves, their cumulative effect shreds already tired legs.

From here on, the marvelous scenery enjoyed earlier is but a memory; any potential views are blocked by throngs of ghostly white aspens and intertwined conifers. Springs seeping from the hillside nourish tall grasses that blanket the lush forest and in turn provide habitat for deer, wild turkeys, and other wildlife.

Intersect a jeep road and follow it uphill for 0.5 mile. Where the road bends right, fork left on the VRRT toward Stucki Spring. One-half mile farther, intersect Webster Flat Road. Legs willing, cross over and take the singletrack up the final climb past Lundell Spring; then freewheel to Deer Haven Campground (**m29.5**). (Alternatively, just take the Webster Flat road around the knoll.)

From the campground's entrance, head north on a doubletrack and go through the wire gate. Check your brakes because you'll drop nearly 1,000 feet over the next few miles. Much of the jeep road ahead is strewn with pebbles, studded with rocks, and punctuated with "kickers." Check your landing pad if you dare launch—no point ruining a perfectly good ride this close to the end. When you intersect an all-weather road, take it right and down to Woods Ranch. Finally, make a beeline to the cooler and propose a toast to this new Utah classic.

Packing fond memories of spectacular views enjoyed earlier, Jim ventures through dense woods on the VRRT's western section.

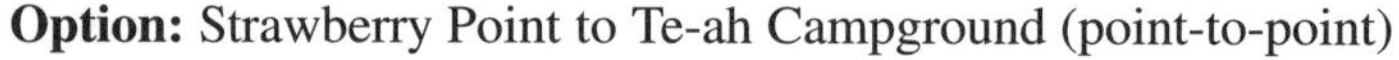

Option: Strawberry Point to Te-ah Campground (point-to-point)

If 33 miles is a big bite to swallow, then this abbreviated 20-mile trek is the perfect alternative. This section of the VRRT offers the best scenery and the best trail-riding conditions. Because there is significant elevation gain, this option is rated advanced level.

Specs.: 20 miles; 3,000-foot gain

Option: Lars Fork–Strawberry Point (double loop)

This intermediate-level, figure-eight loop on the east end of the VRRT boasts captivating scenery and thrilling trail riding, which make it a superior option. To reach the trailhead, drive 4 miles up Strawberry Road from UT 14. Turn up Lars Fork (doubletrack but suitable for passenger cars), and park 0.5 mile farther at one of the several backcountry campsites alongside the road.

The 3-mile, gently-rising Lars Fork jeep road is baby-butt smooth and utterly peaceful (see **m7.1**). When you reach the top, take the VRRT left/east along the rim, up many quick, steep hills to increasingly stellar views of the corrugated cliffs below and of Zion National Park in the distance. Leave the rim and descend on both trails and doubletracks for a of couple miles. (Watch carefully for trail markers.) Fork right on a trail segment that drops you like a pinball through dark, damp woods to a small creek. Cross the doubletrack ahead (posted closed to vehicles), and climb a long-winded section through four turns to another doubletrack. The VRRT follows this jeep road 0.3 mile and then forks from it to the right, continuing as trail. Descend like a dive bomber to Strawberry Road (see **m1.8**).

Had enough? If so, take Strawberry Road 2 miles back to Lars Fork; otherwise, turn right and bike 3 miles up to Strawberry Point to pay homage to the Great Architect. Now backtrack 0.5 mile, peel off the road onto the VRRT, and wiggle and giggle on singletrack to Strawberry Road. Take Strawberry Road 2 miles back to Lars Fork.

Specs.: 15 miles; 1,700-foot gain

Option: Cascade Falls–Navajo Point (loop)

This loop features a short hike to Cascade Falls, challenging riding conditions, and Navajo Lake as the trailhead. It's a close runner up to Lars Fork–Strawberry Point as the best loop option to the VRRT.

Begin at Navajo Lake and take the Navajo Lake road east, forking right on FDR 054 for Cascade Falls. After a fast descent, take the Duck Creek ATV Trail south 1.8 miles to the Cascade Falls trailhead. (See Cascade Falls, also.) After hiking to and from Cascade Falls, climb the VRRT to the plateau above (see **m11.2**). If you fatigue before reaching Navajo Point, simply take one of the three connecting trails back to the lake: Dike, Spruces, or Navajo. Otherwise, descend north from Navajo Point and take Lodge Trail to the Navajo Lake road. Return to your trailhead on the paved road or on the Navajo Lake Loop Trail. Add a few extra miles by descending all the way to Te-ah Campground and looping around the north shore of Navajo Lake on the Navajo Lake Loop Trail. This loop is equally enjoyable counterclockwise.

Specs.: 14.5 miles; 1,700-foot gain

Notes & Precautions:

The VRRT is a huge ride. Plan 6–10 hours riding time plus a couple extra hours for shuttling vehicles. Carry generous amounts of food and water, stock a complete emergency repair kit, and be prepared for afternoon storms. Water is available at Te-ah Campground during the summer. (Contact the Cedar City Ranger District to find out when taps are turned on and off in spring and fall, respectively.) Water is available at Navajo Lodge, located 1.5 miles east of Te-ah. (You may be obligated to buy a snack in return for requesting water.) Deer Haven Organizational Campground is open by reservation only; thus water taps are turned on only when the site is occupied. Cascade Falls is a potential water source but should be purified; it may dry up by late summer.

Trailhead Access:

Woods Ranch: From Brian Head drive 4.0 miles south on UT 143 and then 7.5 miles south on UT 148 through Cedar Breaks National Monument to UT 14. Turn right/west on UT 14 and drive 6.5 miles down Cedar Canyon to Woods Ranch, located between mileposts 11 and 12. (From Cedar City drive 11.5 miles east on UT 14/Center Street to Woods Ranch.)

Strawberry Point: From Woods Ranch shuttle bikes and bodies 21.2 miles east on UT 14 to Strawberry Road/FDR 058, between mileposts 32 and 33. Take the all-weather road 9 miles to the Strawberry Point parking area.

22 Navajo Lake Loop Trail

Location:	Navajo Lake (21 miles southeast of Brian Head, 28 miles east of Cedar City)
Length:	11.7 miles
Configuration:	Loop (either direction)
Tread:	Singletrack (machine-cut)
Physical Difficulty:	Novice (undulating trail with a few very short hill are thrown in for good measure)
Technical Difficulty:	Low (some roots, rocks, and loose tread)
Elevation Changes:	High: 9,200 feet (south side Loop Trail near Navajo Lodge) Low: 9,040 feet (north side Loop Trail near dike) Gain: 200 feet (at most)
Maps:	USGS 1:24,000 scale: Navajo Lake (south side trail is not shown)
Land Status:	Dixie National Forest (Cedar City Ranger District)

There is more to do at Navajo Lake—the aquatic jewel of the Markagunt Plateau—than cast a line from its shore or troll in a sputtering dingy. Hikers, mountain bikers, and equestrians alike can explore the lake's forested perimeter on a non-motorized trail. The Navajo Lake Loop Trail, built by the Dixie National Forest during 1996–1997, is ideal for novice bikers or families with children because of the low grades, groomed tread, and multiple trailheads. Knock off the entire 11.7 mile loop or explore a small portion without fear of pedaling alongside traffic on the paved lake road. Together with the Duck Creek ATV Trail System and Virgin River Rim Trail, the Navajo Lake is a budding haven for fat-tire enthusiasts.

Begin at the Dike parking area and ride counterclockwise; although you can start anywhere on the lake's south side and ride either direction with little change in difficulty. Pedal east on the paved lake road for about one-half mile, fork left on the Navajo Lake Loop Trail, and cross lava beds pock marked with sink holes (**m1.8**). Before the dike was built—an ongoing effort lasting from 1929–1953—the lava flows naturally retained the lake. The dike, however, gave the lake a more consistent water level.

The north-side Loop Trail extends 3.6 miles to Navajo Lake Spring, where it exits to a dirt road, posted "no camping" (**m5.4**). Along the way, the trail steers away from the shoreline, venturing through sun-kissed slopes wooded with aspen and fir and underlain with supple grasses and fragrant wildflowers. But the trail then descends to the lakeshore (opposite Navajo Lodge across the lake) where you can pull up a piece of shoreline and while away the afternoon. Take the dirt road to the paved lake road, and then pedal the road right/west to the Virgin River Rim Trail (VRRT), located just past the entrance to Te-ah Campground (**m6.3**).

The VRRT rises gently to moderately 1.5 miles to the Lodge Trail junction. Careen down Lodge Trail, and then continue eastward on the Loop Trail parallel to the paved road (**m8.9**). The south-side trail, back to the Dike parking area, is easy cruising. Unlike the north-side, the south-side is confined to dense, shadow-filled conifers that obscure all but sporadic views of the lake; however, you can exit the trail at Navajo and Spruces Campgrounds and cross the paved lake road to visit the shore.

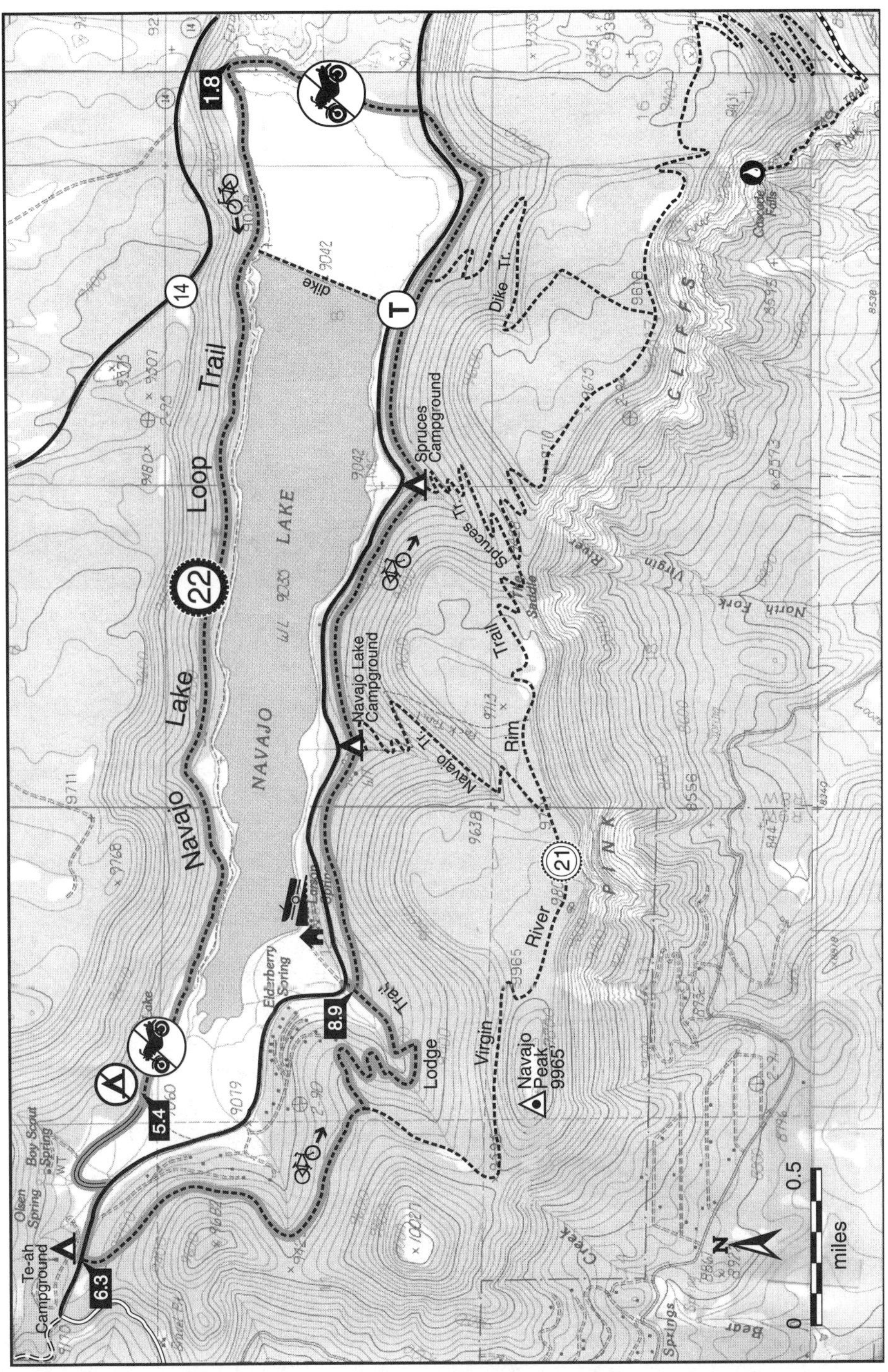

USGS 1:24,000 scale: Navajo Lake (40 foot contour interval).

Tricia takes a spin around Navajo Lake.

Option: Dike Trail, Spruces Trail, and Navajo Trail

If you made easy work of Navajo Lake Loop Trail and crave more miles and vertical, take either Dike, Navajo, or Spruce Trails up to the VRRT. Each is a steeply rising, machine-made path suited for strong intermediate bikers. Expect to dismount and walk many angular and remarkably steep switchbacks. Once on the VRRT, your options are many. When your legs tire, simply descend the next trail back to the lake.

Dike Trail: 1.6 miles one-way; 500-foot gain. The trailhead is near the Dike parking area. It rises to a rim-edge view above Cascade Falls.

Spruces Trail: 0.6 mile one-way; 320-foot gain. The trailhead is at Spruces Campground near campsite 23. This path rises to join the VRRT at the Saddle, where you must continue climbing steeply east or west to the plateau's top to pursue other trails.

Navajo Trail: 1.3 miles one-way; 660-foot gain. The trailhead is Navajo Lake Campground. Begin on the gated dirt road next to the group parking area.

Notes & Precautions:

Navajo Lake Loop Trail is not a race course, so leave your stop watch and heart-rate monitor behind. Naturally, yield the trail to other users with a friendly tip of the helmet.

Trailhead Access:

From Brian Head, drive 4.0 miles south on UT 143 and then 7.5 miles south on UT 148 through Cedar Breaks National Monument to UT 14. Turn left/east and travel 7.6 miles to the Navajo Lake junction. (From Cedar City, travel 18 miles east on UT 14/Center Street to the junction with UT 148 for Cedar Breaks N. M. and then

7.6 miles farther to the Navajo Lake junction. From Panguitch, travel 28 miles south on US 89 and then 14 miles west on UT 14 to the Navajo Lake junction.) The Dike parking area is 1.8 miles along the paved Navajo Lake road.

23 Cascade Falls

Location:	Navajo Lake (21 miles southeast of Brian Head, 28 miles east of Cedar City)
Length:	8.6 miles
Configuration:	Out-and-back
Tread:	All-weather road, ATV trail
Physical Difficulty:	Novice to intermediate (moderately steep 0.5-mile climb on return)
Technical Difficulty:	Low (scattered stones on dirt road, minor obstacles on ATV trail)
Elevation Changes:	High: 9,140 feet (Navajo Lake Road) Low: 8,820 (Duck Creek ATV Trail at Dry Valley) Gain: 540 feet
Maps:	USGS 1:24,000 scale: Henrie Knolls, Navajo Lake, Straight Canyon, and Strawberry Point, Utah
Land Status:	Dixie National Forest (Cedar City Ranger District)

Many passersby have stopped alongside UT 14 to gaze down upon jade-colored Navajo Lake. But few people realize that the 3.5-mile-long lake has no surface outlet. Instead, the lake slowly seeps through fissures and sinkholes in the underground lava beds and then gushes from the face of the Pink Cliffs at Cascade Falls nearly a mile away. There, on the edge of the Markagunt Plateau, the North Fork of the Virgin River maintains its headwaters.

This easy tour takes you from the lakeshore to the Pink Cliffs via dirt roads and the Duck Creek ATV Trail. From the turnaround point, you can hike a short foot trail to Navajo's subterranean outlet. In the distance, the Virgin River's erosive handiwork is manifested in the abysmal chasm of Zion National Park's famed Narrows.

From the Dike parking area, take the Navajo Lake road 1.4 miles east toward UT 14 but not all the way. Turn right on an all-weather road signed "Cascade Falls 4 miles." Descend a half-mile-long lumpy and bumpy hill to Dry Valley and a Y junction, signed "Cascade Falls, FDR 054 (right); UT 14, Duck Creek 2 miles (left)." Hop on the Duck Creek ATV Trail, and take the track 1.8 miles to the parking area for the Cascade Falls National Recreation Trail. (The ATV trail is a fine alternative to riding the washboarded road next to it.) Stash your bike (out of sight, out of mind), and hike the gently descending, half-mile-long footpath to the falls. Keep in mind that Cascades Falls' flow rate peaks during early summer when snowmelt fills the lake and saturates the ground. The Falls are barely a trickle by autumn. Backtrack to Navajo Lake by meandering down the ATV trail and then conquering the hill rising back to Navajo Lake. A few words of encouragement may give youngsters the needed boost.

Option: Dike Trail

Instead of returning to Navajo Lake via the Duck Creek ATV Trail, explore a small section of the Virgin River Rim Trail (VRRT), and then drop to the lake on the

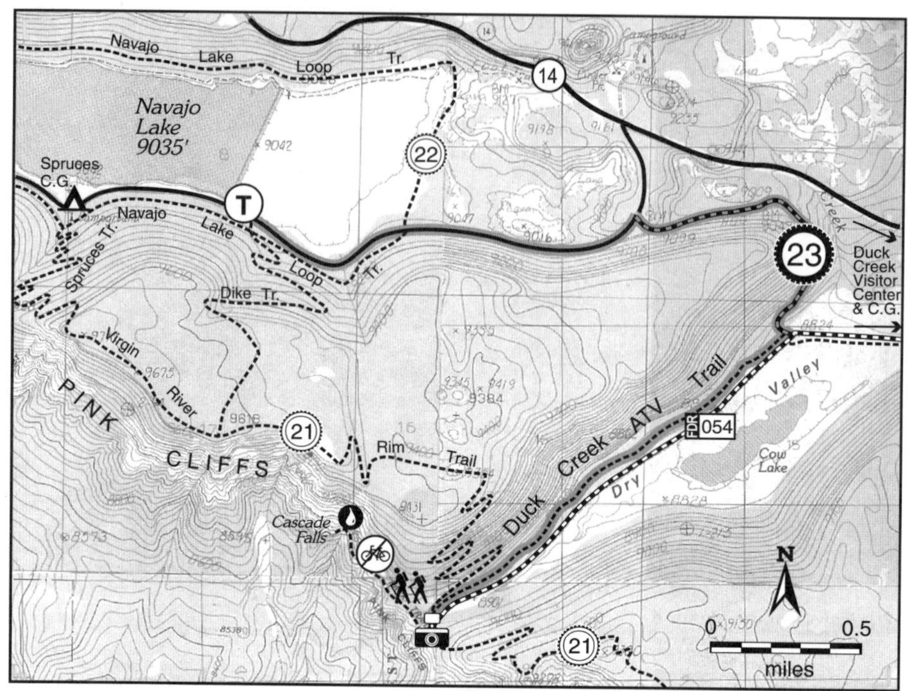

USGS 1:24,000 scale: Henrie Knolls, Navajo Lake, Straight Canyon, and Strawberry Point (40 foot contour interval left half; 20 foot interval right half).

Dike Trail. (See Virgin River Rim Trail, also.) Be forewarned. The 2.5-mile, 700-foot climb from the Cascade Falls trailhead on the VRRT is strenuous. One pitch requires superhuman strength (say "grunt"), but once on top you'll enjoy a glorious view from the plateau's rim to the distant Zion National Park. The Dike Trail drops quickly off the plateau back to Navajo Lake via moderately technical singletrack. (If you legs are still fresh after reaching the Dike Trail on the plateau, keep forging westward on the VRRT. When you legs tire, simply descend Spruces, Navajo, or Lodge Trails and loop back to the Dike parking area. Or, ultimately, descend to Te-ah Campground and loop around the lake on the Navajo Lake Loop Trail.)

Specs.: 8.4 miles (loop); 920-foot gain

Notes & Precautions:

Cascade Falls National Recreation Trail is open to foot traffic only. There is an outhouse at the Cascade Falls N.R.T. parking area but no water tap. Developed campgrounds (Forest Service fee areas) are at Navajo Lake. Limited visitor services are available at nearby Duck Creek Village.

Trailhead Access:

From Brian Head, drive 4.0 miles south on UT 143 and then 7.5 miles south on UT 148 through Cedar Breaks National Monument to UT 14. Turn left/east and

Cascade Falls—birth place of the Virgin River (left).
Cooling off in the Ice Cave (right).

travel 7.6 miles to the Navajo Lake junction. (From Cedar City, travel 18 miles east on UT 14/Center Street to the junction with UT 148 for Cedar Breaks N. M. and then 7.6 miles farther to the Navajo Lake junction. From Panguitch, travel 28 miles south on US 89 and then 14 miles west on UT 14 to the Navajo Lake junction.) The Dike parking area is 1.8 miles along the paved Navajo Lake road.

24 Ice Cave

Location: Duck Creek Visitor Center (21.5 miles southeast of Brian Head; 28 miles east of Cedar City)

Length: 11 miles

Configuration: Loop (counterclockwise)

Tread: All-weather roads, doubletrack, ATV trail

Physical Difficulty: Novice to intermediate (gentle to moderate climbs on good roads and trails)

Technical Difficulty: Low (mostly smooth dirt roads; a few rocks on Duck Creek ATV Trail)

Elevation Changes:
High: 9,015 feet (Duck Creek Ridge)
Low: 8,400 feet (Duck Creek Village)
Gain: 850 feet
Trailhead: 8,555 feet (Duck Creek Visitor Center)

Maps: USGS 1:24,000 scale: Henrie Knolls and Strawberry Point, Utah (Duck Creek ATV Trail is not shown)

Land Status: Dixie National Forest (Cedar City Ranger District)

Many attractions await on this leisurely-paced tour: the quiet forest, the placid alpine ponds, a chilly underground cave, and a country inn. The route embarks from Duck Creek Visitor Center, where you can learn about the region's natural and cultural history. The knowledge you gain will increase your awareness and appreciation of the plateau country through which the route crosses. Nearby campgrounds, fishing holes, trails, and sights offer diverse recreational opportunities.

From Duck Creek Visitor Center, take FDR 370 past Singing Pines Interpretive Trail. Fork left on FDR 059, signed "Ice Cave, Willis Creek, Lars Fork." The modest climb around the switchback ahead is the route's toughest section because the tread is often eroded by vehicles. Thereafter, settle into a steady climbing mode. One mile from the visitor center, fork right to visit the Ice Cave 0.2 mile farther uphill. Although nowhere near national park caliber, the cave is curious just the same because snow and ice can linger inside well into midsummer. Step down into the cavern to escape the heat. Mormon pioneers used the cave as a natural refrigerator to preserve food during the summer.

Return to the previous junction and continue climbing through the aspen, fir, and spruce for about 1 mile to a junction (**m2.3**) signed "Willis Creek and Lars Fork (right), Duck Creek Ridge Road (left)." Take the left fork, and cross the gently sloping Duck Creek ridge. Small imbedded rocks of milky quartzite and limestone make the road lumpy and bumpy, but later on rust-colored sand coats the road and smooths the ride. Regardless, the pedaling is easy and the backcountry is serene. Roll over low undulating hills, and then leave the Dixie National Forest at a horseshoe-shaped junction. Fork right on an all-weather road, and a bit more than one-half mile farther fork right on Color Country Road. (Spruce Road forks left following the power lines overhead.) Pass the Inn at Cedar Mountain and the Pinewoods Inn (or stop in for lunch). Upon intersecting UT 14 (**m6.8**), turn left and pedal the highway 1 mile to Duck Creek Village.

Pick up the Duck Creek ATV Trail on the village's west end near the stop sign. The track quickly swerves away from the highway's edge and winds through tall ponderosa pines. Bounce like a pinball around volcanic boulders scattered about the trail. Cross the access road to Aspen Mirror Lake (or visit the small reservoir to watch anglers cast baited lines). Upon intersecting the next road, take it to the right, cross a metal footbridge over Duck Creek, and continue west on the ATV trail toward Duck Creek Campground. Climb a bit and fork left on a trail that leads to Duck Creek Lake. (The right fork leads to the campground.) Cautiously cross the highway and return to the visitor center.

Option: Virgin River Rim Trail–Duck Creek ATV Trail

If you're right-handed, try this intermediate-level loop (clockwise) via the Virgin River Rim Trail and Duck Creek ATV Trail. Start out as described by stopping first at the Ice Cave. Then, instead of turning left for Duck Creek Ridge Road, continue climbing FDR 059 past Willis Creek to the top of Lars Fork. Hop on the Virgin River Rim Trail and ride the rim west to the Cascade Falls trailhead, ogling the strawberry-colored escarpments scooped from the plateau's edge and Zion's mystical stone

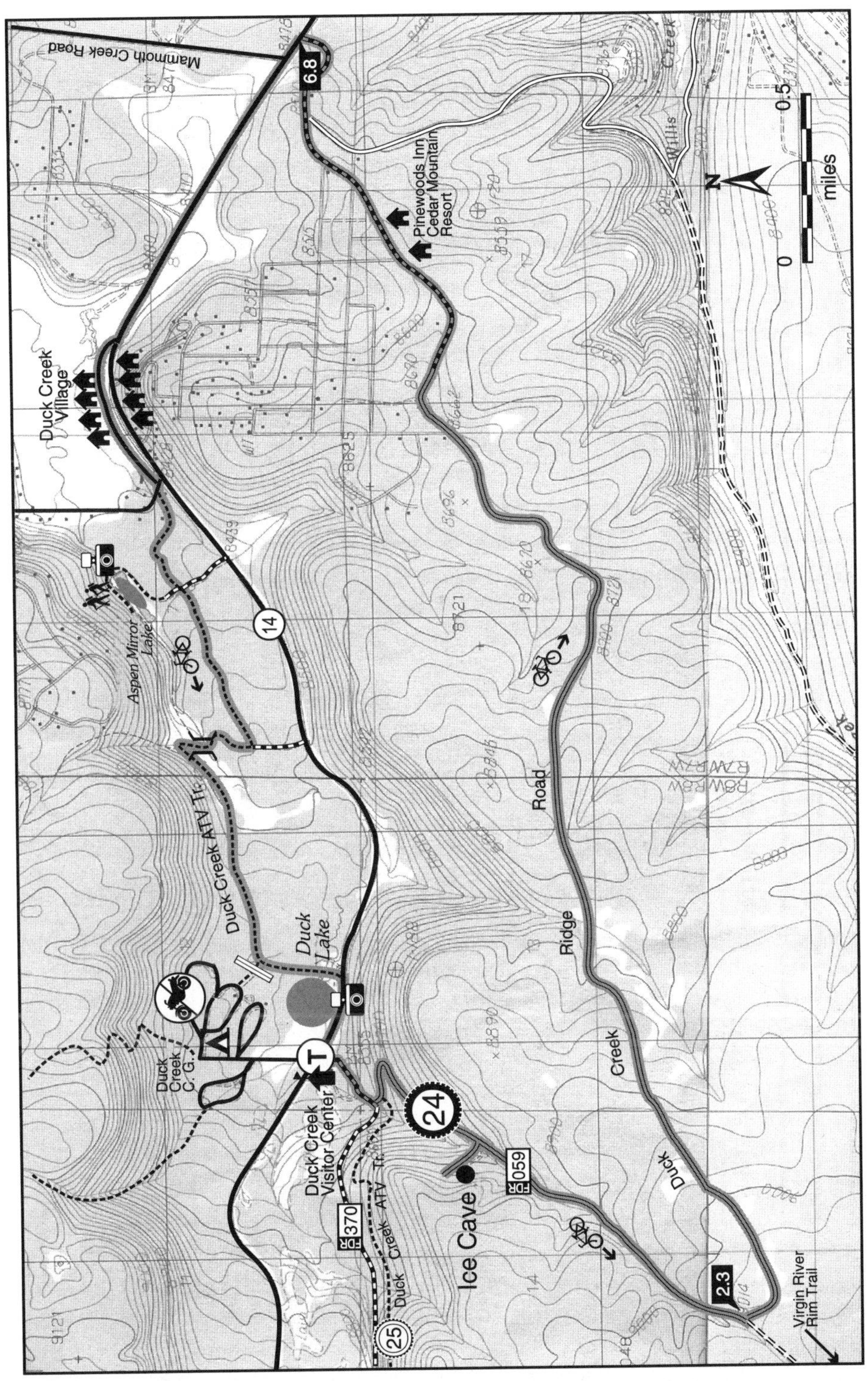

USGS 1:24,000 scale: Henrie Knolls and Strawberry Point (20 foot contour interval).

temples in the distance. Now race 4 miles back to the visitor center on the Duck Creek ATV Trail. (See Duck Creek ATV Trail, also.)

Specs.: 11.5 miles; 800-foot gain

Notes & Precautions:

Use caution crossing and pedaling along UT 14; traffic is frequent. Limited visitor services are available at Duck Creek Village. Duck Creek Visitor Center has a pay phone and a water tap. Duck Creek Campground is a Forest Service fee area.

Trailhead Access:

From Brian Head, drive 4.0 miles south on UT 143 and then 7.5 miles south on UT 148 through Cedar Breaks National Monument to UT 14. Turn left/east and travel 10 miles to Duck Creek Visitor Center, opposite Duck Creek Campground. (From Cedar City, travel 28 miles east on UT 14/Center Street to Duck Creek Visitor Center. From Panguitch, travel 28 miles south on US 89 and then 11.5 miles west on UT 14 to Duck Creek Visitor Center.) Inquire about parking at the visitor center.

25 Duck Creek ATV Trail System

Location:	Duck Creek Village (24 miles southeast of Brian Head; 30 miles east of Cedar City)	
Length:	12 miles	
Configuration:	Out-and-back	
Tread:	ATV trail	
Physical Difficulty:	Novice (gentle hills; one rough section west of Duck Creek Visitor Center)	
Technical Difficulty:	Low (scattered rocks)	
Elevation Changes:	High:	8,900 feet (Cascade Falls parking area)
	Low:	8,400 feet (trailhead: Duck Creek Village)
	Gain:	500 feet
Maps:	USGS 1:24,000 scale: Henrie Knolls and Strawberry Point, Utah (trail is not shown)	
Land Status:	Dixie National Forest (Cedar City Ranger District)	

Granted, ATVs can be deafening and odorous, but they can pack down a fine trail. Hop on the Duck Creek ATV Trail System at one of several trailheads to pedal through stately forests, past reflective lakes stocked with trout, across meadows visited by wildlife, and to other trails that invite bikers and hikers alike. A few hills require a little oomph to surmount, especially for youngsters or first-time bikers. Trying to dodge the scattered boulders can be butt-spankin' fun. Overall, this narrow "doubletrack" is perfect for mountain bikes and is ideal for a family outing.

To take in this entire section of trail, begin at Duck Creek Village. Hop on the ATV Trail at the parking lot's west end next to the stop sign. Bike parallel to the highway, wandering away from traffic and through dispersed ponderosa pines. The trail crosses the access road to Aspen Mirror Lake after 0.4 mile. (To reach the lake, turn right on the road, go to the parking area, and fork right on an ATV track that leads to the lake's dam and footbridge. Note: The trail on the lake's north shore is not recommended for bikes.)

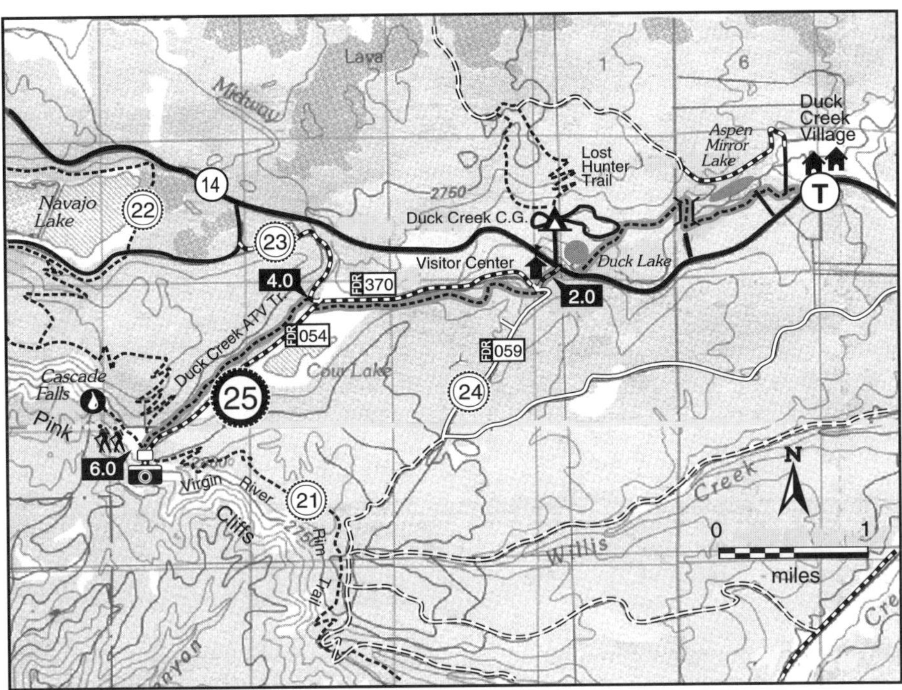

USGS 1:100,000 scale: Panguitch and Kanab (50 meter contour interval).

Back on route, continue 0.5 mile to another road. Take the road to the right, cross a steel footbridge over Duck Creek, and then fork left/west and follow the creek up a narrow, grassy valley. (The trail heading north from the footbridge is unbearably steep and leads to Meadow View Heights Subdivision—hardly worth the effort.)

Climb a bit, and then fork left for Duck Creek Lake. (The right fork leads to Duck Creek Campground, where ATVs are prohibited, and enters near campsite 90. See Options below for additional trails leading from the campground.) Cautiously cross UT 14 and go to the Duck Creek Visitor Center (**m2.0**). Take FDR 370 a few hundred feet to the junction with FDR 059, signed "Ice Cave, Lars Fork," where you continue on the ATV trail. At this point, you'll have to pick your poison. The ATV trail is more difficult over the next mile, and you may have to dismount occasionally because of sharp, steep turns. If you choose to pedal FDR 370 (easier), be aware of truck traffic and stay to the far right side of the road. If you choose the latter, you can hop back on the ATV trail where the road breaks from the forest and enters Dry Valley.

At the junction with FDR 054 (**m4.0**), the ATV trail crosses to the road's west side and continues south parallel to the road for 2 miles to the Cascade Falls National Recreation Trail parking area and trailhead (**m6.0**). This section is particularly joyful because the path wanders through aspens blanketed with wildflowers. (See Cascade Falls, also.) Hike the half-mile path to Cascade Falls, birthplace of North Fork Virgin River, and then return to Duck Creek Village by retracing your path.

The Duck Creek ATV Trail—built for ATVs but ideal for mountain bikes.

Note: From Duck Creek Village, the ATV Trail System extends eastward to Mammoth Creek Road and then for many miles past Strawberry Knolls. Explore if you like.

Option: Virgin River Rim Trail (West)

You can spend all day exploring the Virgin River Rim Trail (VRRT) west of the Cascade Falls trailhead. But you must tackle strenuous climbs onto and along the plateau. Descend to Navajo Lake via Dike, Spruce, Navajo, or Lodge Trails. Each requires adept skills to negotiate sharp turns and steep grades. When you reach Navajo Lake, return to the Duck Creek ATV Trail System by taking Navajo Lake Loop Trail and then turning right on FDR 054, signed "Cascade Falls." You'll intersect the ATV Trail after a half-mile descent on the dirt road (**m4.0** above). (See Virgin River Rim Trail and Cascade Falls, also.)

Specs.: 5 to 15 miles; 800-to 1,000-foot gain

Option: Virgin River Rim Trail (East)

Conversely, explore the VRRT east of the Cascade Falls trailhead and along the plateau's edge. Where the VRRT descends to the head of Lars Fork, loop back to the Duck Creek Visitor Center on FDR 059. Stay left at the junctions for Broad Hollow and Willis Creek roads then descend past the Ice Cave.

Specs.: 16 miles; 1,300-foot gain

Option: Lost Hunter Trail

This short loop from the Duck Creek Campground requires strong legs for climbing, good handling skills for descending, and front suspension for bounding over 100 water bars. Go to the amphitheater parking area at the back of the campground and take Old Ranger Trail to the right. After a short distance, fork right on Lost Hunter Trail. (Old Ranger Trail, an interpretive trail, forks left and is for foot traffic only.) Lost Hunter Trail rises very steeply through a half dozen angular turns to the plateau's top, where it passes a massive ponderosa pine measuring 5 feet in diameter. Pedal through towering aspens to a doubletrack. Take the track left/west 0.25 mile, and fork left on the continued Lost Hunter Trail (before the track crosses the small clearing). Drop off the plateau via the "giant's staircase," and then bear left to return to the amphitheater parking area. How many water bars did you count?

Specs.: 2.4 miles; 500-foot gain

Notes & Precautions:

Be alert to ATVs and bc willing to share the trail. Duck Creek Village offers life's basic necessities: lodging, general store, pizza parlor, gasoline, bait, and bullets—but no Wall Street Journal. Duck Creek Visitor Center, operated by the Dixie National Forest, offers additional regional information. Duck Creek Campground is a Forest Service fee area. The ATV Trail System extends eastward from Duck Creek Village, to Mammoth Creek Road and then for many miles past Strawberry Knolls. Explore if you like.

Trailhead Access:

From Brian Head, drive 4.0 miles south on UT 143 and then 7.5 miles south on UT 148 through Cedar Breaks National Monument to UT 14. Turn left/east and travel 12 miles to Duck Creek Village. (From Cedar City, travel 30 miles east on UT 14/Center Street to Duck Creek Village. From Panguitch, travel 28 miles south on US 89 and then 9.5 miles west on UT 14 to Duck Creek Village.) Other trailheads are at Duck Creek Lake and near Duck Creek Visitor Center (both 2 miles west of Duck Creek Village).

Mike heads up Red Canyon on route to Thunder Mountain.

BRYCE-AREA RIDES

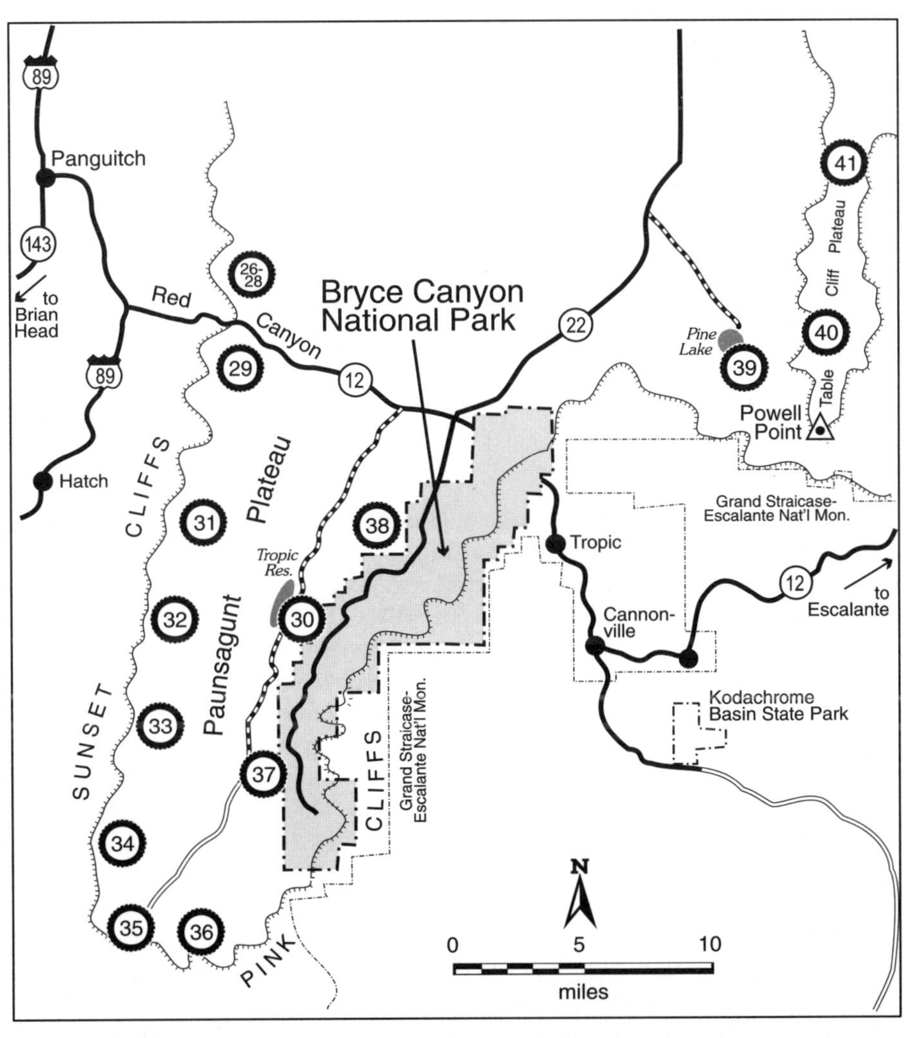

26 Casto Canyon

Location:	12 miles east of Panguitch
Length:	14 miles
Configuration:	Out-and-back with loop
Tread:	ATV track, doubletrack, primitive singletrack
Physical Difficulty:	Intermediate (gentle climb up Casto Canyon; trail crosses the dry, bouldery creek bed many times; moderate climb to Barney Cove)
Technical Difficulty:	Moderate (trail crosses the sandy, boulder-filled creek bed many times; bumpy descent on Sanford Road)
Elevation Changes:	High: 8,255 feet (Barney Cove) Low: 7,080 feet (trailhead: Casto Canyon) Gain: 1,200 feet
Maps:	USGS 1:24,000 scale: Casto Canyon, Utah (Casto Canyon Trail is not shown)
Land Status:	Dixie National Forest (Powell Ranger District)

It would behoove you to visit nearby Bryce Canyon National Park while in the Panguitch area. But take your hiking shoes because bikes are prohibited on all the park's trails. Who cares? Nearby Casto Canyon is the ideal alternative for sprocket heads. Like Bryce Canyon, Casto is a phantasmagoria of peculiar shapes and blazing color etched from the Claron Formation's flesh-toned limestone. Your imagination will run wild. Unlike Bryce, however, Casto welcomes fat tires. Casto Canyon Trail is typically ridden as a 7-mile out-and-back excursion—perfect for novice to intermediate bikers. An extended route, described here, incorporates a side loop up to Barney Cove where you can view Casto from afar and survey the surrounding terrain.

In 1992, the Powell Ranger District upgraded Casto Canyon from an overgrown cattle path to a bonafide multi-use recreational trail. A small parking area, horse staging ramp, and an outhouse were constructed, and the once-primitive trail weaving up Casto was widened to accommodate ATVs. But these improvements do not change Casto's testy demeanor, especially for bicyclists. From the outset, the trail wavers up the canyon in a futile attempt to remain on the creek's bank. However, on nearly every meander, the trail dives off the firm embankment into the creek's bouldery channel. When dry conditions persist and the creek is parched, which is the norm, the channel-bound segments are packed sand and are mostly rideable. But when rain falls, runoff carries loose sand and rocks down the creek, erasing portions of the trail. Then you are forced to dance a technical jig until subsequent travelers pack the trail again. That's how the game is played: pedal easily on terra firma, drop into the dry creek bed, cant-and-ratchet across the rocks, hop onto the solid bank, repeat.

Gradually, the canyon's tall corrugated walls subside to low rounded knolls, and the redrock loses its intricate shapes and flaming color. When you reach the junction signed "Sanford Road (2 miles), Losee Canyon (5 miles), and Red Canyon (9 miles)," fork left and climb the steep, rough ATV track 1.5 miles up a side canyon toward Sanford Road (**m3.6**). (Novice riders may want to backtrack to the trailhead at this point.) At the top of the climb, turn right twice and take Sanford Road/Fremont ATV

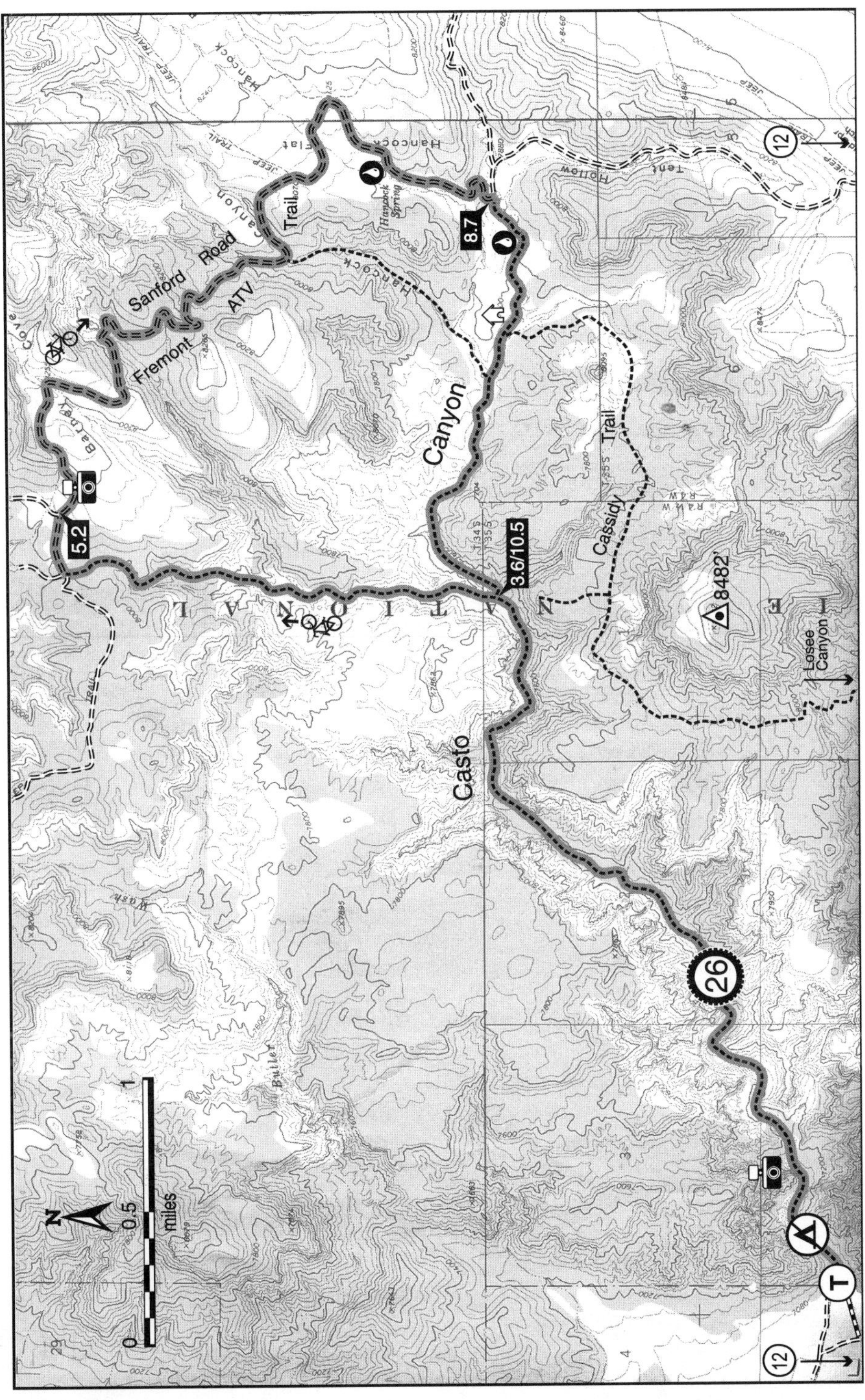

USGS 1:24,000 scale: Casto Canyon and Flake Mountain West (40 foot contour interval).

A wall of lithified lasagne in Casto Canyon.

Trail across Barney Cove—a treeless bench extending from nearby Casto Bluff's ragged volcanic abutment (**m5.2**). Descend the curvy doubletrack nearly 4 miles until it bottoms and bends sharply left across upper Casto Canyon (**m8.7**). Reenter Casto by following the faint doubletrack to the right, which soon narrows to a braided cattle trail. (The lower ATV trail has not been pushed this far up the canyon.) Duck under juniper and pinyon boughs, and then boogie down the drainage—dodging ever-present cow-pies.

Butch Cassidy and the Wild Bunch eluded the law in Casto Canyon. A rock hut that Butch purportedly inhabited has since crumbled and vanished. Pioneers also inhabited Casto. The dilapidated wood-plank structure about one-half mile down Casto Canyon from Sanford Road is a remnant of an old saw mill.

Continue past the signed turnoff for Losee Canyon then the junction for Sanford Road (**m3.6/10.5**). Admire the park-like scenery from a new perspective, while retracing your tracks down Casto Canyon to the trailhead.

Option: Casto Canyon to Losee Canyon via Cassidy Trail

Kill two birds—er, trails—with one stone by linking Casto Canyon and equally scenic Losee Canyon with the 4-mile-long Cassidy Trail in between. Sounds easy enough, but be forewarned. Cassidy Trail is a pack trail at best—it packs a punch to the unsuspecting biker. You'll face a barrage of short leg-burning pulses and eroded technical drops separated by trail segments that range from dreamy to nightmarish. Yet despite these tough riding conditions, this is a killer ride that overflows with scenic wonderment.

Head up Casto Canyon about 5 miles, but pass the junction for Sanford Road after 3.5 miles. Hop out of Casto, following the sign for Cassidy Trail, Losee Canyon, and Red Canyon. Wind through dispersed ponderosa pine and Douglas-fir, watching for tree blazes marking the sometimes indistinct trail. (Don't bother trying to locate yourself on a topographic map because the terrain is utterly confusing. No wonder the Wild Bunch was elusive.) Pass a butte signed "Mexican Hat" after 0.5 mile. Curve left at a solitary wooden post 1.5 miles from Casto, and ignore a faint path branching right/northwest. Forge ahead in a southerly direction. Cross "Little Desert," where bristlecone pines are scattered about limestone dunes that seem scooped from a bucket of Baskin & Robbins orange-vanilla swirl. (This area turns to cement-like mud when wet!) On the other side, veer right and climb a very short steep hill. Then curve sharply left down the other side, and cross more moonscape. (The trail can be difficult to follow here.) After careening down a dry wash, you arrive at the upper Losee Canyon trailhead. (An outhouse to the left is a landmark.)

Losee Canyon Trail is good clean technical fun. Like in Casto, you weave across a mostly dry wash, but Losee Canyon Trail has not been widened for ATVs. It's still a pack trail, so you are constantly on the pegs hopping rocks and tree roots. When you reach the lower trailhead, take the dirt road north to Casto Canyon.

Ride this loop in either direction with little change in difficulty. None of these trails is shown on the USGS 1:24,000 scale Casto Canyon, Utah quadrangle.

Specs.: 13.5 miles; 1,300-foot gain (approximate)

Notes & Precautions:

Casto Canyon is a multi-use trail open to ATVs. Be ready and willing to share the trail, not only with ATVs but with cattle as well. The trailhead has an outhouse but no water tap. Camping is not allowed at the trailhead but is available at nearby Red Canyon Campground (fee area).

Trailhead Access:

From Panguitch, take US 89 south 7 miles; then turn left/east on UT 12 for Bryce Canyon National Park and Escalante. Before entering Red Canyon, turn left/north near milepost 2 for Casto and Losee Canyons. Take the all-weather road 3 miles to the Casto Canyon trailhead, passing Losee Canyon after 2 miles.

27 Losee Canyon

Location:	12 miles east of Panguitch
Length:	6 miles
Configuration:	Out-and-back
Tread:	Singletrack (primitive)
Physical Difficulty:	Intermediate (gentle climb up Losee Canyon; trail crosses dry, rocky creek bed many times)
Technical Difficulty:	Moderate (trail crosses dry creek bed many times, thus a lot of rock-hopping)
Elevation Changes:	High: 7,640 feet (top of canyon) Low: 7,100 feet (trailhead) Gain: 540 feet
Maps:	USGS 1:24,000 scale: Casto Canyon, Utah (trail is not shown)
Land Status:	Dixie National Forest (Powell Ranger District)

Riding among the hoodoos in Losee Canyon. You can't do this in Bryce Canyon National Park.

Try biking any trail in Bryce Canyon National Park and you'll find yourself counting bricks inside the town pokey because, as we all know, it's illegal. Instead, head north by northwest to Losee Canyon to bike through scenery that is positively "arresting," without assuming the risk of being busted.

From the outset, there is no wanting of scenic reward and no anticipation of unforeseen highlights; after a few pedal strokes, you are tightly clenched by Losee's kaleidoscopic glove. As with neighboring Casto Canyon, Losee is a wavering canyon built of wrinkled walls, multi-tiered pillars, and bulbous spires—all the color of glowing embers. But unlike Casto, Losee is closed to ATVs, so you are certain of a peaceful singletrack experience.

The route is straight forward. Just pedal the pack trail up Losee Canyon for 3 miles to the intersection with Cassidy Trail. Then make a U-turn and retrace your tracks to the trailhead, revering the scenery from a new perspective. Along the way, you'll weave back and forth across the dry creek bed on a path that varies from packed dirt and sand to gravel and loose cobbles. Horseback riders travel Losee as

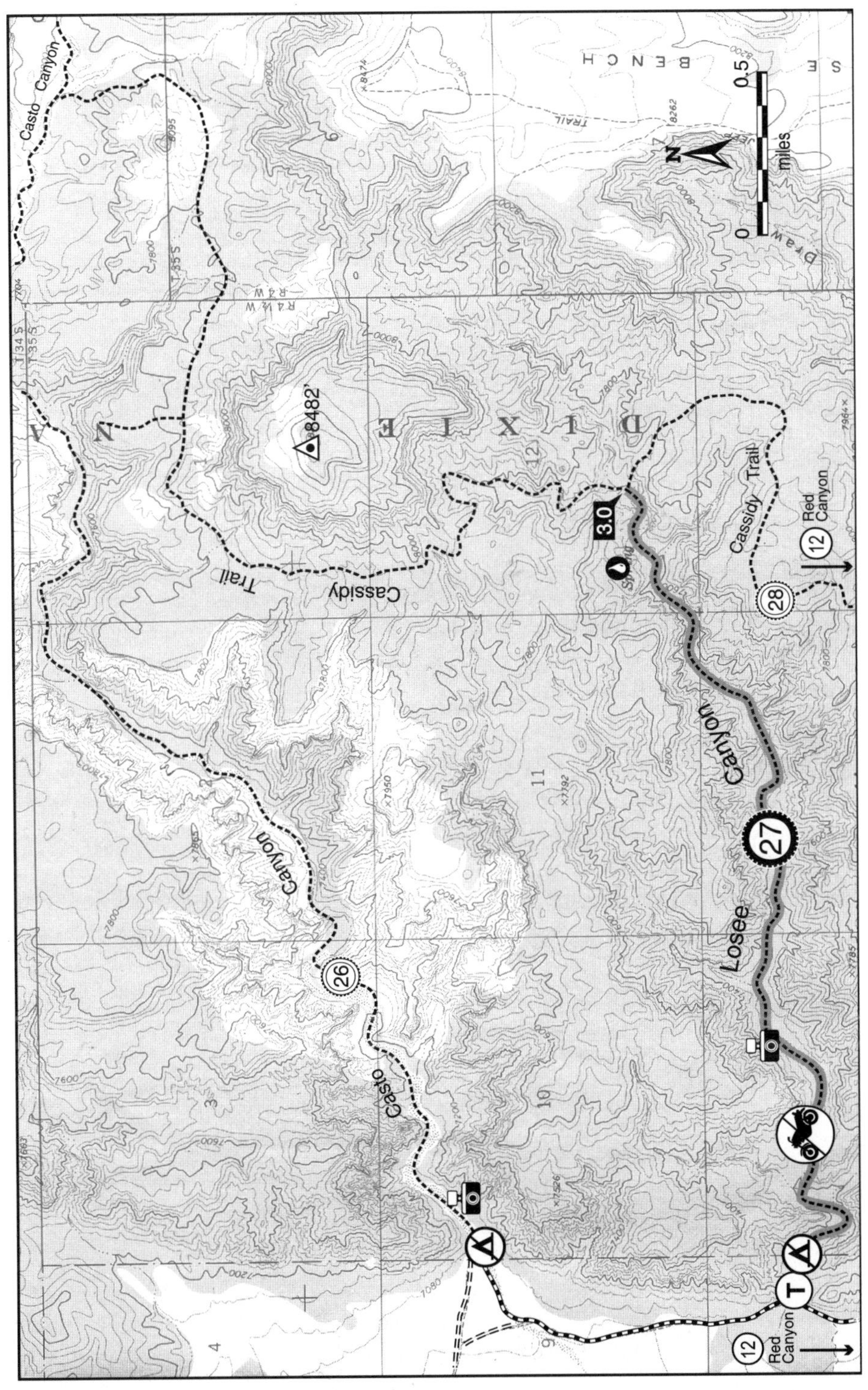

USGS 1:24,000 scale: Casto Canyon (40 foot contour interval).

well, so the trail may be choppy from the horses' hooves. Therefore, earmark Losee for its surreal scenery not for buffed singletrack. Even so, the trail's high-spirited demeanor will gratify those willing to challenge it.

Far to the south, the rim of the Paunsagunt Plateau rises 2,000 feet above the surrounding valleys. There, erosion by water runoff promotes rapid down-cutting and aggressive headward erosion, as evidenced by Sunset Cliff's steeply faced escarpments and Bryce Canyon's deep, fan-shaped amphitheaters. Losee and Casto Canyons, on the other hand, pull up the northern trailing edge of the Paunsagunt where the flesh-colored Claron Formation submerges beneath alluvial fans and volcanic mountains of the Sevier Plateau. Consequently, erosion in Losee Canyon is less brash and more intimate. The coalescing coves, which are filled with intricate features and sprawling aprons, step back gradually from the 3-mile-long canyon.

Option: Losee Canyon to Casto Canyon via Cassidy Trail

See Option under Casto Canyon but ride the loop counterclockwise.

Specs.: 13.5 miles; 1,300-foot gain (approximate)

Notes & Precautions:

Losee Canyon is a multi-use trail open to non-motorized use only. Be willing to share the trail with hikers and equestrians. The trailhead has an outhouse but no water tap. Camping is not allowed at the trailhead but is available at nearby Red Canyon Campground (fee area).

Trailhead Access:

From Panguitch, take US 89 south 7 miles; then turn left/east on UT 12 for Bryce Canyon National Park and Escalante. Before entering Red Canyon, turn left/north near milepost 2 for Casto and Losee Canyons. Take the all-weather road 2 miles to the Losee Canyon trailhead.

28 Cassidy Trail to Losee Canyon

Location:	Red Canyon (10 miles southeast of Panguitch)
Length:	14 miles
Configuration:	Loop (counterclockwise)
Tread:	Singletrack, all-weather road, paved-bike path (proposed)
Physical Difficulty:	Advanced (Cassidy Trail is fraught with steep, eroded sections and is intended for pack horses not mountain bikes; Losee Canyon, also a pack trail, descends gradually; the all-weather road, paved highway, and bike trail are easy)
Technical Difficulty:	Moderate to high (some steep, eroded, pock-marked, unrideable sections; other parts are as sweet as candy)
Elevation Changes:	High: 7,880 feet (Brayton Point)
	Low: 6,980 feet (UT 12 near mouth of Red Canyon)
	Gain: 1,200 feet
	Trailhead: 7,160 feet (Red Canyon Visitor Center)
Maps:	USGS 1:24,000 scale: Casto Canyon and Wilson Peak, Utah (trails are not shown)
Land Status:	Dixie National Forest (Powell Ranger District)

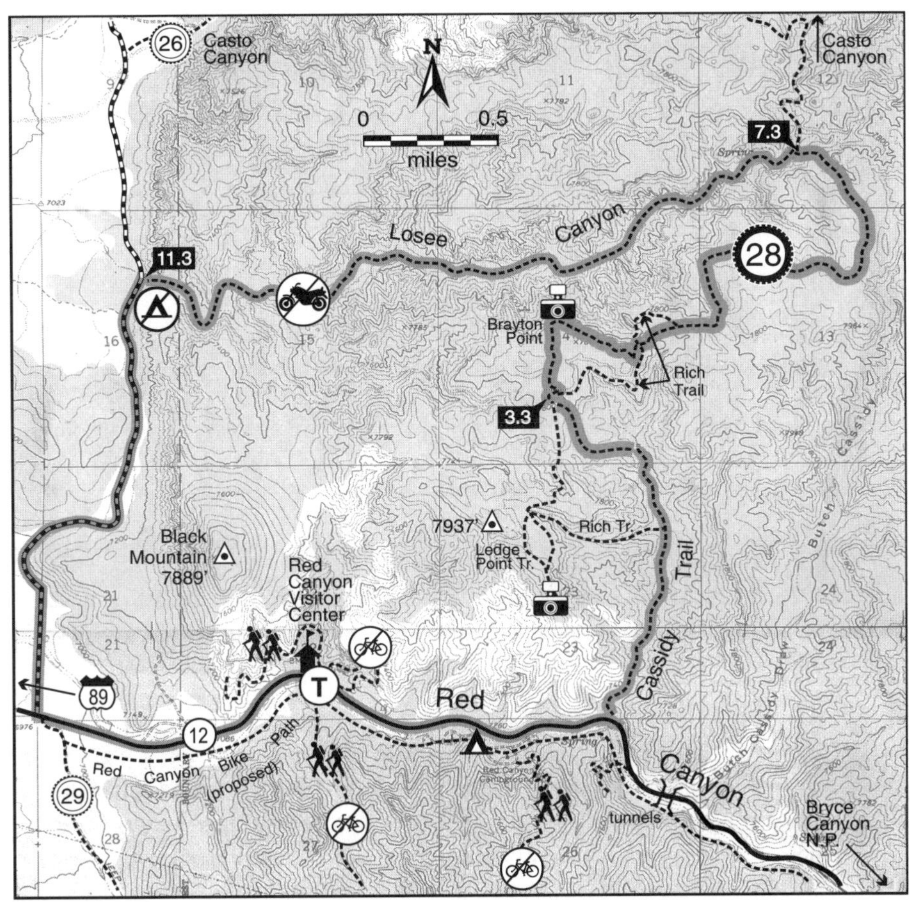

USGS 1:24,000 scale: Casto Canyon and Wilson Peak (40 foot contour interval).

Cassidy Trail gets its name from the wiley bandit, Butch, who eluded the posse time and again amidst Red Canyon's labyrinthine tucks and folds. This route takes you from the rent-a-car highway in Red Canyon to reclusive, confounding, and utterly mesmerizing terrain, of which most passersby are oblivious. That's good for mountain bikers. Be forewarned. Cassidy Trail is intended for boots and hooves not fat tires, so even intrepid bikers will struggle on many sections. But the lure of Losee Canyon, when first viewed from Brayton Point, compels you to press on across contentious terrain to a fairyland of imaginative shapes bathed with irradiant color. Riding conditions are challenging but rewarding, and the scenery is categorically spellbinding.

Embark from the Dixie National Forest's Red Canyon Visitor Center, and pedal 1.5 miles up UT 12 through glowing Red Canyon to the Red Canyon Trailhead. If you reach the highway tunnels, you missed the trailhead by one-quarter mile. Be

Overlooking Losee Canyon from Brayton Point.

cautious of rubberneck motorists gawking at the canyon's bewildering sights along the way.

Cassidy Trail #093 follows the dry creek bed, crossing it several times, so sections are sand and gravel. Soon, the path stays on the west bank, where pedaling is more efficient. Pass Rich Trail forking left (steep and rough) and stay on Cassidy Trail. Thereafter, you must creep up the eroded trail to a subtle ridge peppered with ponderosa pines and manzanita ground cover.

Fork right at a T junction to continue on Cassidy Trail, dragging your bike up a set of impossible switchbacks (**m3.3**). (Rich Trail heads south and connects with Ledge Point Trail. These are highly technical trails, but if you persist, you'll reach a spectacular overlook of Red Canyon.) Upon surmounting the switchbacks, stay left on Cassidy Trail (Rich Trail, eroded and rough, forks right), and wander along the bluff's crest to Brayton Point.

Losee Canyon, beneath your feet, is a confusing spread of convolute coves embossed with ornately eroded shapes. This "badlands" topography results from variable weathering of mud and silt layers interfingered in the pervasive limestone. Consequently, rock layers more resistant to erosion protrude over recesses, form hats atop pillars, and give wavy relief to the canyon's walls and free-standing fins.

Leave Brayton Point by following Cassidy eastward along the bluff's edge, kicking up crunchy pine needles that have fallen from towering ponderosas. Suddenly, the trail plunges off the bluff's rim down a hellish dugway then intersects Rich Trail. Stay straight on Cassidy Trail toward Losee Canyon. Stay straight on Cassidy again at a second junction with Rich Trail, one-half mile farther, and cross terrain as bleak as the moon but as bright as the sun. Watch for tree blazes, rock cairns, hoof prints, and other telltale signs suggesting the trail. At times the trail is upbeat and utterly blissful; other times, it mimics weathered concrete and compels you to perform a repertoire of technical stunts. Descend a small canyon, where the trail is a jumble of rocks, and arrive at the upper Losee Canyon trailhead (**m7.3**). It's 3 miles of sometimes-technical, other-times-easy-going singletrack to the lower Losee Canyon trailhead (**m10.3**). Like tourists driving through Red Canyon, you too will be rubbernecking the whole way and gasping at the astounding display of fanciful shapes.

Take the all-weather road 2 miles south to Red Canyon, and then pedal up UT 12 a couple of miles to complete the loop. Or hop on the paved Red Canyon Bike Trail to avoid the traffic (construction to begin summer 1998). Just before you enter Red Canyon, look at the hillside to the left; you'll see how an ancient flow of black lava has attempted to conceal the canyon's gateway.

Notes & Precautions:

Use caution when pedaling UT 12 through Red Canyon; motorists, including lumbering RVs, are frequent. (You can avoid traffic on the proposed Red Canyon Bike Trail—construction to begin summer 1998.) Equestrians may be encountered on Cassidy and Losee Trails; yield the right of way in all instances. Red Canyon Visitor Center offers ample parking, a soft drink vending machine, water tap, restrooms, and an information center where you can purchase additional maps and literature or visit with a forest information specialist.

Trailhead Access:

From Panguitch, take US 89 south 7 miles; then turn left/east on UT 12 for Bryce Canyon National Park and Escalante. Park at the Dixie National Forest Red Canyon Visitor Center, approximately 1 mile up Red Canyon, between mileposts 3 and 4.

29 Thunder Mountain

Location:	Red Canyon (13 miles southeast of Panguitch)
Length:	8 miles
Configuration:	Point-to-point
Tread:	Singletrack
Physical Difficulty:	Intermediate to advanced (countless intermittent climbs require short bursts of power)
Technical Difficulty:	Moderate (trail twists through innumerable hollows requiring short radius turns and rapid shifting; tread is rough at times; precipitous switchbacks off Thunder Mountain require periodic dismounts)
Elevation Changes:	High: 8,280 feet (west side of Thunder Mountain)
	Low: 7,080 feet (trail end in Red Canyon)
	Trailhead: 8,040 feet (Coyote Hollow)
	Gain 1,200 feet (approximate because of incremental climbs)
Maps:	USGS 1:24,000 scale: Wilson Peak, Utah (trail is not shown)
Land Status:	Dixie National Forest (Powell Ranger District)

Hats off, rather, helmets off, to the Powell Ranger District for the Thunder Mountain Trail, the newest addition to the district's trails inventory. This non-motorized trail, built in 1996, explores Red Canyon's hinterlands beyond the stream of "take-a-photo-

Dancing with the hoodoos on Thunder Mountain Trail.

and-run" tourists who are making a beeline for Bryce Canyon National Park. Once off the highway, tranquility abounds.

On route to Thunder Mountain from the Coyote Hollow trailhead, the machine-cut trail crosses undulating hillsides populated with dispersed pines, and scenic value grows from lackluster to intriguing. Past Thunder Mountain, you'll negotiate a hand-carved, sometimes-treacherous trail threaded through dazzling erosional features.

In a valiant attempt to make Thunder Mountain Trail user friendly, the first few miles roughly contour at the 8,000-foot level. But don't misconstrue that the trail is flat and mellow. On the contrary, the bumpy trail slightly descends immediately before each hollow through which it curves; bends sharply through the wooded cleft; and then rises, often times abruptly, when exiting the hollow. You'll work your gears constantly, perfect your short-radius turns, and pump out a dozen interval-like climbs.

About 3 miles out, the trail crosses a more prominent ridge, affording provocative views of flat-topped Thunder Mountain with its tiered limestone columns. (Ironi-

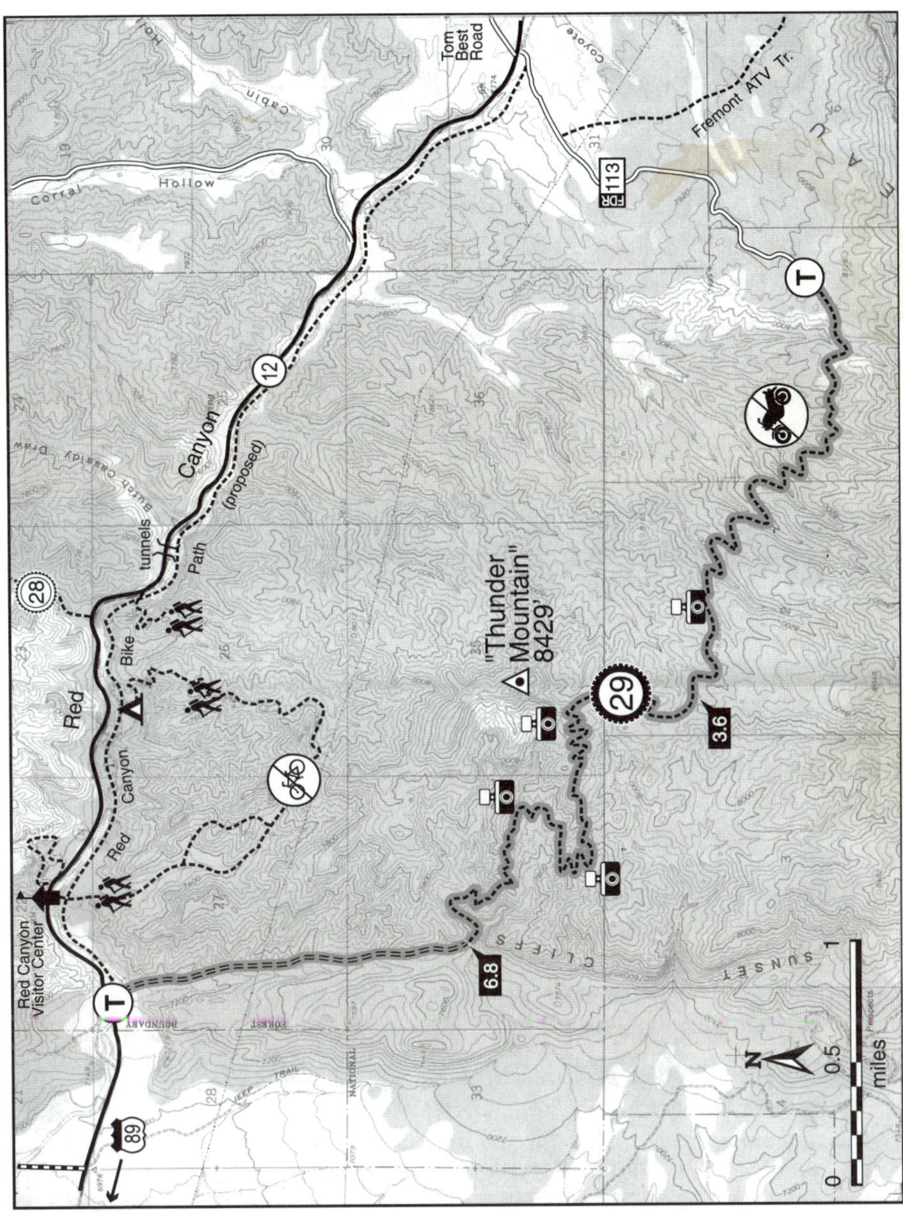

USGS 1:24,000 scale: Casto Canyon and Wilson Peak (40 foot contour interval).

cally, there is no "Thunder Mountain." It's just a name the Powell Ranger District conjured up. But if there was a Thunder Mountain, this prominent butte, wrapped in a shawl of glowing limestone, would be it.) Cross a flat bench (**m3.6**) overshadowed by pines (outhouse on left), and then bend north to climb Thunder Mountain's south flank to the route's high point, both in elevation and scenery.

Riding out a ridge between competing canyons.

The path clips the rim of a horseshoe-shaped bowl adorned with ornate and delicate erosional features carved from the cream-and salmon-colored limestone. The path then coils and plunges down the slope. Even intrepid bikers will be stymied by these audacious switchbacks. The trail's precarious routing takes you through the heart of the bowl you peered into earlier and out along a barren ridge, where rust-colored formations fill deep, craggy canyons on both sides. Pass a spur trail to the right, unless you care to hike a short way up to an overlook of sibling canyons. With the Sunset Cliffs rapidly approaching from the west, the trail is forced off the divide into a chasm drenched in fiery hues. Upon breaching the cliffs (**m6.8**), climb briefly northward through scattered pines; then freewheel more than a mile on a doubletrack alongside a sandy wash to the trail's end at the mouth of Red Canyon.

Option: Thunder Mountain–Red Canyon loop

No car shuttle? No problem. Ride Thunder Mountain Trail as a 15-mile loop by pounding the pavement up Red Canyon and then taking the dirt road to the Coyote Hollow trailhead. The highway rises gently for 5 miles through terrain that begs national-park status. Like motorists in their rentals, you too will be rubbernecking at all the sights and snapping photos of rock formations that seduce your camera's lens. To avoid mingling with traffic, ride the proposed Red Canyon Bike Trail. Construction of this 4-mile paved path is scheduled to commence during the summer of 1998.

Specs.: 15 miles; 2,200-foot gain

Notes & Precautions:

Use caution if pedaling UT 12 through Red Canyon. Motorists are frequent, and their attention is easily distracted by the captivating scenery. Trailheads have outhouses but no water taps. Red Canyon Campground is a Forest Service fee area. A pay telephone, a soft drink vending machine, and restrooms are available at the Dixie National Forest Red Canyon Visitor Center. Be alert to hikers and equestrians, especially when downhilling to the trail's end. Yield the trail in all instances.

Trailhead Access:

From Panguitch, take US 89 south 7 miles; then turn left/east on UT 12 for Bryce Canyon National Park and Escalante. Thunder Mountain's western (lower) trailhead is at the mouth of Red Canyon at the Dixie National Forest boundary. To reach the eastern (upper) trailhead, drive 5 miles through Red Canyon. Turn right on FDR 113, just east of milepost 7 and opposite Tom Best Road, signed "Fremont ATV/ Great Western Trail." Take the all-weather road southwest 2.2 miles to the Coyote Hollow trailhead, passing a left turn for the Fremont ATV/GWT.

30 Tropic Reservoir

Location:	East Fork Sevier River valley (25 miles southeast of Panguitch)	
Length:	4.3 miles	
Configuration:	Loop (clockwise)	
Tread:	All-weather road, doubletrack	
Physical Difficulty:	Novice (short, modest climbs on west lake road)	
Technical Difficulty:	Low (gravel on East Fork road, some rocks and ruts on west lake road)	
Elevation Changes:	High:	7,960 feet (Kings Creek Campground)
	Low:	7,835 feet (trailhead: Tropic Reservoir)
	Gain:	200 feet
Maps:	USGS 1:24,000 scale: Bryce Point and Tropic Reservoir, Utah	
Land Status:	Dixie National Forest (Powell Ranger District)	

Tropic Reservoir is an oasis on the Paunsagunt Plateau. Its shimmering surface absorbs the cerulean sky while reflecting the creamsicle-colored slopes breaking from verdant forests. The loop around the reservoir is gauged for first-time bikers and for families with children, although caution should be used on the East Fork road where truck traffic may be encountered. The rest of the loop is peaceful. Kings Creek Campground is a perfect base camp if you choose to explore the many routes nearby.

From the boat dock, pedal north around the Kings Creek bay and cross the dam. Turn right on the East Fork road/FDR 087 and pedal south alongside the reservoir. There are several spurs from the road that lead to overlooks of the reservoir—each makes a fine picnic stop. Pass the Tropic Water Stop where artesian spring water flows from a tap supported by a small rock pillar. Thereafter, turn right on FDR 109 for Badger Creek and Proctor Canyon (**m2.1**). Weave through towering conifers set among grass meadows, and then fork right on the west lake road. The pebble- and rock-studded road rises gradually along the interface between the forested hills and the reed-lined shore. Waterfowl congregate on the lake's marshy edge, snapping up aquatic snacks and then taking to synchronous flight. If luck prevails, you'll spy a

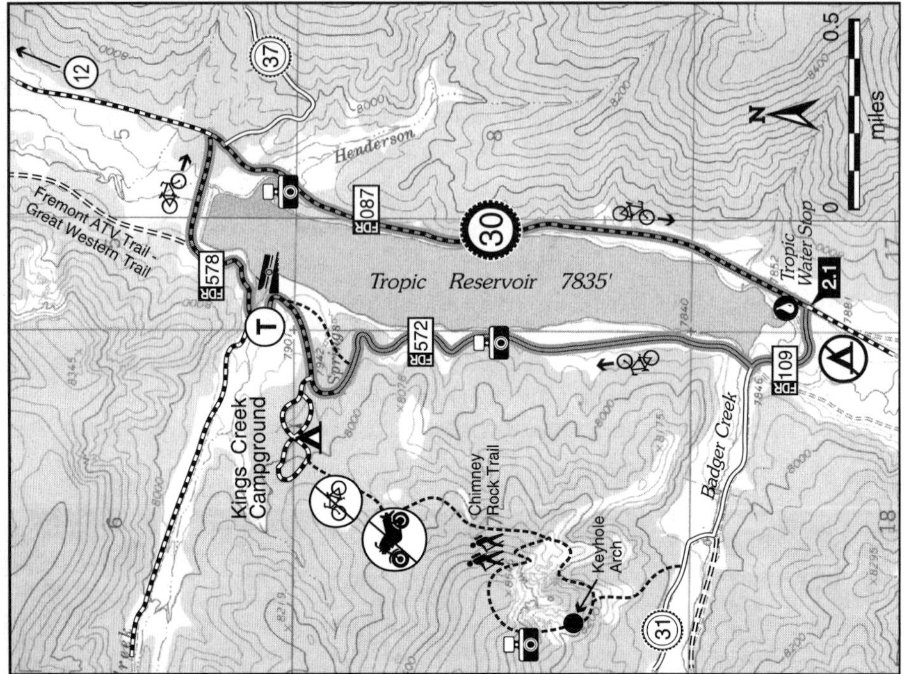

USGS 1:24,000 scale: Tropic Reservoir and Bryce Canyon (40 foot contour interval).

blue heron poised with its neck crooked. Stay right at the entrance to Kings Creek Campground to return to the boat dock, or take a short cut on the ATV trail.

Option: Chimney Rock Trail (foot traffic only)

This 2.5-mile trail takes you from Kings Creek Campground through pine forests to an isolated amphitheater stuffed with hoodoo formations. You'll view Keyhole Arch from afar and brush by Chimney Rock and other bewildering shapes. Since it's centrally located in the East Fork Sevier River valley, your cohorts can tally the miles while you go for a stroll or vice versa.

The signed trailhead is located next to campsite 20 in Kings Creek Campground. (Day-use parking requires a fee.) Take the trail south a few hundred feet, passing a trail branching sharply right and leading to the group area. Upon intersecting a doubletrack, take the road uphill about 100 yards to a multiple junction. The footpath branches left and might be marked with a small rock pile. Hike up through pine and fir, passing an overlook of Tropic Reservoir, to the rim of a redrock amphitheater. Circle counterclockwise around a wooded knoll and descend the steep, narrow path toward the Badger Creek valley. Watch for daylight shining through Keyhole Arch, tucked neatly in the cliffs. About half way down the slope, fork left on a faint path that hugs the base of the hoodoo-filled bowl. (If you reach the Badger Creek road, you've gone too far and missed the turn.) Now climb back uphill to a sunny barren ridge, pass Chimney Rock and assorted erosional features, and then rejoin the trail you hiked out from the campground.

Keyhole Arch—Chimney Rock Trail (left); reflective Tropic Reservior (right).

Notes & Precautions:

The Tropic Reservoir loop can be ridden in either direction with little change in difficulty. Watch for thundering log trucks on the East Fork road. The west lake road may be a bit bumpy for child trailers. Kings Creek Campground is a Forest Service fee area.

Trailhead Access:

From Panguitch, take US 89 south 7 miles; then turn left/east on UT 12 for Bryce Canyon National Park and Escalante. Drive 11 miles through Red Canyon and across the Paunsagunt Plateau. Between mileposts 10 and 11, turn right on FDR 087 (all-weather road), signed "Kings Creek Campground, Tropic Reservoir." Follow FDR 087 for 7 miles to Tropic Reservoir, cross the dam on route to Kings Creek Campground, and park at the boat dock.

31 Sunset Cliffs I (Blue Fly Creek)

Location:	East Fork Sevier River valley (25 miles southeast of Panguitch)
Length:	19.5 miles
Configuration:	Loop (counterclockwise)
Tread:	Doubletracks
Physical Difficulty:	Intermediate to advanced (gradual climbing up Left Fork Blue Fly; steep, rough hills up to and off of Left Fork Blue Fly–Badger Creek divide)
Technical Difficulty:	Low to moderate (mostly packed dirt, but loose pebbles and rocks on steep hills up to and off of Left Fork Blue Fly–Badger Creek divide)
Elevation Changes:	High: 9,160 feet (Left Fork Blue Fly–Badger Creek divide) Low: 7,700 feet (bottom of Left Fork Blue Fly road) Gain: 1,740 feet Trailhead: 7,840 feet (Tropic Reservoir)
Maps:	USGS 1:24,000 scale: Bryce Canyon, Bryce Point, Tropic Reservoir, and Wilson Peak, Utah (doubletrack from Tropic Reservoir to Left Fork Blue Fly road is not shown)
Land Status:	Dixie National Forest (Powell Ranger District)

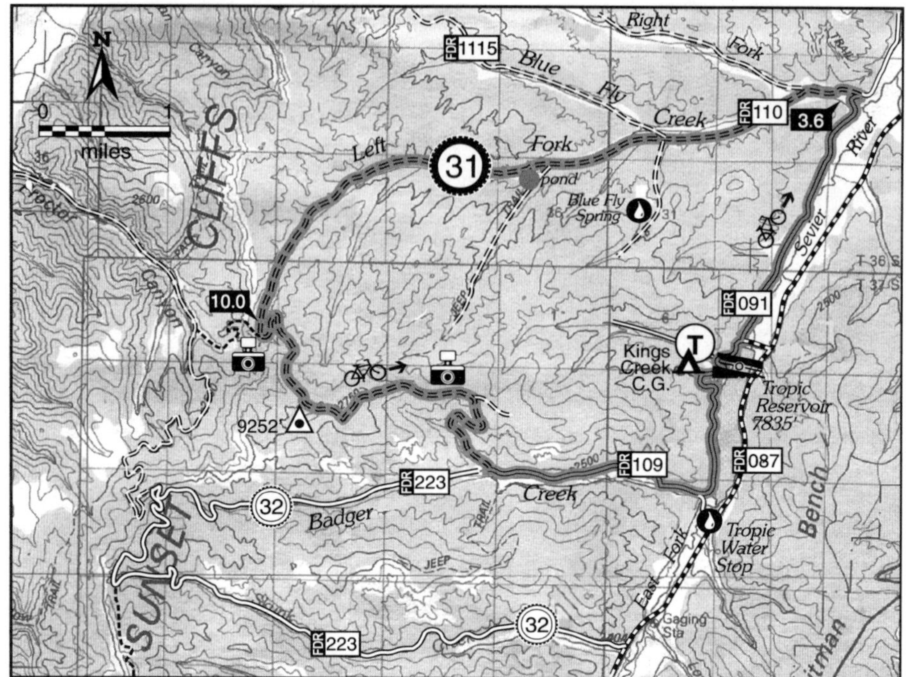

USGS 1:100,000 scale: Panguitch (50 meter contour interval).

This medium-distance loop offers both a variety of riding conditions and scenery. It begins with easy pedaling alongside the fertile East Fork Sevier River valley followed by gradual climbing to the always-dazzling Sunset Cliffs. A rough, demanding hill rises to the loop's summit (Left Fork Blue Fly–Badger Creek divide) and to a sweeping panorama of the colorful Paunsagunt Plateau. A sketchy descent off the divide is followed by an idle cruise down a broad valley and along the shore of the scenic Tropic Reservoir.

Pedal to the Tropic Reservoir dam and fork left on FDR 091, tagged "Fremont ATV/Great Western Trail." Follow the meandering East Fork Sevier River along the interface of the grass-filled valley and the pine-forested hills. A few modest hills are offset by relaxing, freewheeling descents. Fork left on FDR 110 for Left Fork Blue Fly, Proctor Canyon, and Badger Creek (**m3.6**).

Although Left Fork Blue Fly Creek valley may not be postcard quality, the wide sage-covered hollow, ringed by salmon-colored hills dotted with pines, captures the eye with its subtle form. Stay straight on the main road (unsigned), 2 miles up the valley, where FDR 1115 forks right across the valley and a doubletrack to Blue Fly Spring forks left up a hollow. When you reach a cattle pond 1 mile farther, take the right fork (to the north side of the pond), which is actually the Left Fork road. Quickly, the valley narrows, and ponderosa pines, underlain with manzanita, succumb to fir and aspen.

The Left Fork road tops out at a small clearing on the rim of Sunset Cliffs (**m10.0**). Park your rig, take to foot, and hike north up the knoll for a unimpeded view of the cliffs, wavering past Wilson Peak to Red Canyon. Beneath your feet, Proctor Canyon funnels to a narrow passage between blocky, honey-blond sandstone cliffs before opening to the Sevier River Valley. Brian Head Peak atop the Markagunt Plateau is but a bump on the horizon. Munch some snacks and gulp some fluids because you might need an energy boost for the upcoming climb.

Back at the clearing, follow the road uphill into the trees and across sun-baked slopes dotted with bristlecone pines. The limestone's crumbly surface coats the road with marble-size pebbles that compound the effort needed to surmount the protracted grade. But the cliffs' fleshy color coupled with captivating views of ever-deepening Proctor Canyon ease the effort. Enter cool shadows cast by a thicket of trees, and then power up one last pitch that finishes you off like a heavyweight's upper cut. Breathe a sigh of relief; it's all downhill from here, but the road's roughness prevents unencumbered rejoicing. Beyond the tree tops to the north, the Paunsagunt Plateau's rolling, orange-colored hills speckled with pines resemble schools of salmon eagerly hunting for spawning grounds.

About 1.5 miles out the ridge, you'll reach a Y junction; fork right and descend the steep, gravelly switchbacks to the Badger Creek road (FDR 109). Cruise down the valley toward Tropic Reservoir, scanning nearby slopes for hoodoo formations. Fork left on the west lake road (**m17.5**), ride past King Creek Campground, and return to the boat dock.

Option: "No-Name Trail" (Proctor Canyon loop)

Strong, fearless types, who relish venturing where others dare not, can extend the loop a few miles by dropping (literally) over the Sunset Cliffs into Proctor Canyon and then circling back to the rim. Consequently, you'll culminate the loop by racing down the length of Badger Creek at Mach speed.

The most difficult part of this option is not the technically demanding descent on "No Name Trail" but being able to actually find the trail. When you reach Sunset Cliffs at the head of Left Fork Blue Fly (**m10.0** above), don't continue the loop by rounding the bend and climbing into the trees; instead, go to the pass's absolute lowest point. Here you'll find an old ponderosa pine with a small, weathered, inscription-less wooden plaque tacked to it, no doubt denoting the long-forgotten trailhead. You'll scratch your head, befuddled, because there appears to be no trail. Now look *very* closely over the rim and to your right. You should be able to see a faint line angling down from the saddle, roughly north by northwest, where horses trod many moons ago. That's it! (Amazingly, the trail is accurately located on the USGS 1:24,000 scale quadrangle: Tropic Reservoir, Utah, 1966.)

Slip and slide down the crumbly, eroded slope, using your right foot as an outrigger and dismounting with rapid grace at the most treacherous spots—that's provided you get in the saddle to begin with. Five minutes down from the pass, you reach a gray sand bench surrounded by manzanita and pines. Bend sharply left to continue descending through the trees. (Watch for token tree blazes marking the trail.) Fork right upon intersecting a doubletrack and descend to Proctor Canyon (lightly im-

Climbing Proctor Canyon back to the Sunset Cliffs after dropping over the rim on "No Name Trail."

proved doubletrack), which may be marked by an unsigned wooden post. The deed is done, time to climb.

The 1,500-foot, 3.5-mile ascent back to the Sunset Cliffs takes about one hour, so gear down and treasure the interludes of rich forest and blazing-orange palisades. You'll no doubt shake your head as you glance over your shoulder to the cliffs over which you tumbled. When you gain the rim, fork left on FDR 109, and race down the Badger Creek road 6 miles to Tropic Reservoir to end this little jaunt.

Specs.: 22 miles; 2,500-foot gain

Notes and Precautions:

Doubletracks turn to sloppy goo when wet. Kings Creek Campground at Tropic Reservoir is a developed Forest Service fee area.

Trailhead Access:

From Panguitch, take US 89 south 7 miles; then turn left/east on UT 12 for Bryce Canyon National Park and Escalante. Drive 11 miles through Red Canyon and across the Paunsagunt Plateau. Between mileposts 10 and 11, turn right on FDR 087 (all-weather road), signed "Kings Creek Campground, Tropic Reservoir." Follow FDR 087 for 7 miles to Tropic Reservoir, cross the dam on route to Kings Creek Campground, and park at the boat dock near the campground's entrance.

32 Sunset Cliffs II (Badger Creek)

Location:	East Fork Sevier River valley (27 miles southeast of Panguitch)		
Length:	17.5 miles		
Configuration:	Loop (counterclockwise)		
Tread:	Doubletrack		
Physical Difficulty:	Intermediate (gentle to moderate climb on packed dirt and pebbly jeep roads)		
Technical Difficulty:	Low (jeep roads are packed dirt with pebbly sections; a couple of rough, steep switchbacks)		
Elevation Changes:	High:	9,200	feet (Sunset Cliffs)
	Low:	7,860	feet (trailhead: Tropic Reservoir)
	Gain:	1,340	feet
Maps:	USGS 1:24,000 scale: Tropic Reservoir, Utah		
Land Status:	Dixie National Forest (Powell Ranger District)		

Sunset Cliffs II (Badger Creek to Skunk Creek) is a fine introduction to the wonderful mountain biking opportunities in the East Fork Sevier River valley. You'll begin this route at the shore of placid Tropic Reservoir, and then pedal up a narrow valley neighbored by miniature Bryce Canyon-esque formations that are masked by pine-forested slopes. The ride's highlight comes at its summit where you can hike to a viewpoint overlooking luminescent cliffs, incised canyons, broad valleys, and distant plateaus. You'll culminate the loop with a blazing-fast descent back to the East Fork valley. As the cliff's name implies, early evening is prime time to ride this route.

From Tropic Reservoir's boat dock, pedal up past the entrance to Kings Creek Campground. Then roll along the west lake road for 1 mile to the junction with FDR 109, signed "Badger Creek, Proctor Canyon." Head up Badger Creek, forking right after 0.5 mile, and cross the broad valley to its north side. Search the slopes above you for hoodoo formations. Stay straight (left) on FDR 233 for Skunk Creek and Proctor Canyon, where FDR 109 forks right for Blue Fly Creek (**m3.6**). Gradually, the grassy valley tightens to a narrow canyon filled with pine, fir, and aspen. Simultaneously, the road begins rising in stair-step fashion, in that each short, moderately steep ascent is offset by a gently rising recovery zone. Swing around a pair of steep, rough turns and then through a second set 0.5 mile farther. Shortly thereafter, you reach a junction on the ridge (**m7.1**).

Stay left on FDR 233 toward Skunk Creek, contouring around knolls that conceal Sunset Cliffs. (The right fork descends Proctor Canyon to Hatch.) A mile farther, the road brushes the cliff's edge. Don't be content with the limited view from the road; rather, hike northward up the knoll to survey these colorful escarpments and the encompassing plateaus. Did you find the small arch below the rim?

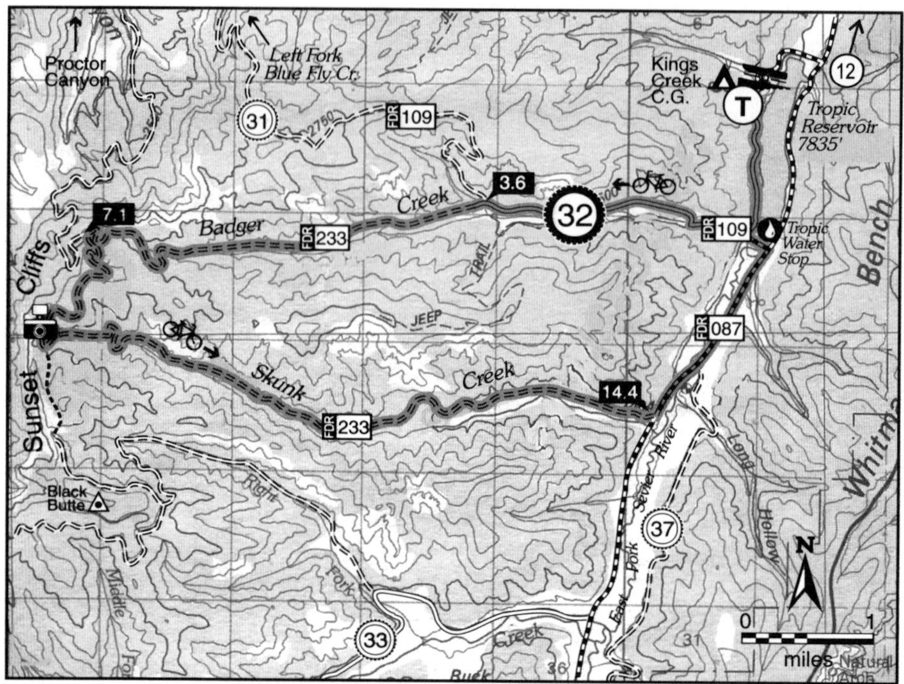

USGS 1:100,000 scale: Panguitch (50 meter contour interval).

The ride down Skunk Creek is a giant slalom course made for fat tires. Lean your bike into the swooping turns, letting your tire's knobs dig into the roadbed, but watch out for ruts and rocks that invariably booby trap unsuspicious curves. After a few miles of mad descending, the road mellows as the valley floor flattens to a carpeted meadow. Turn left on the East Fork road/FDR 087 (**m14.4**) and then left again for Badger Creek. Finally, take the west lake road back to the trailhead.

Notes & Precautions:

Use caution hiking along Sunset Cliffs. The crumbly surface may be unstable and break away. Kings Creek Campground at Tropic Reservoir is a developed Forest Service fee area.

Trailhead Access:

From Panguitch, take US 89 south 7 miles; then turn left/east on UT 12 for Bryce Canyon National Park and Escalante. Drive 11 miles through Red Canyon and across the Paunsagunt Plateau. Between mileposts 10 and 11, turn right on FDR 087 (all-weather road), signed "Kings Creek Campground, Tropic Reservoir." Follow FDR 087 for 7 miles to Tropic Reservoir, cross the dam on route to Kings Creek Campground, and park at the boat dock.

Setting out for the Sunset Cliffs (left); a view upon reaching the rim (right).

33 Sunset Cliffs III (Blubber Creek)

Location:	East Fork Sevier River valley (32 miles southeast of Panguitch)		
Length:	15.0 miles		
Configuration:	Loop (counterclockwise) with out-and-back		
Tread:	Doubletrack		
Physical Difficulty:	Intermediate (moderate climb, undulating along the rim, freewheeling descent)		
Technical Difficulty:	Low (doubletracks are hard-packed dirt with pebbly sections; good cruising)		
Elevation Changes:	High:	9,100	feet (Sunset Cliffs)
	Low:	8,300	feet (trailhead: Blubber Creek)
	Gain:	900	feet
Maps:	USGS 1:24,000 scale: Tropic Reservoir, Utah		
Land Status:	Dixie National Forest (Powell Ranger District)		

This is the third is a series of rides that rises from the fertile East Fork Sevier River valley to the glowing Sunset Cliffs. You'll pass hoodoo formations that peak from wooded knolls and stop at two captivating displays of the Sunset Cliffs. The route follows smooth doubletracks throughout and is part of the East Fork ATV Trail System. You'll start with a moderate climb, roll along the rim, and end with a blazing descent—all on smooth doubletracks. Double your distance if you tack on the optional tour to the Right Fork Upper Kanab Creek.

From the junction of FDR 211 and FDR 868, fork left and pedal up FDR 211 alongside the Left Fork Blubber Creek's broad meadows. Scan the hillsides above for fleshy Bryce Canyon-esque outcrops. (FDR 868 also rises to the rim, but the climb is tedious and uneventful.) After **2.5** miles, FDR 211 ends at a Y junction with FDR 106. Fork right to begin the climb up Middle Fork Blubber to the Sunset Cliffs. You'll return on the Left Fork. Ignore two doubletracks forking right and continue climbing up the main valley. After the road bends across the valley's head, your

USGS 1:100,000 scale: Panguitch (50 meter contour interval).

eye's will be drawn to the fine view of Blubber Creek valley below and of salmon-colored hills flecked with pines.

Intersect the rim road and take it left/south following ATV decals (**m6.7**). (FDR 106, which you just ascended, is tagged "Thru Road" at this junction. The rim road is now FDR 106 as well.) Less than 1 mile ahead, the road clips the Sunset Cliffs for a pretty view. (Ignore the doubletrack forking left, unless you want to bail out to Left Fork Blubber Creek.) The second viewpoint is 1.5 miles farther along the rim road. Thereafter, the road descends steeply to a junction signed "Right Fork Blubber" in reverse and "Kanab Creek" to the right (**m10.2**). Fork left on the unsigned Left Fork Blubber Creek road to descend 4.3 miles back to the trailhead.

Option: Right Fork Upper Kanab Creek

If you want to log extra miles and behold a dazzling view of the Sunset Cliffs that pales those viewed previously, then head over to Sand Pass at the head of the Right

Taking a closer look at the effects of differential erosion.

Fork Upper Kanab Creek instead of descending to the trailhead. It's 3 miles to Sand Pass, and the first mile rises at a crushing 15-percent grade. But the rest is a breeze. At Sand Pass, you might grumble that the immediate view is not worth the effort. Now hike up the wooded knoll to the south and then along the cliff's edge for one-quarter mile. There your jaw will drop to your toes as you gaze into a gaping amphitheater of crinkled walls plastered with corrugated columns. If you dare, you can walk out a rock platform atop coalescing spires for a more intimate view. Below, Kanab Creek canyon stretches southward toward Alton.

To reach Sand Pass, descend to the junction where FDR 106 is signed "Right Fork Blubber, Kanab Creek" (**m10.2** above), but do not fork left and descend to the trailhead. Instead, fork right and downshift in preparation for the hill climb. There's not much sightseeing over the next mile, so drop your head to your handlebar and grind away. (This road is not on topographic maps.) One-half mile up, stay right while ignore a logging road forking left and crossing the upper canyon. Soon thereafter the road levels, curves south, and enters the woods. At a T junction just past a cattle guard, fork right on FDR 106. Stay on FDR 106 for 1.5 miles to where the road turns left and begins descending Right Fork Upper Kanab Creek. Sand Pass is to the right, within spitting distance of the junction.

You'll have to decide how to return to the trailhead. The quickest way is to backtrack and descend Left Fork Blubber Creek as described above. But if you want to log still more miles, then rocket down Right Fork Upper Kanab Creek, cruise alongside the fertile meadows of "lower" Upper Kanab Creek, and then circle back to Blubber Creek via the East Fork road, all on fast doubletracks and smooth dirt roads.

Specs.: 23.5 miles; 1,700-foot gain

Notes & Precautions:

Use caution hiking along Sunset Cliffs. The crumbly surface may be unstable and break away. Kings Creek Campground at Tropic Reservoir is a developed Forest Service fee area. Backcountry camping is allowed in both Blubber Creek and Upper Kanab Creek valleys.

Trailhead Access:

From Panguitch, take US 89 south 7 miles; then turn left/east on UT 12 for Bryce Canyon National Park and Escalante. Drive 11 miles through Red Canyon and across the Paunsagunt Plateau. Between mileposts 10 and 11, turn right on FDR 087 (all-weather road), signed "Kings Creek Campground, Tropic Reservoir." Follow FDR 087 for 7 miles to Tropic Reservoir then 4.8 miles farther to the Blubber Creek road/ FDR 211. Drive 2 miles up Blubber Creek to the junction with FDR 868. Park off the road. (Along the way, ignore a doubletrack forking right and signed FDR 106. Although the described route follows FDR 106 in part, this particular road leads to destinations unknown and may be signed erroneously.)

34 Sunset Cliffs IV (Robinson Canyon)

Location:	East Fork Sevier River valley (40 miles southeast of Panguitch)
Length:	8 miles
Configuration:	Loop (clockwise)
Tread:	Doubletrack
Physical Difficulty:	Intermediate (steep half-mile climb followed by gentle hills, rolling terrain, and a brisk descent)
Technical Difficulty:	Low (hard-packed and soft dirt with scattered pebbles and occasional ruts)
Elevation Changes:	High: 9,000 feet (top of Horse Hollow)
	Low: 8,400 feet (bottom of Robinson Canyon)
	Gain: 600 feet
Maps:	USGS 1:24,000 scale: Alton and Podunk Creek, Utah
Land Status:	Dixie National Forest (Powell Ranger District)

This is the forth in a series of trips to the always-charming Sunset Cliffs. If not for a rather audacious half-mile climb at the outset, this would be the easiest trip to the Sunset Cliffs as well. Still, novice riders should not be deterred. The climb is over quickly, and when your eyes fall upon the Sunset Cliffs, all memories of your effort will be erased. The viewpoint you are striving for is perhaps the most glorious along the cliffs. You can hike along the level rim and peer into the horseshoe-shaped bowl

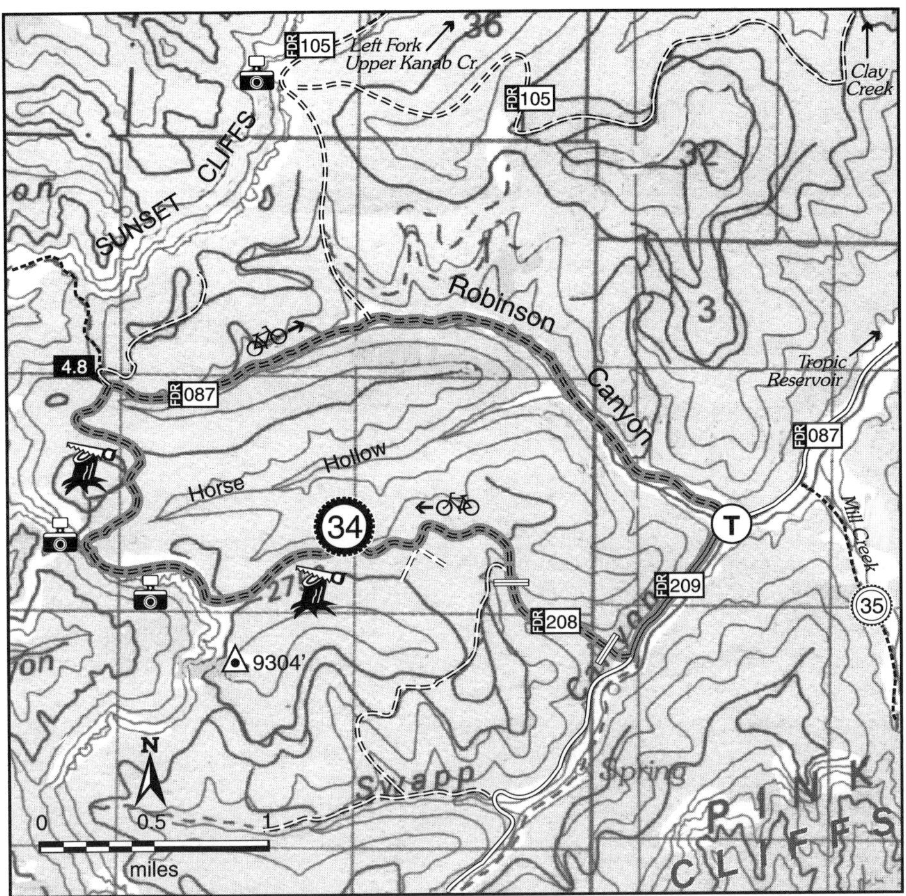

USGS 1:100,000 scale: Panguitch (50 meter contour interval).

from many angles. From each vantage, you'll discover new and peculiar shapes etched from the blinding Claron Formation. Sunset Cliffs IV is also the starting line for the 37 mile Grand Tour of the Sunset Cliffs.

Start out from Robinson Canyon with 0.7 mile of very gentle climbing on FDR 209; then fork right on FDR 208 and go around a steel gate. Shift down to your granny gear and attack the half-mile-long 15-percent-grade hill. When you reach the second gate, breathe a sigh of relief because the tough part is over. Continue straight following ATV decals. At a four-way junction amidst sapling aspens, fork right and climb gently through woods that have been logged in years past. Bisect a grove of spindly aspens while contouring across the head of Horse Canyon, and then enter mixed conifers. As the road begins to descend, stop, dismount, and walk 100 feet through the manzanita and common juniper ground cover to the rim of the Sunset Cliffs. This is a colossal viewpoint, one that combines intricate erosional forms with

On the edge (left); lower Robinson Canyon (right).

sweeping vistas. The cliffs, with their fluted columns, arched alcoves, and ornately carved entablatures, are a veritable study of the classical order of architecture blended with Romanesque and Gothic themes.

Back on your bike, descend to the pass, and check out the view of Water Canyon below, of Kanab Creek canyon in the middle ground, and of Zion's sandstone temples on the hazy horizon. Then veer eastward away from the cliffs and climb the pebbly doubletrack around a knoll that has been denuded of timber. Ignore doubletracks forking left and right at the top; follow the ATV decals that lead you downhill to the head of Robinson Canyon/FDR 087 (**m4.8**). (Ignore the singletrack and doubletrack to the left. Neither is worth pursuing.)

The rest of the route is a free-flowing coast for those who prefer a casual pace or a rip-roaring rampage for those who charge at race pace. Pass FDR 105 forking left, unless you're bound for the Grand Tour (see Options), and cruise down lower Robinson Canyon where the creek makes gooseneck meanders through a pristine meadow.

Option: Grand Tour of Sunset Cliffs (Robinson Canyon to Tropic Reservoir)

Go for broke on this expert-level tour. Tie together Sunset Cliffs I-IV by riding 37 miles from Robinson Canyon to Tropic Reservoir. The route follows hard-packed dirt doubletracks with intermittent sections coated with silt and native limestone gravel. Pedaling is fast-paced overall, but there are a few significant climbs along the way. The first climb is the half-mile grind up FDR 208 from the trailhead. Going anaerobic right of the start line no way to begin a day-long tour, so go easy and spin if you can. The second, and harshest, is the mile-long climb out of Robinson Canyon to the top of Left Fork Upper Kanab Creek. The 10-percent grade will test your power output, and the rock-infested ruts redline the technical difficulty meter. Third is the half-mile ascent out of upper Left Fork Blubber Creek. Here the grade is steep and steady, but the technical difficulty is low, thankfully. The last notable hill is the chug up an ATV trail between Black Butte and upper Skunk Creek. In between these challenging sections, there are generous descents where you can speed as fast as you dare. But the real reason you should pursue this route is to rank the half dozen viewpoints of the Sunset Cliffs. Each overlook reveals the Sunset Cliffs' ever-changing character but and never tiresome character.

This route requires a shuttle between Tropic Reservoir and Robinson Canyon; otherwise, you'll have to tack on 15 miles along the East Fork road.

Your only source from which to purify water along the tour is at the confluence of Left and Right Forks of Upper Kanab Creek. Thereafter, the route stays near the rim and above water sources until it descends Badger Creek to Tropic Reservoir.

Specs.: 37 miles; 3,600-foot gain

Notes & Precautions:

Use caution when hiking along Sunset Cliffs. The crumbly surface may be unstable and break away. Kings Creek Campground at Tropic Reservoir is a developed Forest Service fee area.

Trailhead Access:

From Panguitch, take US 89 south 7 miles; then turn left/east on UT 12 for Bryce Canyon National Park and Escalante. Drive 11 miles through Red Canyon and across the Paunsagunt Plateau. Between mileposts 10 and 11, turn right on FDR 087 (all-weather road), signed "Kings Creek Campground, Tropic Reservoir." Follow FDR 087 (a Scenic Backway) for 21.7 miles to Robinson Canyon. (From UT 12 you'll pass Tropic Reservoir after 7 miles, fork right at the Y junction for Podunk Creek after 15.3 miles, pass the Podunk Guard Station after 16.5 miles, and fork right at the Y junction for Crawford Pass after 18 miles. The "Scenic Backway" ends at the Podunk Guard Station where the all-weather road becomes a single-lane lightly improved dirt road that is suitable for passenger cars when dry.)

35 Mill Creek Trail

Location:	East Fork Sevier River valley (40 miles southeast of Panguitch)
Length:	8.0 miles
Configuration:	Loop (counterclockwise)
Tread:	Doubletrack, ATV trail, singletrack (primitive)
Physical Difficulty:	Intermediate (mostly gentle hills, one occurrence of route finding)
Technical Difficulty:	Low to moderate (mostly smooth doubletracks; steep, loose descent on ATV trail; little-used singletrack often has deadfall and wet areas)
Elevation Changes:	High: 9,040 feet (top of ATV trail above Mill Creek pass) Low: 8,340 feet (Mill Creek trailhead on FDR 087) Gain: 700 feet Trailhead: 8,600 feet (Straight Canyon trailhead)
Maps:	USGS 1:24,000 scale: Podunk Creek, Utah (middle section of route is not shown)
Land Status:	Dixie National Forest (Powell Ranger District)

If you're a singletrack purist, then sneak down the East Fork Sevier River valley to the very tip of the Paunsagunt Plateau. Here you'll find a serendipitous trail that is seldom tickled by knobby tires. As an added bonus, you'll be entertained by a couple of grand vistas from the plateau's rim and descend a wild ATV trail through dark, creepy woods. With only 1.5 miles of singletrack to offer, Mill Creek Trail is a long

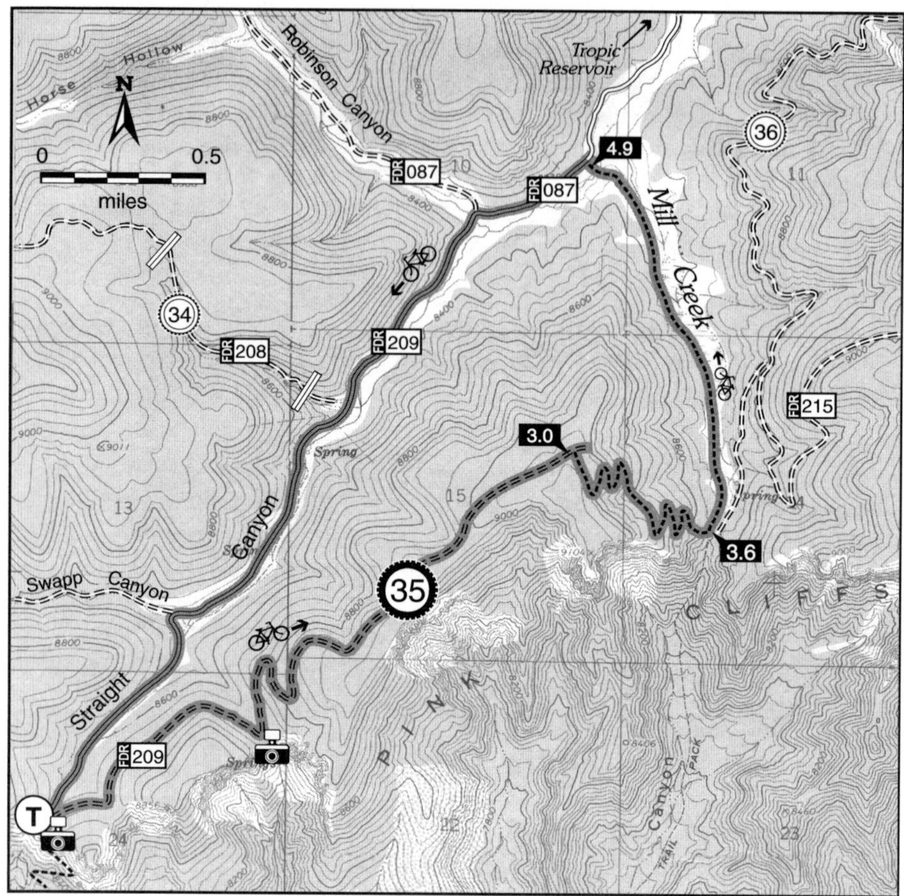

USGS 1:24,000 scale: Podunk Creek (40 foot contour interval).

haul from the paved world, unless, of course, you crave solitude, huge vistas, and interludes with four-legged creatures. Mum's the word.

At the Straight Canyon trailhead, peer over the edge of the Pink Cliffs, and then embark by following the doubletrack northeastward. After 1 mile, the road curves up to a scenic viewpoint enclosed by a fence—good thing because the earth drops nearly 500 feet beneath your feet as the Pink Cliffs break from the plateau's forested rim. Far below, the western province of the Grand Staircase–Escalante National Monument stretches toward the horizon as mammoth stratigraphic steps. If your sole objective is panoramic views, then retreat to the trailhead. If you want to explore these backwoods, then press on.

Scramble up steep, gravelly curves; then cruise along the hilltop into an eerie stand of charred trees that burned in 1994. Nearing the east edge of the mount, fork right on an ATV trail (**m3.0**). (The road ends shortly beyond the turnoff.) Hold on tight, and bounce down the rough switchbacking track to Mill Creek Canyon Pass.

Rays of sunlight cast commingling shadows on the Mill Creek Trail.

But don't dally or you might be ambushed by conniving Ewoks lurking amongst the timbers' commingling shadows.

Stop as soon as you leave the darkened woods and reach the saddle (**m3.6**). Mill Creek Trail heads left into the sapling aspens and along the *west* side of the drainage. If you continue on the doubletrack across the saddle, you'll intersect the Pink Cliff loop along its "back nine" and wind up miles off course near Crawford Pass.

In years past, the trail was unsigned and virtually unidentifiable, which means you might ride aimlessly at first while searching for the trail. Once in the woods, the tread is obvious. You will soon be hopping roots and deadfall with eager anticipation; dodging rocks, cow pies, and eye-poking tree limbs; slogging past trail-side springs; and careening comically down the accidental path.

All good things come to an end when the trail exits to the East Fork road (**m4.9**). Circle back to the Straight Canyon trailhead towing memories of this secretive jaunt.

Notes & Precautions:

This is no place for a mechanical breakdown (to bike or vehicle) because you are miles from nowhere. The Straight Canyon trailhead has no water tap and no outhouse.

Trailhead Access:

From Panguitch, take US 89 south 7 miles; then turn left/east on UT 12 for Bryce Canyon National Park and Escalante. Drive 11 miles through Red Canyon and across the Paunsagunt Plateau. Between mileposts 10 and 11, turn right on FDR 087 (all-weather road), signed "Kings Creek Campground, Tropic Reservoir." Follow FDR 087 18 miles to a Y junction, signed "Crawford Pass, Meadow Canyon (left); Robinson Canyon (right)," passing Tropic Reservoir and the Podunk Guard Station after 7 and 16.5 miles, respectively. Stay right on FDR 087 (lightly maintained but usually suitable for passenger cars under dry conditions) for nearly 4 miles to the lower Mill Creek trailhead. Park here alongside the road, or continue on FDR 087 and then on FDR 209 for 3 miles total to the Straight Canyon trailhead.

36 Pink Cliff

Location:	East Fork Sevier River valley (35 miles southeast of Panguitch)
Length:	15 miles
Configuration:	Loop (clockwise)
Tread:	Doubletrack
Physical Difficulty:	Intermediate (moderate climbs, plenty of cruising)
Technical Difficulty:	Low (sections have sand, loose and embedded pebbles, and ruts)
Elevation Changes:	High: 9,394 feet (Pink Cliff)
	Low: 8,100 feet (trailhead: East Fork road)
	Gain: 1,600 Feet
Maps:	USGS 1:24,000 scale: Podunk Creek, Utah (most of route is not shown)
Land Status:	Dixie National Forest (Powell Ranger District)

The Pink Cliffs are what make this region of southern Utah so spectacular and utterly peculiar. As their name suggests, these naked limestones are a dazzling orange-pink, layered with chalk white and rich salmon hues. The cliffs' propensity for what geologists call differential weathering results in scalloped escarpments stuffed with "hoodoos," or rock formations of irregular if not fantastic form. This tour takes you to the Cliffs' namesake viewpoint, where you peer into rock amphitheaters nearly the scenic equal to nearby Bryce Canyon National Park, minus the pressing crowds and double-decker tour buses. The route's "back nine" rambles through peaceful forests populated with deer and elk.

From the East Fork road/FDR 087, take FDR 092 toward Crawford Pass. Pass the junction with FDR 215, just shy of 1 mile up and signed "Loop Road, Mill Hollow," and continue climbing to Crawford Pass (**m2.2/12.8**). (You'll conclude the loop on FDR 215.) At the pass, turn right on FDR 203 for "Loop Road and Pink Cliffs" to knock off the majority of the route's elevation gain. A gentle descent there-

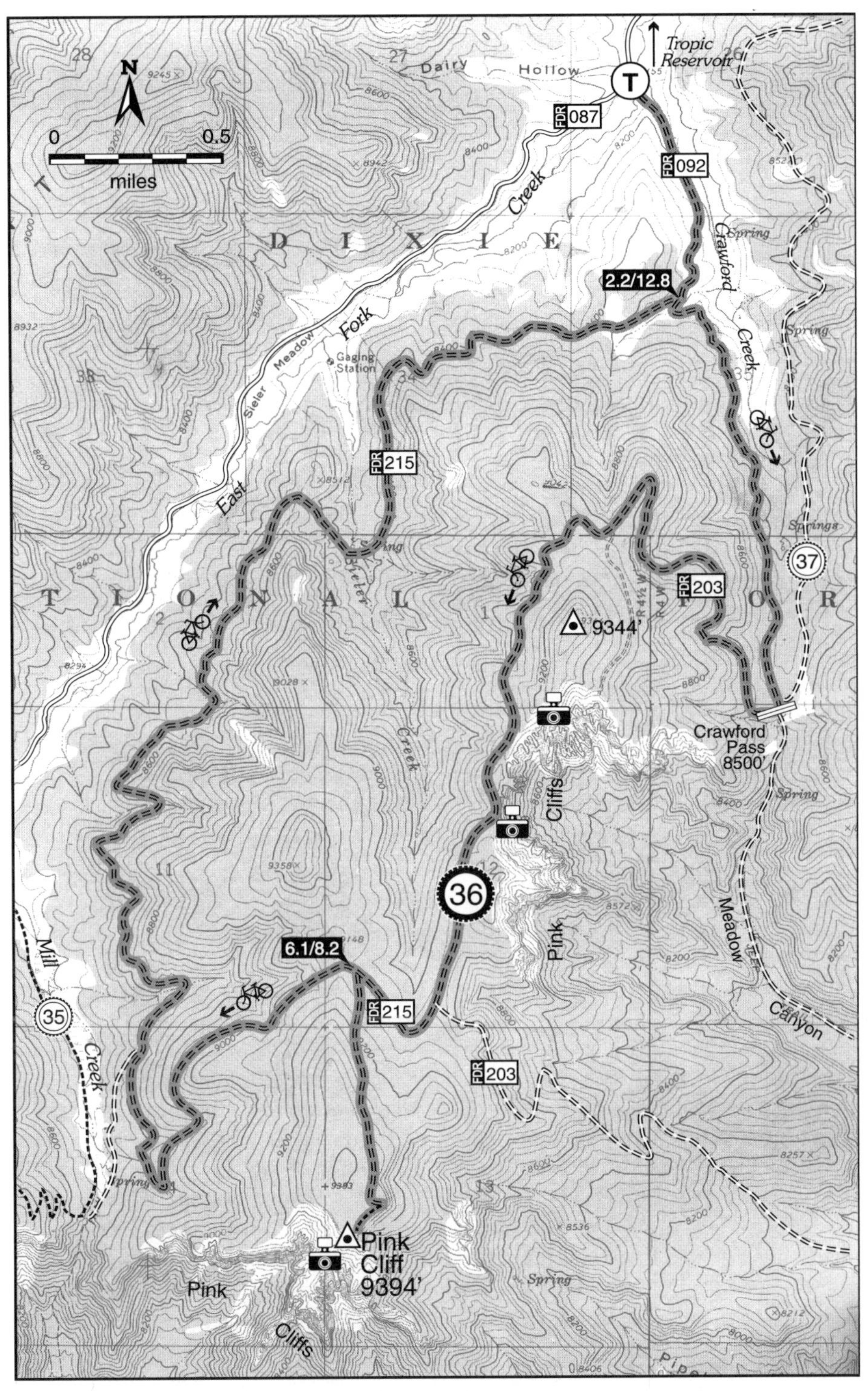

USGS 1:24,000 scale: Podunk Creek (40 foot contour interval).

A view John Wesley Powell enjoyed over a century ago.

after takes you to the rim of the Pink Cliffs. Dismount and hike northward up the forested knoll for a gaping view of an amphitheater of Bryce Canyon quality.

At the upcoming Y junction, stay straight (right) on FDR 215, signed "Pink Cliffs." (FDR 203 forks left and drops over the rim. FDR 215 will take you back to the Crawford Pass road.) One-half mile farther (**m6.1/m8.2**), turn left for the spur to the Pink Cliffs. You'll climb moderately for 1 mile and then come to a T junction. Fork left and take the ATV track to the plateau's terminus.

John Wesley Powell's survey crew stood at this very spot over a century ago, while surveying these plateaus. Below your feet, the flesh-colored Pink Cliffs have eroded to arthritic appendages jutting from the rim's edge. The erosional expression of these limestones is ever-changing, from fanciful to grotesque but always engaging. Beyond the rim lies the Grand Staircase, where eons of uplift and erosion have cut dendritic canyons into the table lands. Stash your rig and bushwhack by foot westward along the rim and then down the slope toward Mill Creek Canyon Pass. If you walk far enough, you'll gain an impressive low-angle view of the rim.

Return to FDR 215, and continue the loop on a raging downhill through high speed turns. Beyond a right-hand hairpin curve, the road loops northward and roughly contours above Mill Creek and East Fork Creek for 5 miles. Some stretches are baby-butt smooth; others are lumpy and bumpy. Elk inhabit these lush woods, and rousing a bedded herd electrifies the calm air with rampaging hooves and slashing antlers. Upon intersecting the Crawford Pass road/FDR 092 (**m12.8**), turn left and glide back to your vehicle.

Notes & Precautions:

Do not get suckered into descending from Crawford Pass to Meadow Canyon along the Great Western Trail. You'll encounter private property (a locked gate) and be forced to backtrack to the pass—an abusive endeavor. Portions of the East Fork road/FDR 087 south of Tropic Reservoir may be impassable to passenger cars when wet. Kings Creek Campground at Tropic Reservoir is a developed Forest Service fee area.

Trailhead Access:

From Panguitch, take US 89 south 7 miles; then turn left/east on UT 12 for Bryce Canyon National Park and Escalante. Drive 11 miles through Red Canyon and across the Paunsagunt Plateau. Between mileposts 10 and 11, turn right on FDR 087 (all-weather road), signed "Kings Creek Campground, Tropic Reservoir." Take FDR 087 for 18 miles to a Y junction, signed "Crawford Pass, Meadow Canyon (left); Robinson Canyon (right)," passing Tropic Reservoir and the Podunk Guard Station after 7 miles and 16.5 miles, respectively. Park at your discretion alongside the road.

37 Great Western Trail (East Fork Sevier River Section)

Location:	East Fork Sevier River valley (27 miles southeast of Panguitch)
Length:	20.5 miles
Configuration:	Point-to-point (see Options for loop rides)
Tread:	Doubletracks
Physical Difficulty:	Intermediate (gentle and moderate climbs combined with lots of easy cruising; see Options for novice-level rides)
Technical Difficulty:	Low (some loose and imbedded stones plus minor sand and ruts on mostly hard-packed doubletracks)
Elevation Changes:	High: 8,500 feet (Crawford Pass) Low: 7,880 feet (trail end: near Tropic Reservoir) Gain: 1,000 feet Trailhead: 8,155 feet (East Fork road)
Maps:	USGS 1:24,000 scale: Podunk Creek and Tropic Reservoir, Utah (Crawford Pass to Podunk Creek section is not shown)
Land Status:	Dixie National Forest (Powell Ranger District)

The East Fork Sevier River section of the Great Western Trail captures the trail's multi-use concept. Here, motorized and non-motorized users can travel undulating doubletracks through elk-populated woods, while gaining views of the long, narrow, lush valley below and of the colorful Bryce Canyon-esque cliffs breaking from slopes across the valley. Pedaling is easy because the route contours the hillsides on a near-level keel. And although Bryce Canyon National Park is merely a stone's-throw away, few travelers visit the fertile East Fork valley. Thus, tranquility abounds, even with the route's ATV designation.

The route begins with a perfect little warmup. The steady 2-mile climb to Crawford Pass fires up your power plant but doesn't produce buckets of perspiration, unless, of course, you charge at race pace and go anaerobic. At Crawford Pass (**m2.2**), turn

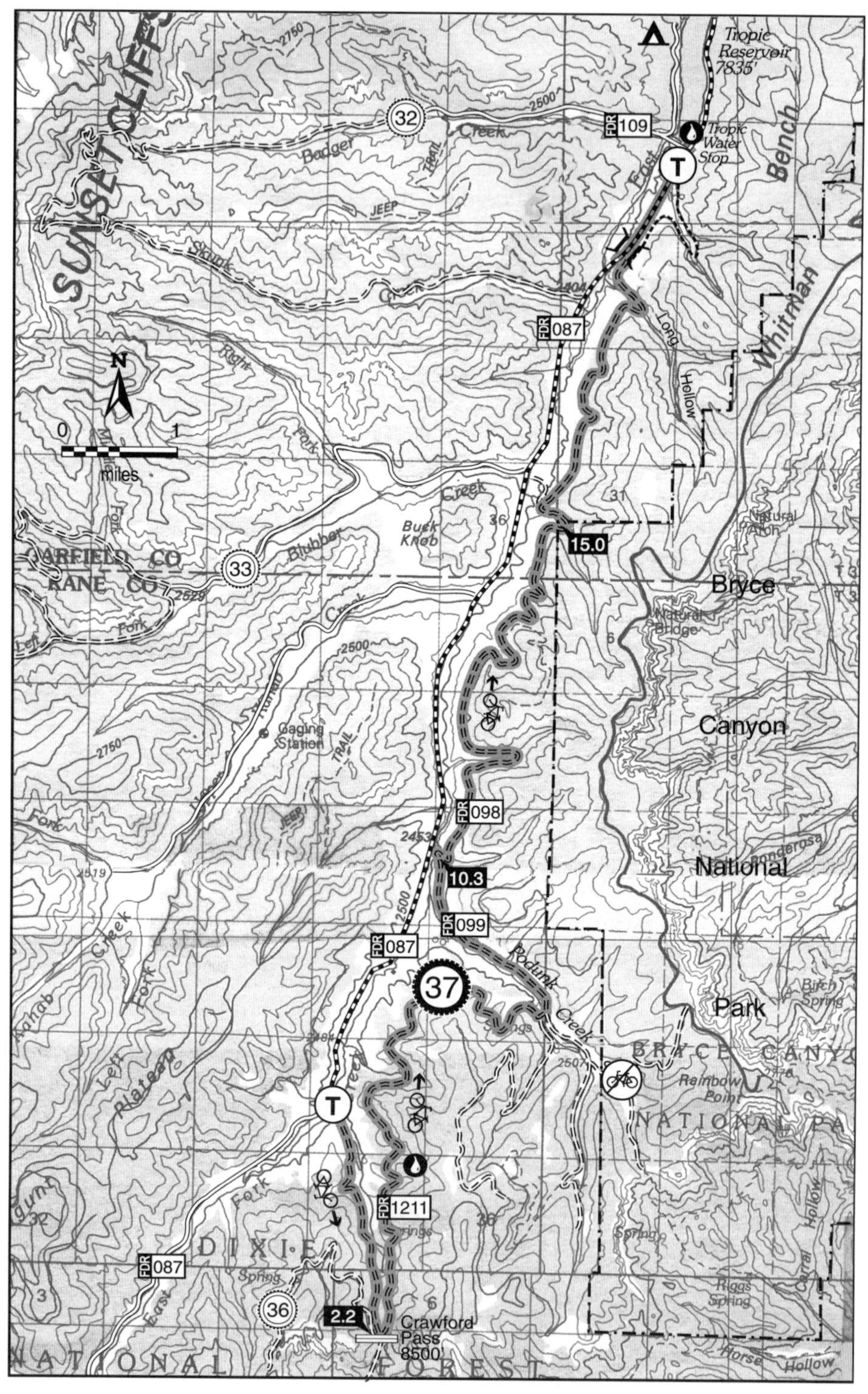

USGS 1:100,000 scale: Panguitch (50 meter contour interval).

left on FDR 1211/Great Western Trail (GWT) for Podunk Creek. Climb a bit more; then contour high above Crawford Creek and the East Fork Sevier River valley. You'll catch a retreating glimpse of hoodoo outcrops, pass springs bubbling from grassy wells, and curve through numerous hollows creasing the hillsides. The doubletrack is mostly smooth after an initial pebbly section, so the pedaling is easy. Elk find cover in these heavily wooded slopes, and during rutting season bulls seduce mates with eerie bugling. Bend through Coyote Hollow, cross Podunk Creek, and descend like the wind 2 miles on FDR 099. Just before the road crosses the East Fork Sevier River, fork right on FDR 098 to continue the GWT (**m10.3**).

This section from Podunk Creek to Long Hollow requires a bit more effort because the doubletrack's tread varies between packed dirt and soft silt mixed with grassy, lumpy, bumpy, rocky stints. Still, there is plenty of requisite cruising during which wandering eyes can spy hoodoo-stuffed escarpments scooped from timbered slopes across the valley.

The track swings far from the East Fork valley as it wraps through Puma Hollow and arcs through lesser hollows. In Bridge Hollow (**m15.0**), the road nips the fenced boundary of Bryce Canyon National Park. You'll have an opportunity to bail out to the East Fork road or continue on the GWT as you exit Bridge Hollow. After bending through Long Hollow, 2 miles later, take the left-hand doubletrack down to the East Fork road and back to Tropic Reservoir. (Ignore the ATV track leading to Ingram Hollow—it's hardly worth the effort.)

Option: East Fork GWT (loop)

If you're hankering for a long-distance, low-intensity ride, then the loop version of the East Fork Great Western Trail fits the bill. You'll warm up with 9.2 miles of nearly imperceptible climbing on the East Fork road/FDR 087 and culminate the loop on the GWT, as described above. During prolonged dry spells, the East Fork road may develop washboards, but they never reach teeth-chattering, bolt-loosening magnitudes. Also, be willing to share the road with occasional vehicles that can kick up clouds of dust. Most of the time, you'll have the road to yourself.

Specs.: 29.7 miles; 1,300-foot gain

Option: East Fork GWT (Podunk Creek–Long Hollow loop)

No shuttle available? Then knock off the bottom half of the GWT as an intermediate-level loop. Start near Tropic Reservoir (see Trailhead Access), and pedal 6.6 miles up the East Fork road to Podunk Creek. You may rattle over some washboards, but they are rarely of consequence. Fork left on FDR 099, signed "Podunk Creek, Park Boundary," and then left again on FDR 098, tagged "GWT." Now follow the main description above from **m10.3** back to Tropic Reservoir.

Specs.: 17 miles; 750-foot gain

Option: East Fork GWT (Crawford Pass–Podunk Creek loop)

This option is well suited for novice riders. Drive to and park at the Podunk Creek junction on the East Fork road, located 6.6 miles south of Tropic Reservoir. Pedal up the East Fork Road nearly 3 miles to the junction for Crawford Pass. Ride the main route, described above, 10 miles back to Podunk Creek. The farther you

In search of elk along the Great Western Trail.

venture out the East Fork valley, the less likely you are to encounter humanoids and the more likely you are to rustle up deer and elk.

Specs.: 13 miles; 500-foot gain

Note & Precautions:

Be aware of sporadic traffic on the East Fork road, especially log trucks. Kings Creek Campground at Tropic Reservoir is a Forest Service fee area.

Trailhead Access:

From Panguitch, take US 89 south 7 miles; then turn left/east on UT 12 for Bryce Canyon National Park and Escalante. Drive 11 miles through Red Canyon and across the Paunsagunt Plateau. Between mileposts 10 and 11, turn right on FDR 087 (all-weather road), signed "Kings Creek Campground, Tropic Reservoir." Follow FDR 087 for 8 miles to the southern edge of Tropic Reservoir. Drop one vehicle near the junction with FDR 109 (Badger Creek road). In the shuttle vehicle, drive 9.2 miles south on the East Fork road (FDR 087), and park at the junction signed "Crawford Pass, Meadow Canyon (left)." (You'll pass the Podunk Creek junction and the Podunk Guard Station 6.6 miles and 7.8 miles south of Tropic Reservoir, respectively.)

38 Daves Hollow–Whiteman Bench

Location:	0.5 mile north of Bryce Canyon National Park
Length:	8 miles (Daves Hollow); 21.5 miles (Whiteman Bench)
Configuration:	Loop (counterclockwise)
Tread:	Doubletracks, all-weather road
Physical Difficulty:	Daves Hollow: Novice (gentle hills); Whiteman Bench: Intermediate to advanced (gentle hills; steep, 1-mile climb to Whiteman Bench; need a good sense of direction to navigate the numerous road junctions)
Technical Difficulty:	Daves Hollow: Low (packed dirt with sporadic rocks); Whiteman Bench: Low to moderate (same as Daves Hollow but add gravel and washboards on the East Fork road plus a steep, rocky descent past Whiteman Spring)
Elevation Changes:	High: 8,400 feet (top of Whiteman Bench) Low: 7,700 feet (bottom of Daves Hollow) Gain: 350 feet (Daves Hollow loop) Gain: 1,400 feet (Whiteman Bench loop) Trailhead: 7,720 feet
Maps:	USGS 1:24,000 scale: Bryce Canyon and Bryce Point, Utah
Land Status:	Dixie National Forest (Powell Ranger District)

If you've had your fill of eyeball-popping vistas in Bryce Canyon National Park, take an afternoon off from hiking and pedal through the adjacent Dixie National Forest. Granted, the scenery is not staggering like in Bryce Canyon, but you'll find these two woodland tours satisfying and utterly peaceful.

Daves Hollow loop is ideal for novice bikers or families towing a child in a tag-along trailer. This 8-mile loop winds idly through tranquil stands of ponderosa pines and across broad grass-filled meadows visited by small and big game. Those craving a longer ride can extend Daves Hollow by venturing to Tropic Reservoir in the East Fork Sevier River valley, climbing Whiteman Bench, and cruising back to the trailhead on fast-paced doubletracks. Although a Global Positioning Satellite (GPS) receiver is not required, you will have to navigate many road junctions. Portions of these routes follow the Great Western Trail.

Head west from the Gateway Trailhead, following the Great Western Trail (GWT) markers. Pass FDR 1175/GWT and FDR 1174, both branching left, and stay straight on FDR 1173. (You'll culminate both Daves Hollow and Whiteman Bench loops on FDR 1175.) Crest a low knoll and wander to a junction. Stay straight on what is now FDR 103. (Fork left on FDR 109 for a shortened version of Daves Hollow loop.)

Drop to Daves Hollow itself and arrive at the junction with FDR 088 (**m3.0**). Turn left and take FDR 088 up grassy Daves Hollow for 0.5 mile; then fork right to continue on the main road up a small wooded dale. (The less-traveled track forking left up Daves Hollow, proper, tends to be lumpy and bumpy.) When you intersect FDR 090/GWT (**m5.3**), you have two choices. Those opting for the shorter Daves Hollow loop should turn left, take FDR 090 across the mile-wide vale, and complete the ride on FDR 1175 back to the trailhead. If you're game for the longer Whiteman Bench loop, then read and ride on.

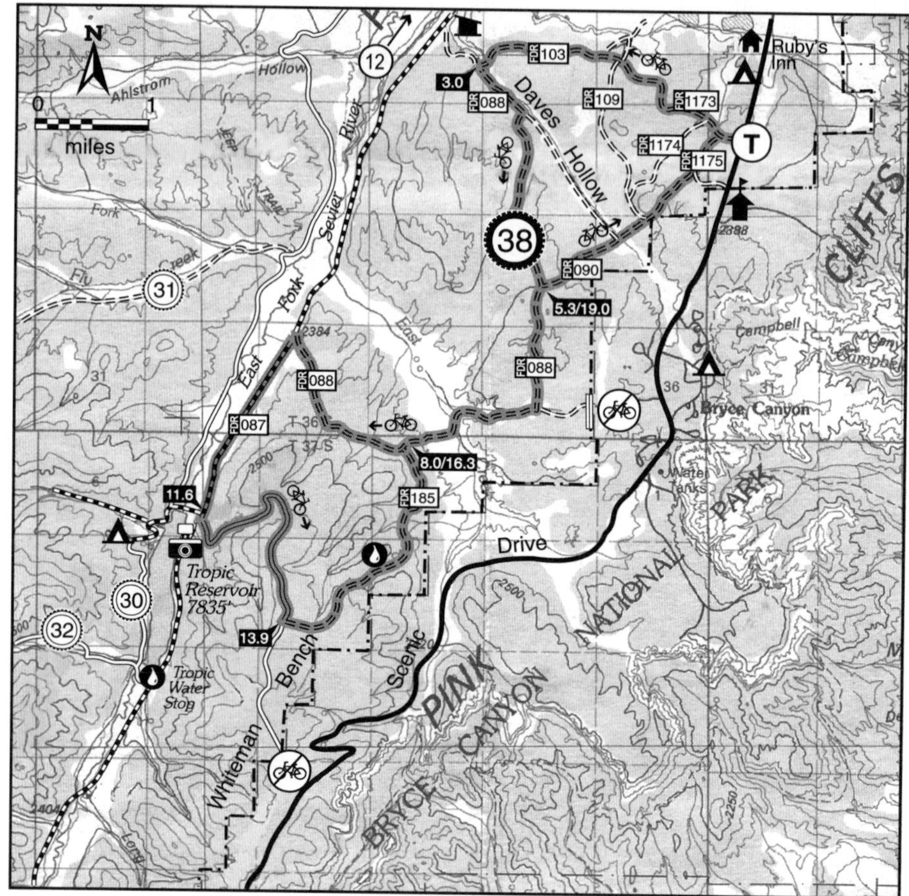

USGS 1:100,000 scale: Panguitch (50 meter contour interval).

Continue south on FDR 088 up the gently rising hollow; then blaze downhill to a T junction. Turn right, staying on FDR 088/GWT. (The road to the left ends at the park boundary after 0.5 mile.) Less than 1 mile farther, fork left on FDR 088 and bend right to cross the East Creek valley (not to be confused with the upcoming East Fork Sevier River valley). At the junction with FDR 185, signed for Whiteman Spring (left), stay right on FDR 088/GWT toward the East Fork road (**m8.0/16.3**). Later, you'll loop back on FDR 185 from Whiteman Spring. Scattered pebbles and sinuous ruts in Johnson Hollow may prevent you from opening up the throttle, but you will freewheel the entire way. When you reach the East Fork road, take it south 1.8 miles to the edge of Tropic Reservoir (**m11.6**).

So far this ride has been a piece of cake. Well, you just might burp up that cake on the gravelly 10-percent climb to Whiteman Bench (FDR 185). One mile up (note the blue "1" marker on the road's edge), the doubletrack curves right and levels. Watch for where the plateau necks to a subtle ridge. Immediately thereafter, you'll pass a

Winding through stately ponderosa pines on the Daves Hollow loop.

doubletrack forking left and pass a blue "2" marker, meaning 2 miles from the East Fork road. One-half mile farther (**m13.9**), fork left on an unsigned doubletrack (FDR 185 continued). Roll through the woods, and drop down the steep, rocky hill past Whiteman Spring (wooden trough). Beyond, the road mellows, and you arc around graceful turns to the junction with FDR 088 (**m16.3/8.0**). Now retrace your outbound tracks to the junction with FDR 090/GWT (**m19.0/5.3**). Turn right, cross breezy Daves Hollow, and, after entering the wooded knolls, take FDR 1175 back to the trailhead. Whew!

Notes & Precautions:

Be alert to motorists on the East Fork road, especially barreling log trucks—you might get sand-blasted by their billowing wakes. Water taps are at Kings Creek Campground on the west side of Tropic Reservoir. Tropic Water Stop is also a source of refreshment. Whiteman Spring flows perennially, but the water should be purified just to be safe.

Trailhead Access:

From Panguitch, take US 89 south 7 miles; then turn left/east on UT 12 for Bryce Canyon National Park and Escalante. Drive 13 miles through Red Canyon and across the Paunsagunt Plateau to Bryce Junction. Turn right/south on UT 63 for Bryce Canyon National Park. Gateway Trailhead (Great Western Trail) is 0.8 mile past Ruby's Inn/Best Western and 0.5 mile before the park's entrance.

The Table Cliff Plateau catches the last rays of the evening.

39 Henderson Canyon Overlook

Location:	18 miles northeast of Bryce Canyon National Park
Length:	6.5 miles
Configuration:	Out-and-back
Tread:	All-weather road
Physical Difficulty:	Novice (gradual climb, free-flowing descent)
Technical Difficulty:	Low (packed dirt with pebbles)
Elevation Changes:	High: 8,850 feet (turnaround at overlook)
	Low: 8,175 feet (trailhead: Pine Lake)
	Gain: 675 feet
Maps:	USGS 1:24,000 scale: Pine Lake, Utah
Land Status:	Dixie National Forest (Escalante Ranger District)

If the 2,000-foot ascent from Pine Lake to the Powell Point trailhead is too much to ask of either your vehicle or your legs, then enjoy this easy, equally scenic ride. Henderson Canyon Overlook proves that short rides are great rides, indeed. Granted, you won't toe the edge of Powell Point, but you will have a spectacular view of the Pink Cliffs' Romanesque ramparts upholding the Table Cliff Plateau. Schedule this ride for late in the day when the sun's waning rays reflect off the furrowed cliffs.

Circle around the west side of Pine Lake, and then head up the road between two low-rising knolls. The pedaling is easy as you cross the flats above Pine Lake. Pass the junctions for the Great Western Trail and start chugging up Pole Canyon. Dispersed pine, fir, and aspen underlain by green, glossy manzanita and tenacious oak lend comfort and tranquility. Suddenly, the Pink Cliffs rear above the pines, blocking the sky with a massive corrugated rampart splashed with hues of chalk-white, orange, and pink. A log fence marks the overlook and the all-too-obvious end of the

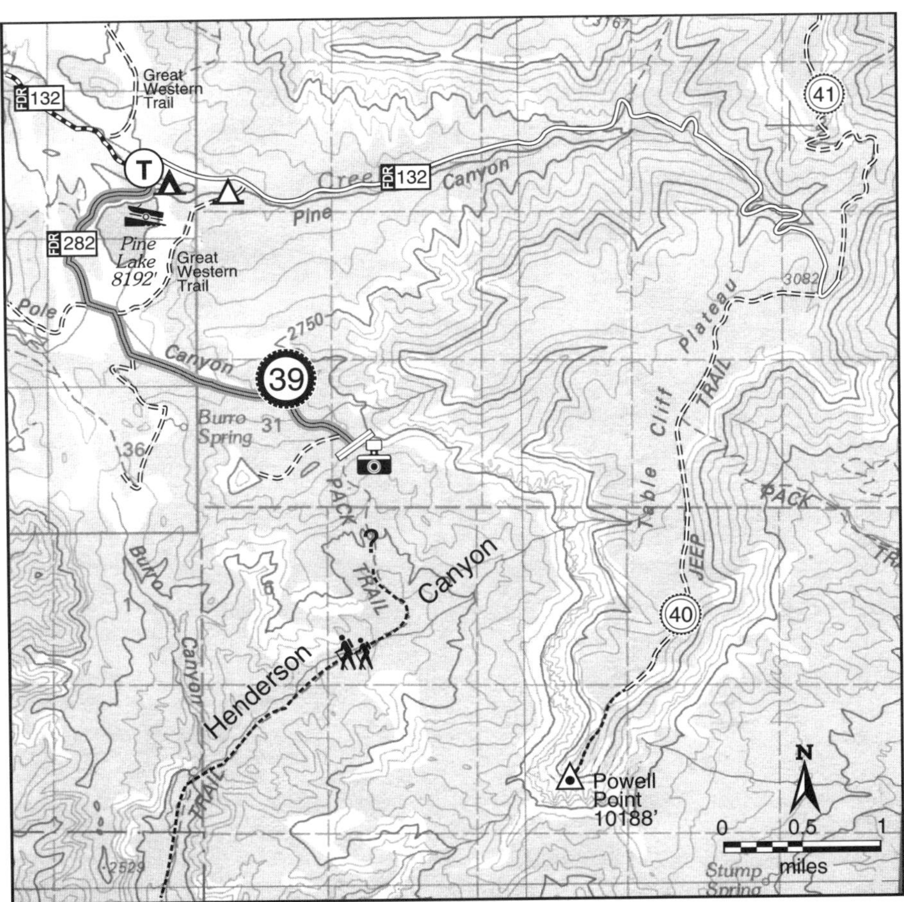

USGS 1:100,000 scale: Escalante (50 meter contour interval).

road. Those who struggled while climbing to Henderson Canyon Overlook can breath a sigh of relief; the return leg is a freebie with a lot of coasting. But before you make an about face, hike up the hill to the left and pick your way out along the rock face to claim rights to your own perch for viewing or meditation.

If you've been poking around Brian Head–Bryce Country, you'll quickly note the striking similarity between the white, orange, and pink crenelated limestones bolstering the Table Cliff Plateau and those shaping Bryce Canyon National Park, Strawberry Point, and Cedar Breaks National Monument. In fact, these rocks all belong to the pervasive Tertiary-age Claron Formation. The Claron Formation was deposited in a shallow basin lake that covered much of southwestern Utah about 60 million years ago. The eroded edge of the Table Cliff reveals the Claron's two prominent members or stratigraphic subsets: the lower Pink Limestone Member, which forms the massive pastel skirt flaring down to Henderson Canyon, and the upper White Limestone Member, which caps the plateau with meringue-white vertical cliffs.

Notes & Precautions:

Use extreme caution when viewing from or hiking along the edge of cliffs. The limestone substrate may be unstable and crumble. Pine Lake Campground is a forest service fee area.

Trailhead Access:

From Bryce Junction (2 miles north of Bryce Canyon National Park), drive 11 miles north on UT 22 toward Antimony. Turn right on FDR 132 (all-weather road) for Pine Lake and Table Cliff Plateau and drive 5.5 miles to the reservoir and campground. Just before the entrance to Pine Lake Campground, turn right on FDR 282 for Pine Lake and Henderson Canyon Viewpoint. Day-use parking is near the dam.

40 Powell Point

Location:	23 miles northeast of Bryce Canyon National Park
Length:	9.2 miles
Configuration:	Out-and-back
Tread:	Doubletrack, singletrack
Physical Difficulty:	Novice to intermediate (nearly flat with one short steep hill near the trail's end; high elevation can be taxing on lungs and legs)
Technical Difficulty:	Low (packed dirt, mud holes and ruts, a couple of switchbacks, occasional deadfall)
Elevation Changes:	High: 10,260 feet (mid-route) Low: 10,120 feet (trailhead: top of Pine Canyon) Gain: 500 feet
Maps:	USGS 7.5 minute: Pine Lake, Sweetwater Creek, and Upper Valley, Utah
Land Status:	Dixie National Forest (Escalante Ranger District)

Powell Point is more than just another yawning overlook from the edge of the High Plateaus: it is a Titanic viewpoint, a salient where the Great Architect oversees its handiwork in the Grand Staircase–Escalante National Monument. The point forms a blunt terminus to the peninsular Table Cliff Plateau. When viewed from afar the point resembles the bow of an ocean tanker crashing through a sea of white, pink, and salmon-hued breakers. The ride to Powell Point is every bit as enjoyable as the staggering view from the turnaround. The initial doubletrack rolls through damp, muffled forests across the Table Cliff's broad summit. A mile before the plateau's terminus, the doubletrack ends and a playful singletrack takes you to the point.

Before embarking for Powell Point, take a gander eastward from the trailhead to the Kaiparowits Plateau province of the Grand Staircase–Escalante National Monument. Sprawling beneath the rim of the Table Cliff and Aquarius Plateaus, Upper

Valley steers countless tributaries toward the Escalante River, which flows out of sight. But the Escalante's down-cutting temperament is evident in the incised, naked sandstones of the Box–Death Hollow Wilderness and the Escalante Canyons beyond. The ruler-straight rampart running southeastward on the horizon, appropriately called the Straight Cliffs, marks the dividing line between the Kaiparowits Plateau section in the foreground and the Escalante Canyons section afar.

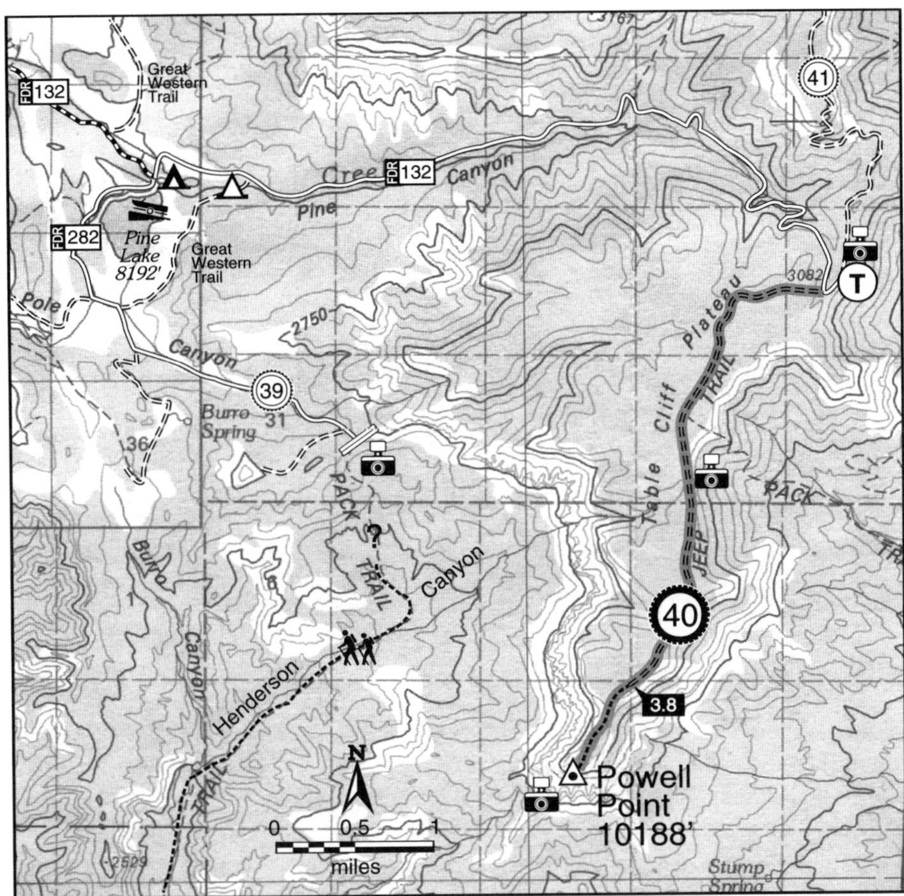

USGS 1:100,000 scale: Escalante (50 meter contour interval).

From the outset, the doubletrack rises gently for about one mile then flattens as it crosses the plateau. Twice, the Table Cliff necks to a narrow divide where opposing slopes attempt to merge through the efforts of headward erosion. Continual views of Upper Valley and the Aquarius flash through a curtain of tree boughs.

The jeep road ends at the singletrack trailhead, signed "Scenic Viewpoint 3,000 feet" (**m3.8**). (The trail is closed to motorized travel.) As you round the first turn, you will sneak a peek of the colossal views yet to come. Cross a neck in the plateau, which affords sights of the crumbling cliffs, and then struggle up a steep slope. Finally, ramble through the trees to Powell Point (**m4.6**). You'll know when to stop!

Imagine the exultation of John Wesley Powell's survey crew in 1880 when they too gazed from this divine perch. Clarence Dutton, Powell's protégé, described the point as ". . . the aspect of a vast Acropolis crowned with a Parthenon."

At the trailhead, you sighted across the monument's Kaiparowits Plateau and Escalante Canyons sections. Here, at the point, your eyes fall upon the namesake

Limestone colonnades of the Claron Formation support the Table Cliff Plateau.

Grand Staircase section. Powell Point combined with Bryce Canyon to the west define the Staircase's colorful top rung. The Paria River, due south, along with its attendant tributaries has effectively sliced deeply into the province's subsequent step—the Gray and White Cliffs. The stratigraphic succession continues across the Utah–Arizona border until it culminates in the depths of the Grand Canyon. When you are through admiring the sights, return to the trailhead by backtracking. Savor the sweet singletrack and then charge across the table top.

Option: Pine Lake to Powell Point

If rough road conditions in Pine Canyon stymie your vehicle, you'll have to begin pedaling from Pine Lake. The climb to the Table Cliff Plateau is a steady, strenuous 2,000-foot grind. The first few miles may have gravel and ruts because rains easily wash the unconsolidated limestone soil from adjacent slopes across the road. Farther up, dense timber stabilizes the hillsides, and the road is packed dirt and rock. Find the Powell Point trailhead where the road bends 90 degrees left/north atop the plateau (6.2 miles from Pine Lake). The huge vista eastward from the forested rim is a telltale sign. If you mistakenly continue north, you'll be following the lengthy Barney Top loop.

Specs.: 22 miles (out-and-back); 2,300-foot gain

Notes & Precautions:

The dirt road up Pine Canyon to the trailhead is lightly maintained and may be rough for passenger cars. High clearance is recommended. Use extreme caution along cliff edges near Powell Point. The loose, crumbly limestone is unstable and may break away. Pine Lake Campground is a Forest Service fee area. The singletrack to Powell Point is sensitive to knobby tires. Pedal softly and "Leave no Trace" to ensure continued bike access to Powell Point.

Trailhead Access:

From Bryce Junction (2 miles north of Bryce Canyon National Park), take UT 22 north 11 miles toward Antimony. Turn right on FDR 132 (all-weather road) for Pine Lake and Table Cliff Plateau, and drive 5.5 miles to the reservoir and campground. Continue on FDR 132 for 6.2 miles to the plateau's top, where the road bends 90 degrees left/north. (High clearance is recommended.) Park at the viewpoint just around the bend

41 Barney Top

Location: 18 miles northeast of Bryce Canyon National Park
Length: 31 miles
Configuration: Loop (counterclockwise)
Tread: Doubletrack, all-weather dirt roads, pavement
Physical Difficulty: Advanced to expert (steady, strenuous climb to Barney Top with a few tough switchbacks near the top; large elevation gain; very gradual climb upon returning to Pine Lake)
Technical Difficulty: Low to high (periodic washboards and gravel on the Escalante Canyon and Pine Canyon roads; steep switchbacks with loose rocks on the final climb to Barney Top; highly technical, bouldery doubletrack dropping off Barney Top followed by less-threatening conditions)
Elevation Changes: High: 10,520 feet (Barney Top)
Low: 7,500 feet (UT 22)
Trailhead: 8,200 feet (Pine Lake Reservoir)
Gain: 3,200 feet
Maps: USGS 1:24,000 scale: Flake Mountain East, Pine Lake, Sweetwater Creek, and Upper Valley, Utah
Land Status: Dixie National Forest (Escalante Ranger District)

Barney Top is an alpine seque between the steep-walled Table Cliff Plateau and the rolling Escalante Mountains, which in turn meld with the expansive Aquarius Plateau. This loop takes you from high sage plains surrounding Pine Lake to Barney Top's 10,500-foot crest, where you view distant lands that hold promise for untold mountain bike adventures. Later on, you pass the ghost town of Widtsoe. Its century-old cemetery is a monument to courageous Mormon pioneers.

This is a long ride that offers a variety of riding conditions: You begin with a steady, strenuous climb up Pine Canyon to Table Cliff Plateau; rise up through steep, rough switchbacks to Barney Top; descend through vicious boulders off the rim; freewheel endlessly down Escalante Canyon; and pedal easily on dirt and paved roads.

Start up Pine Canyon at a steady, conservative pace because there is plenty of climbing ahead. Colorful coalescing escarpments etched high in the Table Cliff Plateau float above the crowns of dispersed pine and fir. As you rise in elevation, the canyon narrows and the timber thickens until the once panoramic route is tightly

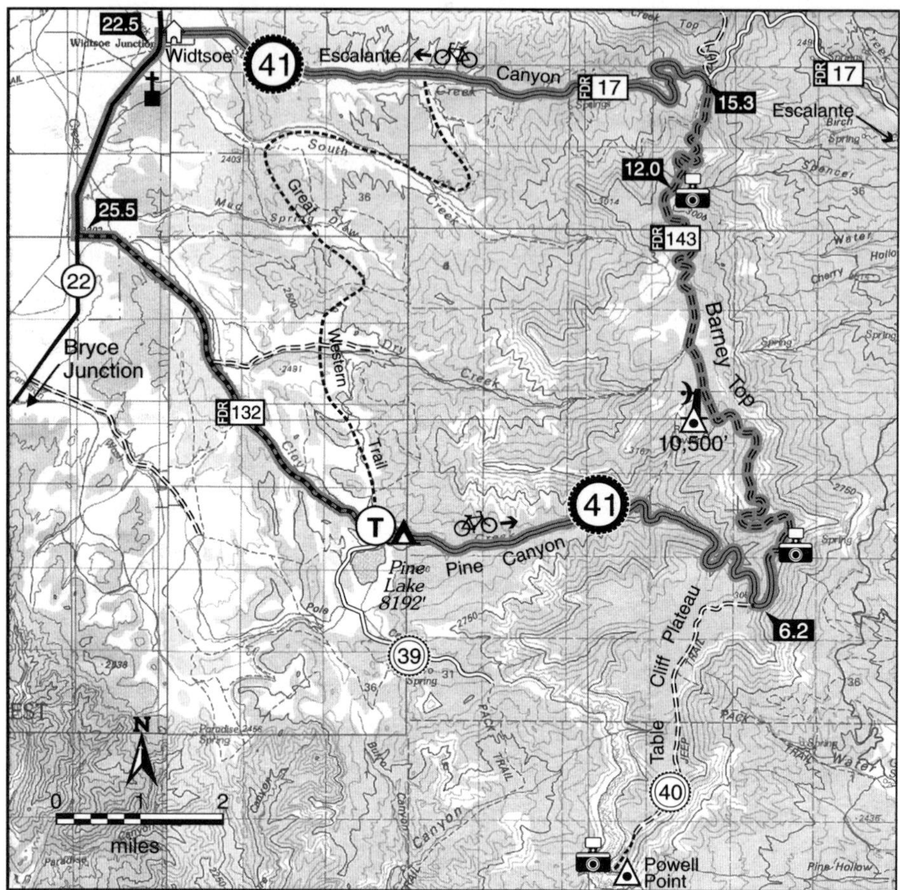

USGS 1:100,000 scale: Escalante (50 meter contour interval)

grasped by a wooded glove. When you gain the Table Cliff Plateau, scenery makes a grand re-appearance (**m6.2**). The eastern edge of the Table Cliff can be seen blending with the Barney Top and then the Escalante Mountains to the north. The later then curve east and become the volcanic bluffs rimming the Aquarius Plateau. The Upper Valley basin beneath the Aquarius' rim funnels a dozen tributaries toward the distant Escalante River. Of these headwater creeks, Sand and Pine Creeks have gouged deep canyons into the Box-Death Hollow Wilderness. To the southeast, the 50-mile-long Straight Cliffs define the edge of the Kaiparowits Plateau, the central province of the Grand Staircase-Escalante National Monument. If you opt to pedal to Powell Point, you'll again gaze across the monument but to where the Paria River has sliced deep, dark canyons into the distant White Cliffs.

Cruise north atop the Table Cliff Plateau with scenes of the Aquarius flashing through the trees. Where the road swings west and begins rising to Barney Top, you'll find a complimentary view across the Paunsagunt Plateau. Brian Head Peak

A headstone chronicles the hardships of Pioneer Life.

on the distant Markagunt Plateau, which rises 1,000 feet higher than you're current elevation, is a mere bump on the horizon.

Ahead, a series of rough, steeply rising switchbacks may make you sigh with exasperation, but the effort is eased by the composite panorama of forested highlands and incised sandstone wilderness off to the east. The pedaling is generally fast and easy across Barney Top until you reach the sign warning "four-wheel-drive only" (**m12.0**).Hunker down for a violent drop on a bouldery dugway scratched into the plateau's volcanic rim. Then race north for several miles off Barney Top on exciting doubletrack until you reach the crossroads atop Escalante Canyon (**m15.3**). (Untold adventures await atop the Escalante Mountains to the north, including the infamous Gap Trail and intriguing portions of the Great Western Trail.)

Turn left/west toward Widtsoe on FDR 17 and drop rapidly through switchbacks marred with washboards and loose dirt chewed up by vehicles. Thereafter, it's a straight shot down Escalante Canyon to UT 22. You'll descend quickly from cool subalpine slopes to warm sagebrush plains. Pass the turnoff for the Great Western Trail along the way. (Although the GWT appears to be a shortcut back to Pine Lake on a map, it crosses many hills and vales on dubious doubletracks.)

After pedaling through miles of unproductive land, you pass ghostly shacks of the Widtsoe town site (**m22.5**). Widtsoe was settled at the turn of the twentieth century by a trio of families. The town prospered for two decades and grew to a modest population of 1,100. But then World War I seized two dozen of the town's prominent young men from their laborious tasks of tending the land and building the town. The community quickly faltered, families moved away (many without even selling their land), and Widtsoe succumbed to the sage and juniper. If you stop at the Widtsoe

The ghostly remains of Widtsoe.

cemetery, located a short way up UT 22, you can reflect on the pioneer lifestyle. Elegantly carved granite headstones outline polygamous lineages, whereas driftwood crosses at the head of small earthen mounds attest to the harsh environment that took the lives of many infants.

A couple miles past the cemetery, turn left on FDR 132 (**m25.5**). The 5.5-mile ride back to Pine Lake is slightly uphill and may seem utterly monotonous. But the growing views of the distant Table Cliff Plateau and Barney Top rekindle memories of the glorious vistas encountered earlier on this adventuresome tour.

Option: Powell Point

If you made easy work of the 2,000-foot, 6-mile climb up Pine Canyon to the Table Cliff Plateau, then visit Powell Point. You'll tack on 9 miles (round-trip) and trivial elevation gain. Your effort will be rewarded when you toe the edge of southern Utah's great power spot. The lasting memories of the sweet singletrack to and from the point just might soften the palm-bruising descent off Barney Top that you'll experience later on.

Specs.: 9 miles (out-and-back); 500-foot gain

Notes & Precautions:

Travel well equipped; Barney Top is infrequently traveled. Be aware of motorists and truck traffic on the Escalante Canyon road. Pine Lake Campground is a Forest Service fee area.

Trailhead Access:

From Bryce Junction (2 miles north of Bryce Canyon National Park), drive 11 miles north on UT 22 toward Antimony. Turn right on FDR 132 (all-weather road) for Pine Lake and Table Cliff Plateau, and drive 5.5 miles to the reservoir and campground. Park and embark.

Sometimes there is more to mountain biking than just mountain biking.

APPENDIX I

Rides According to Difficulty

Featured Trail **pg #**
Optional Trail pg #

Brian Head-Area Rides

Novice:

Brian Head Resort:
(Color Country Trail) 76
(Wildflower Trail) 78
Brian Head Town Trail 56
Cascade Falls 127
Dead Lake 110
Duck Creek ATV Trail 132
Ice Cave 129
Navajo Lake Loop Trail 124
Pioneer Cabins 65

Intermediate:

Birch Spring Knoll 107
Brian Head Resort:
(Color Country Trail) 76
(Lightning Point Trail) 79
C Trail 48
Cascade Falls–Dike Trail loop 127
Dark Hollow Trail–Second Left Hand Canyon 71
Dark Hollow–Scout Camp loop 75
Dike Trail (Navajo Lake) 126
Duck Creek ATV trail-VRRT (west loop) 134
Ice Cave–VRRT-Duck Creek ATV Trail loop 130
Left Fork Bunker Creek 85
Lowder Ponds 81
Navajo Trail (Navajo Lake) 126
Right Fork Bunker Creek 89
Red Desert–Tippets Valley 113
Scout Camp Loop 68
Spruces Trail (Navajo Lake) 126
The Three Peaks 44
Twisted Forest–High Mountain 59
Twisted Forest (Sugarloaf Mountain Road) 61
VRRT–Cascade Falls-Navajo Point loop 123
VRRT–Lars Fork-Strawberry Point loop 122
Yankee Meadow Reservoir 53

Advanced:

Brian Head Resort:
(Timberline Trail) 77
(Mace's Run Trail) 80
(Uphill Route) 80
Blowhard Mountain 62
C Trail—out-and-back 49
C Trail—Cedar Canyon loop 50
C Trail—Greens Lake Drive loop 50
Dark Hollow–Brian Head Peak Trail loop 75
Duck Creek ATV trail-Lost Hunter Trail loop 134
Duck Creek ATV trail-VRRT (east loop) 134
Left Fork–Right Fork Bunker Creek loop 87
Lowder Ponds–Bunker Creek (one-way) 84
Lowder Ponds–Bunker Creek (loop) 84
Red Creek Reservoir 51
Three Peaks Loop Trail 46
Virgin River Rim Trail (VRRT) 116
VRRT–Strawberry Point-Te-ah Campground 122

Expert:

Brian Head Resort: (Z Trail) 79
Brian Head to Panguitch 92
Dark Hollow-Parowan Canyon loop 75
Spruce Trail (Horse Valley Peak) 104
Tour de Frog 97

Bryce-Area Rides

Novice:

Casto Canyon (out-and-back) 138
Chimney Rock Trail 152
Daves Hollow 175
Great Western Trail–Crawford Pass-Podunk Creek loop 173
Henderson Canyon Overlook 178
Tropic Reservoir 151

Intermediate:

Casto Canyon (loop) 138
Great Western Trail (East Fork Sevier River Section) 171
Great Western Trail–Podunk Creek-Long Hollow loop 173
Losee Canyon 141
Mill Creek Trail 165
Pink Cliff 168
Powell Point 180
Sunset Cliffs II (Badger Creek) 157
Sunset Cliffs III (Blubber Creek) 159
Sunset Cliffs IV (Robinson Canyon) 162
Whiteman Bench 175

Advanced:

Cassidy Trail to Losee Canyon 144
Casto Canyon to Losee Canyon 140
Great Western Trail–East Fork loop 173
Losee Canyon to Casto Canyon 144
Pine Lake to Powell Point 182
Sunset Cliffs I (Blue Fly Creek) 153
Sunset Cliffs III–Right Fork Upper Kanab Creek 160
Thunder Mountain 147
Thunder Mountain–Red Canyon loop 150

Expert:

Barney Top 183
Grand Tour of Sunset Cliffs 164
Sunset Cliffs I–No Name Trail 155

APPENDIX II

Master List of Rides

Featured Trail **pg #**
Optional Trail pg #

Barney Top **183**
Birch Spring Knoll **107**
Blowhard Mountain **62**
Brian Head Resort **76**
Brian Head Resort:
Color Country Trail 76
Lightning Point Trail 79
Mace's Run Trail 80
Timberline Trail 77
Uphill Route 80
Wildflower Trail 78
Z Trail 79
Brian Head to Panguitch **92**
Brian Head Town Trail **56**

C Trail **48**
C Trail—out-and-back 49
C Trail—Cedar Canyon loop 50
C Trail—Greens Lake Drive loop 50
Cassidy Trail to Losee Canyon **144**
Cascade Falls **127**
Cascade Falls–Dike Trail loop 127
Casto Canyon **138**
Casto Canyon to Losee Canyon 140
Chimney Rock Trail 152
Color Country Trail 76

Dark Hollow Trail–Second Left Hand Canyon **71**
Dark Hollow–Brian Head Peak Trail loop 75
Dark Hollow-Parowan Canyon loop 75
Dark Hollow–Scout Camp loop 75
Daves Hollow **175**
Dead Lake **110**
Dike Trail (Navajo Lake) 126

Duck Creek ATV Trail **132**
Duck Creek ATV trail-Lost Hunter Trail loop 134
Duck Creek ATV trail-VRRT (east loop) 134
Duck Creek ATV trail-VRRT (west loop) 134
Grand Tour of Sunset Cliffs 164
Great Western Trail (East Fork Sevier River Section) **171**
Great Western Trail–Crawford Pass-Podunk Creek loop 173
Great Weastern Trail–East Fork loop 173
Great Western Trail–Podunk Creek-Long Hollow loop 173

Henderson Canyon Overlook **178**

Ice Cave **129**
Ice Cave–VRRT-Duck Creek ATV Trail loop 130

Left Fork Bunker Creek **85**
Left Fork–Right Fork Bunker Creek loop 87
Lightning Point Trail 79

Losee Canyon **141**
Losee Canyon to Casto Canyon 144
Lowder Ponds **81**
Lowder Ponds–Bunker Creek 84
Lowder Ponds–Bunker Creek loop 84

Mace's Run Trail 80
Mill Creek Trail **165**

Navajo Lake Loop Trail **124**
Navajo Trail (Navajo Lake) 126

Pine Lake to Powell Point 182
Pink Cliff **168**
Pioneer Cabins **65**
Powell Point **180**

Red Creek Reservoir **51**
Red Desert–Tippets Valley **113**
Right Fork Bunker Creek **89**

Scout Camp Loop **68**
Spruce Trail (Horse Valley Peak) **104**
Spruces Trail (Navajo Lake) 126
Sunset Cliffs I (Blue Fly Creek) **153**
Sunset Cliffs I–No Name Trail 155
Sunset Cliffs II (Badger Creek) **157**
Sunset Cliffs III (Blubber Creek) **159**
Sunset Cliffs III–Right Fork Upper Kanab Creek 160
Sunset Cliffs IV (Robinson Canyon) **162**
Sunset Cliffs–Grand Tour 164

The Three Peaks **44**
Three Peaks Loop Trail 46
Thunder Mountain **147**
Thunder Mountain–Red Canyon loop 150
Timberline Trail 77
Tour de Frog **97**
Tropic Reservoir **151**
Twisted Forest–High Mountain **59**
Twisted Forest (Sugarloaf Mountain Road) 61

Uphill Route 80

Virgin River Rim Trail (VRRT) **116**
VRRT-Cascade Falls–Navajo Point loop 123
VRRT-Lars Fork–Strawberry Point loop 122
VRRT-Strawberry Point–Te-ah Campground 122

Whiteman Bench **175**
Wildflower Trail 78

Yankee Meadow Reservoir **53**

Z Trail 79

APPENDIX III

Sources of Additional Information and Services

Dixie National Forest

Supervisor's Office
82 N. 100 East
Cedar City, UT 84721
(435) 865-3700

Cedar City Ranger District
82 N. 100 East
P.O. Box 627
Cedar City, UT 84721
(435) 865-3700

Powell Ranger District
225 E. Center Street
P.O. Box 80
Panguitch, UT 84759
(435) 676-8815

Escalante Ranger District
755 W. Main
P.O. Box 246
Escalante, UT 84726
(435) 826-5400

Red Canyon Visitor Center
5375 E. Hwy 12
Panguitch, UT 84759
(435) 676-2676

Panguitch Lake Ranger Station
(435) 676-2649

Bureau of Land Management

Cedar City District
176 E. Sargent Dr.
Cedar City, UT 84720
(435) 586-2401

National Park Service

Bryce Canyon National Park
Park Headquarters
Bryce, UT 84717
(435) 834-5322

Cedar Breaks National Monument
P.O. Box 749
Cedar City, UT 84720
(435) 586-9451

Zion National Park
Park Headquarters
Springdale, UT 84767
(435) 772-3256

Tourism Bureaus

Brian Head Chamber & Visitor Services
259 S. Hwy 143
P.O. Box 190325
Brian Head, UT 84719
(435) 677-2810
www.brianheadutah.com

Garfield County Travel Council
P.O. Box 200
Panguitch, UT 84759
(801) 676-8826
(800) 444-6689

Iron County Tourism & Convention Bureau
286 N. Main
P.O. Box 1007
Cedar City, UT 84720
(435) 586-5124
(800) 354-4849
tourism@netutah.com
http://www.ted.net~iron

Kane County Travel Council
78 S. 100 East
Kanab, UT 84741
(800) 733-5263

Utah Travel Council
Council Hall
Capitol Hill
Salt Lake City, UT 84103
(435) 538-1030
(800) 200-1160
http://www.utah.com

Panguitch Chamber of Commerce
P.O. Box 400
Panguitch, UT 84759
(435) 676-8585
http://www.infowest.com/panguitch

Cedar City Chamber of Commerce
286 N. Main
Cedar City, UT 84720
(435) 586-4484

Law Enforcement, Emergency Services, & Hospitals

All Emergency Services: 911

Utah State Highway Patrol
2130 N. Main
Cedar City, UT 84720
Emergency Calls: 911
Or (435) 586-9445
Non-emergency calls
(435) 586-2786
Statewide Road Conditions
(800) 492-2400

Garfield County Sheriff
55 N. Center St.
Escalante, UT 84726
(435) 826-4647

Iron County Sheriff
2132 N. Main
Cedar City, UT 84720
(435) 586-6511

Brian Head Police, Ambulance, & Fire Department
Brian Head, UT 84719
(435) 677-2043
(435) 677-2029

Cedar City Police
110 N. Main
Cedar City, UT 84720
(435) 586-2956

Panguitch City Police
45 S. Main
Panguitch, UT 84759
(435) 676-8807

To Report a Forest Fire:
1748 Kitty Hawk Dr.
Cedar City, UT 84720
(435) 586-4215

Brian Head Medical Clinic
Navajo Lodge
(435) 677-2700

Garfield Memorial Hospital
224 N. 400 East
Panguitch, UT 84759
(435) 676-8811

Parowan Medical Clinic
450 E. Clinic Way
Parowan, UT 84
(435) 477-3344
(435) 438-2531

Valley View Medical Center
595 S. 75 East
Cedar City, UT 84720
(435) 586-6587

Bike Shops

Brian Head Cross Country Ski & Bike
233 Hunter Ridge Dr.
(Lodge at Brian Head)
Brian Head, UT 84719
(435) 677-2012
(800) BIKESKI (245-3754)

Brian Head Resort
P.O. Box 19008
369 S. Hwy 143
Brian Head, UT 84719
(435) 677-2035

High Mountain Outfitter
223 Hunter Ridge Dr.
(Cedar Breaks Lodge)
Brian Head, UT 84719
(435) 677-2035

Brian Head Sports, Inc.
329 S. Hwy 143
Brian Head, UT 84719
(435) 677-2014

Georg's Ski Shop & Bikes
612 S. Hwy 143
Brian Head, UT 84719
(435) 677-2013

Bike Route
70 W. Center
Cedar City, UT 84720
(435) 586-4242

Cedar Cycle
38 E. 200 South
Cedar City, UT 84720
(435) 586-5210

Color Country Cyclery
491 S. Main
Cedar City, UT 84720
(435) 586-7433

Mountain Bike Heaven
25 E. Center
Panguitch, UT 84759
(435) 676-2880

Ruby's Inn (Rentals only)
Bryce Canyon
Bryce, UT 84717
(435) 834-5341

Mountain Bike Clubs and Associations

International Mountain Bike Association (IMBA)
PO Box 7578
Boulder, CO 80306
5541 Central Ave, #201
Boulder, CO 80301
(303) 545-9011
http://www.imba.com

Utah Mountain Bike Association (UMBA)
P.O. Box 573657
Murray, UT 84157-3657
(801) 968-1269
http://www.redrocks.com/local/umba/

Color Country Cycling Club
P.O. Box 416
Cedar City, UT 84720
(435) 586-7567

Other Businesses, Groups, and Organizations

Brian Head Resort
P.O. Box 19008
369 S. Hwy 143
(Giant Steps Lift)
Brian Head, UT 84719
(435) 677-2035
http://www.Aminews.com/BrianHead

Utah Summer Games (USG)
P.O. Box 71
Cedar City, UT 84721
(435) 865-8421

Utah Shakespearean Festival
Cedar City, UT 84720
(435) 586-1944

APPENDIX IV

References

Bromka, Gregg. *Mountain Biking Utah.* Helena: Falcon Press Publishing Company, Inc., 1998.

———. *Mountain Biking Utah's Canyon & Plateau Country.* Salt Lake City: Off-Road Publications, 1992.

———. *Mountain Biking Utah's Wasatch & Uinta Mountains.* Salt Lake City: Off-Road Publcations, 1996.

Buchanan, Dr. Hayle. *Wildflowers of Southwestern Utah: A Field Guide to Bryce Canyon, Cedar Breaks and Surrounding Communities.* Bryce, Utah: Bryce Canyon Natural History Association, 1992.

Burt, William H. and Richard P Grossenheider. *The Peterson Field Guide Series: A Field Guide to the Mammals--North American north of Mexico.* Boston: Houghton Mifflin, 1980.

Chronic, Halka. *Roadside Geology of Utah.* Missoula: Mountain Press Publishing, Co., 1990.

Clark, Herbert, and Arnold Small. *Birds of the West.* Cranberry, New Jersey: A. S. Barnes and Co., Inc., 1976.

Crampton, C. Gregory. *Land of Living Rock. The Grand Canyon and the High Plateaus: Arizona, Utah, Nevada.* New York: Alfred A Knopf, Inc., 1972.

Dalton, Luella Adams. *History of the Iron County Mission, Parowan, Utah.* n.p., n.d.

DeCourten, Frank. *Shadows of Time: The Geology of Bryce Canyon National Park.* Bryce Canyon, Utah: Bryce Canyon Natural History Association, 1994.

Gray, Mary Taylor. *Watchable Birds of the Southwest.* Missoula: Mountain Press Publishing Co., 1995.

Johnsgard, Paul A. *Birds of the Rocky Mountains.* Lincoln, Nebraska: University of Nebraska Press, 1992.

Johnson, Carl M. *Common Native Trees of Utah.* Logan, Utah: College of Natural Resources, Utah State University, 1970.

Roylance, Ward J. *Utah: A Guide to the State.* Salt Lake City: Utah: A Guide to the State Foundation, 1982.

Shaw, Richard J. *Utah Wildflowers: A Feild Guide to Northern and Central Mountains and Valleys.* Logan, Utah: Utah State University Press, 1995.

Smart, William B. *Old Utah Trails.* Salt Lake City: Utah Geographical Series, Inc., 1988.

Stokes, William Lee. *Geology of Utah.* Salt Lake City: Utah Museum of Natural History, University of Utah, 1986.

Van Cott, John W. *Utah Place Names.* Salt Lake City: University of Utah Press, 1990.

Weir, Bill, and W. C. McRae. *Utah Handbook.* Chico, California: Moon Publications, Inc., 1997.

Wharton, Tom, and Gayen Wharton. *Utah.* Oakland, California: Compass American Gudies, Inc., 1995.

Zeveloff, Samual I. *Mammals of the Intermountain West.* Salt Lake City: University of Utah Press, 1988.

WHERE DO YOU WANT TO RIDE TODAY?

LET OFF-ROAD PUBLICATIONS TAKE YOU THERE

Tired of the same old dirt? Then saddle up with a guidebook from Gregg Bromka and Off-Road Publications.

Mountain Biking Utah's Brian Head - Bryce Country: 41 rides in southern Utah's spectacular high plateaus: $14.95

Mountain Biking Utah's Wasatch & Uinta Mountains: 101 rides in northern Utah's mountainlands: $18.95

Mountain Biking Utah: 80 classic rides throughout the entire state: $14.95

But wait, there's more: These guidebooks plus dozens of additional guidebooks for the entire U.S.A. are available through Off-Road Publications
1590 S. 1400 East
Salt Lake City, Utah 84105
(801) 486-0698
http://www.OffRoadPub.com.

A native of upstate New York, author Gregg Bromka ventured west to pursue higher education and a career in geology. Instead he became captivated by Utah's stunning natural setting and took to the trail on his mountain bike. Searching for enticing mountain biking trails became Gregg's obsession, and writing about his pursuits was a natural progression. Today, Gregg makes his home in Salt Lake City, Utah.